Inclusion and Exclusion in Competitive Sport

Society is obsessed with categorising and treating individuals and groups according to their physical and non-physical differences, such as sex, gender, disability and race. This treatment can lead to the inclusion or exclusion of an individual from the tangible and intangible benefits of society. Where this practice becomes discriminatory, legal frameworks can protect human rights and ensure that people are treated with due respect for their similarities and differences. In a sporting context, the inclusion and exclusion of athletes based upon their differences is often a necessary part of the essence of competitive sporting activity, arranged around rules and categories that can have an unequal exclusionary impact on certain classes of individual. Dominant sporting cultures can also have exclusionary effects.

This important and innovative book seeks to investigate the socio–legal and regulatory balance between inclusion and exclusion in competitive sport. It critically analyses a range of legal and non-legal cases concerning sport-specific inclusion and exclusion in the areas of sex, gender, disability and race, including those cases involving Oscar Pistorius, Caster Semenya and Luis Suarez, to identify the extent to which the law and sport adopt a justifiable and legitimate inclusive or exclusive approach to participation. The book explores national and international regulatory frameworks, identifying deficiencies and good practice, and concludes with recommendations for regulatory reform.

Inclusion and Exclusion in Competitive Sport is important reading for anybody with an interest in the relationship between sport and wider society, sports development, sport management, sports law or socio–legal studies.

Seema Patel is a Senior Lecturer in Law and Deputy Director of the Centre for Sports Law at Nottingham Law School, Nottingham Trent University, UK. She teaches across a range of subjects, but focuses on sports law (in which she holds a PhD), the law of torts and street law. Her particular area of expertise is discrimination in sport and the regulatory balance between inclusion and exclusion in competitive sport. Seema has frequently attended and presented her research at a number of national and international conferences, and has also published in the area and provided expert comment to local press on news stories relating to sports law.

Routledge Research in Sport, Culture and Society

1 **Sport, Masculinities and the Body**
Ian Wellard

2 **India and the Olympics**
Boria Majumdar and Nalin Mehta

3 **Social Capital and Sport Governance in Europe**
Edited by Margaret Groeneveld, Barrie Houlihan and Fabien Ohl

4 **Theology, Ethics and Transcendence in Sports**
Edited by Jim Parry, Mark Nesti and Nick Watson

5 **Women and Exercise**
The body, health and consumerism
Edited by Eileen Kennedy and Pirkko Markula

6 **Race, Ethnicity and Football**
Persisting debates and emergent issues
Edited by Daniel Burdsey

7 **The Organisation and Governance of Top Football Across Europe**
An institutional perspective
Edited by Hallgeir Gammelsæter and Benoît Senaux

8 **Sport and Social Mobility**
Crossing boundaries
Ramón Spaaij

9 **Critical Readings in Bodybuilding**
Edited by Adam Locks and Niall Richardson

10 **The Cultural Politics of Post-9/11 American Sport**
Power, pedagogy and the popular
Michael Silk

11 **Ultimate Fighting and Embodiment**
Violence, gender and mixed martial arts
Dale C. Spencer

12 **The Olympic Games and Cultural Policy**
Beatriz Garcia

13 **The Urban Geography of Boxing**
Race, class, and gender in the ring
Benita Heiskanen

14 **The Social Organization of Sports Medicine**
Critical socio-cultural perspectives
Edited by Dominic Malcolm and Parissa Safai

15 **Host Cities and the Olympics**
An interactionist approach
Harry Hiller

16 **Sports Governance, Development and Corporate Responsibility**
Edited by Barbara Segaert, Marc Theeboom, Christiane Timmerman and Bart Vanreusel

17 **Sport and Its Female Fans**
Edited by Kim Toffoletti and Peter Mewett

18 **Sport Policy in Britain**
Barrie Houlihan and Iain Lindsey

19 **Sports and Christianity**
Historical and contemporary perspectives
Edited by Nick J. Watson and Andrew Parker

20 **Sports Coaching Research**
Context, consequences, and consciousness
Anthony Bush, Michael Silk, David Andrews and Hugh Lauder

21 **Sport Across Asia**
Politics, cultures, and identities
Edited by Katrin Bromber, Birgit Krawietz, and Joseph Maguire

22 **Athletes, Sexual Assault, and 'Trials by Media'**
Narrative immunity
Deb Waterhouse-Watson

23 **Youth Sport, Physical Activity and Play**
Policy, interventions and participation
Andrew Parker and Don Vinson

24 **The Global Horseracing Industry**
Social, economic, environmental and ethical perspectives
Phil McManus, Glenn Albrecht, and Raewyn Graham

25 **Sport, Public Broadcasting, and Cultural Citizenship**
Signal lost?
Edited by Jay Scherer and David Rowe

26 **Sport and Body Politics in Japan**
Wolfram Manzenreiter

27 **The Fantasy Sport Industry**
Games within games
Andrew C. Billings and Brody J. Ruihley

28 **Sport in Prison**
Exploring the role of physical activity in penal practices
Rosie Meek

29 **Sport and Nationalism in China**
Lu Zhouxiang and Fan Hong

30 **Rethinking Drug Use in Sport**
Why the war will never be won
Bob Stewart and Aaron Smith

31 **Sport, Animals, and Society**
Edited by James Gillett and Michelle Gilbert

32 **Sport Development in the United States**
Edited by Peter Smolianov, Dwight Zakus and Joseph Gallo

33 **Youth Olympic Games**
Edited by Dag Vidar Hanstad, Barrie Houlihan and Milena Parent

34 **Safeguarding, Child Protection and Abuse in Sport**
International perspectives in research, policy and practice
Edited by Melanie Lang and Mike Hartill

35 **Touch in Sports Coaching and Physical Education**
Fear, risk, and moral panic
Edited by Heather Piper

36 **Sport, Racism and Social Media**
Neil Farrington, Lee Hall, Daniel Kilvington, John Price and Amir Saeed

37 **Football and Migration**
Perspectives, places, players
Edited by Richard Elliott and John Harris

38 **Health and Elite Sport**
Is high performance sport a healthy pursuit?
Edited by Joe Baker, Parissa Safai and Jessica Fraser-Thomas

39 **Asian American Athletes in Sport and Society**
Edited by C. Richard King

40 **Pierre Bourdieu and Physical Culture**
Edited by Lisa Hunter, Wayne Smith and Elke Emerald

41 **Reframing Disability?**
Media, (dis)empowerment, and voice in the 2012 Paralympics
Edited by Daniel Jackson, Caroline E. M. Hodges, Mike Molesworth and Richard Scullion

42 **Sport and the Social Significance of Pleasure**
Richard Pringle, Robert E. Rinehart and Jayne Caudwell

43 **A Sociology of Football in a Global Context**
Jamie Cleland

44 **Gambling with the Myth of the American Dream**
Aaron M. Duncan

45 **Inclusion and Exclusion in Competitive Sport**
Socio–legal and regulatory perspectives
Seema Patel

Inclusion and Exclusion in Competitive Sport

Socio–legal and regulatory perspectives

Seema Patel

Routledge
Taylor & Francis Group
LONDON AND NEW YORK

First published 2015
by Routledge
2 Park Square, Milton Park, Abingdon, Oxfordshire OX14 4RN

and by Routledge
711 Third Avenue, New York, NY 10017

First issued in paperback 2016

Routledge is an imprint of the Taylor & Francis Group, an informa business

British Library Cataloguing-in-Publication Data
A catalogue record for this book is available from the British Library

Library of Congress Cataloging-in-Publication Data
Patel, Seema, author.
Inclusion and exclusion in competitive sport : socio-legal and regulatory perspectives / Seema Patel.
pages cm. — (Routledge Research in Sport, Culture and Society ; 45)
Includes bibliographical references and index.
1. Sports—Law and legislation. 2. Discrimination in sports—Law and legislation. 3. Sports—Moral and ethical aspects. I. Title.
K3702.P39 2015
344'.099—dc3
2014042331

ISBN 13: 978-0-415-37711-9 (pbk)
ISBN 13: 978-1-138-02551-6 (hbk)

Typeset in Times New Roman
by FiSH Books Ltd, Enfield

This book is dedicated to Rob, Dad, Mum and Asha.

Contents

Figures and tables

Figure

Tables

Cases

Adams by Adams v Baker, 909 F. 2d. 643 (1990)
Bellinger v Bellinger [2003] 2 ALL ER 593
Bennett v The Football Association Ltd, 28 July 1978. Court of Appeal (Civil Division) Transcript No. 591
British Judo Association v Petty [1981] ICR 660, CA
CAS 2008/A/1480 *Pistorius v IAAF*
Clinton v Nagy, 411 F. Supp. 1396 (N.D. Ohio 1974)
Corbett v Corbett [1970] 2 ALL ER 33
Couch v British Boxing Board of Control (1997 unreported, IT no. 2304231/97)
Cruz v Pennsylvania Interscholastic Athletic Association, 157 F. Supp. 2d. 485 (E.D. Pa. 2001)
Darrin v Gould, 540, P. 2d 882 (Wash. 1975)
de Freitas v Permanent Secretary of Ministry of Agriculture [1999] 1 AC 69
Dennin v Connecticut Interscholastic Athletic Conference Inc. 913 F. Supp. 3d 663. (D. Ct. 1996)
Dogru v France [2008] ECHR 1579
Dr Renee Richards v Unites States Tennis Association 93 Misc. 2d 713, 400 NYS 2d 267
Emily South v Royal Victorian Bowls Association [2001] VCAT 207 (28 February 2001)
Equal Authority v Portmarnock Golf Club & Others [2005] IEHC 235 (H. Ct. June 10 2005)
Ferneley v Boxing Authority of New South Wales [2001] FCA 1740
Force by Force v Pierce City R-VI School District, 570 F. Supp. 1020 (S.W. Mo, 1983)
Fortin v Darlington Little League, 514 F. 2d 344 (1975)
Goodwin v UK (2002) 35 EHRR 18
Greater London Council v Farrar [1980] 1 W.L.R 608
Hardwick v FA, IT case, unreported. Case no. 2200651/96
Hollenbock v United States Olympic Committee, 513 F. 3d. 1191 (10th Cir. 2008)
Hussaney v Chester City FC, 15 January 2011 No. EAT/203/98
Knapp v Northwestern University, 101 F. 3d 473 (7th Cir. 1996)
Kuketz v Petronelli, 821 NE 2.d 473 (Mass. 2005)

Lafler v Athletic Board of Control, 536 F. Supp. 104 (W.D. Mich. 1982)
Lana Lawless v the Ladies Professional Golf Association and the Long Driver's of America United States District Court Case Number CV10 4599 DMR
Lantz by Lantz v Ambach, 620 F. Supp 663 (1985)
Martin v PGA Tour, Inc., 994 F. Supp. 1242 (D. Or. 1998)
Martin v International Olympic Committee (1984) 740 F. 2d 67
McPherson v Michigan High School Athletics Association, 119 F. 3d. 453 (6th Cir. 1997)
Meca-Medina and Majcen v Commission (Case C-519/04 P) [2006] ECR I-699
Mercer v Duke University, 181 F. Supp. 2d. 525, 531 (M.D.N.C. 2001)
Modahl v British Athletic Federation Ltd (No 2) [2002] 1 WLR 1192
Moore v The Squash Rackets Association Ltd IT case, case no. 50482/94, May 9th 1995
Nordenfelt v Maxim Nordernfelt Guns and Ammunition Co. Ltd [1894] AC 535
Olinger v United States Golf Association 205 F. 3d 1001 (2000)
Panesar v Nestle Co Ltd [1980] ICR 144n
Pottgen v Missouri State High School Activities Association, 40 F 3.d 926 (8th Cir. 1994)
Robertson v Australian Ice Hockey Federation [1998] VADT 112 (26 March 1998)
R v John Terry, Westminster Magistrate's Court, 13 July 2012, unreported). Available at: www.judiciary.gov.uk/wp-content/uploads/JCO/Documents/Judgments/r-v-john-terry.pdf
Sagen v Vancouver Organising Committee for the 2010 Olympic and Paralympic Winter Games [2009] BCSC 942 (Sup Ct (BC))
Sandison v Michigan High School Athletics Association, 64 F 3.d 1026 (6th Cir. 1995)
Saunders v Richmond Borough Council (1977) IRLR 362, [1978] ICR 75, EAT
Schultz v Hemet Youth Pony League, 943 F. Supp. 1222 (C.D. Cal. 1996)
Shepherd v United States Olympic Committee, 464 F. Supp. 2d 1072 (D. Colo. 2006)
Singh v Rowntree MacKintosh Ltd [1979] ICR 554
Singh v The Football League, The Football Association and Others (unreported, December 2001, ET Case No. 5203953/99)
Sterling v Leeds Rugby League Club [2001] ISLR 201
Taylor v Moorabbin Saints Football League and Football Victoria [2004] VCAT 158 (17 February 2004)
Walrave and Koch v Association Union Cycliste Internationale (Case 36/74) [1974] ECR 1405

Statutes

American Declaration of the Rights and Duties of Man 1948
American Convention on Human Rights 1970
Beijing Platform for Action 1995
Boxing and Wrestling Control Act (NSW Act) 1986 (AUS)
Brighton Declaration on Women and Sport 1994
Canadian Charter of Rights and Freedoms 1982
Charter of the United Nations 1945
Civil Rights Act 1964 (USA)
Convention on the Elimination of All Forms of Discrimination Against Women (CEDAW) 1979
Convention on the Rights of Persons with Disabilities (CRPD) 2009
Disability Discrimination Act 1995 (UK)
Education Amendments Act 1972 (USA)
Equal Opportunity Act (EOA) 1995 (AUS)
Equal Status Act (ESA) 2000 (IRE)
Equal Treatment Between Men and Women in Access to and the Supply of Goods and Services Directive 2004/113 (OJ 2004 L373/37)
Equal Treatment Directive 2006/54 (OJ L204/23)
Equality Act (EA) 2010 (UK)
European Convention on Human Rights (ECHR) 1950
European Social Charter 1996
Framework Employment Directive 2000/78 (OJ 2000 L303/16)
Gender Recognition Act (GRA) 2004 (UK)
Grundgesetz 1949 (GER)
Human Rights Act (HRA) 1998 (UK)
International Convention on the Elimination of All Forms of Racial Discrimination (ICERD) 1969
International Covenant on Civil and Political Rights (ICCPR) 1976
International Covenant on Economic, Social and Cultural Rights (ICESCR) 1976
Physical Activity and Sport Act 2003 (CAN)
Race Equality Directive 2000/42 (OJ 2000 L180/22)
Race Relations Act (RRA) 1976 (UK)
Sex Discrimination Act (SDA) 1984 (AUS)

Sex Discrimination Act (SDA) 1975 (UK)
Sports Act 30/2004 (PORT)
The Americans with Disabilities Act (ADA) 1990 (USA)
The Lisbon Treaty 2009
The Treaty on the Functioning of the European Union (TFEU) 2009
UNESCO International Convention against Doping in Sport 2005
UNESCO International Declaration on Human Genetic Data 2003
UNESCO Universal Declaration on the Human Genome and Human Rights 1997
Universal Declaration on Human Rights (UDHR) 1948
White Paper on Sport 2007 (EU)
Yogakarta Principles 2006

Acknowledgements

Many thanks to Austen Garwood-Gowers and Simon Boyes for their continuous help and support. I would also like to thank Simon Whitmore and Will Bailey at Routledge for their advice and guidance throughout this process.

Introduction

Context

This book aims to investigate the regulatory balance between inclusion and exclusion in competitive sport. Society is obsessed with categorising and treating individuals and groups according to their physical and non-physical differences, such as sex, gender, disability and race. This treatment can lead to the inclusion or exclusion of an individual from the tangible and intangible benefits of society.

One of the areas which individuals seek inclusion is within sport, a field that has the potential to foster the recognition of aspects of being human, and override divisions (Rojek, 2005: 50). However, the oppositional force of exclusion can limit their inclusion. Inclusion and exclusion exists on a scale from reasonable to unreasonable, arbitrary to justifiable.

This book considers these inclusionary and exclusionary forces, and the existing legal framework in light of the special nature of competitive sports participation. It offers conceptual thinking around sport-specific inclusion and exclusion. Sport possesses a degree of 'specificity' because of its unique essence and institutional core values. The essence of sporting activity is concerned with challenging our physical and non-physical differences by creating conditions which separate winners and losers on the basis of these differences. The core of competitive sport is ultimately about being the best athlete; however, it is a contested realm where positive and negative values continually conflict and contrast with each other.

In order to protect this essence, rules and regulations concerning eligibility and selection are imposed to match ability, preserve competition, ensure safety, provide the best possible entertainment and generate revenue. Rules also exist to maintain its complex network of traditions, cultures and values that provide it with a degree of social exclusivity and cultural distinctiveness (Brackenridge *et al.*, 2000: 18; Sugden and Tomlinson *in* Coakley and Dunning, 2000: 319). The application of these rules can at times have an unequal exclusionary impact on certain classes of individual. The result of this is the potential incompatibility of sport with the existing legal framework of equality legislation in circumstances where there is no justification for differential treatment.

With this in mind, this book critically analyses a range of legal and non-legal cases concerning sex, gender, disability and race to identify when sporting exclusion is justifiable for the protection of the essence, and when it is unjustifiable and incompatible with equality legislation. For instance, the exclusion of South African female sprinter Caster Semenya by the International Association of Athletics Federations (IAAF) will be evaluated to determine whether the IAAF were justified in their approach. This position will be contrasted with the case of South African runner Oscar Pistorius who was excluded from competing in mainstream competitions on the grounds of his disability. Less well-known examples, such as the Iran women's football team, will also be analysed to evaluate whether a justified, evidence-based, legitimate inclusive or exclusive approach is employed by sport and/or the law.

This book acts as a practical tool for sports governing bodies and decision-makers by offering a framework for effectively balancing inclusion and exclusion in competitive sport *across* the areas of sex, gender, disability and race. It will also propose the most appropriate method of regulation within sport and/or law in this area to stimulate improvements in rule making and encourage good governance in this field. In turn, this will equip these parties with a reference for consistently ensuring that their rules and actions pursue legitimate sporting aims and objectives which are focused on matching ability, preserving competition and ensuring safety and, furthermore, that these are compatible with legal provisions which protect fundamental freedoms.

On a broader level, the book raises general awareness of the underlying issues and themes which appear to be restricting individuals from participating in sport. It is important to break down unnecessary barriers which have thus far prevented many minority groups from competing in competitive sport. At the same time, individuals need to be aware of the legitimate boundaries to their participation based upon justifiable reasoning.

Aims and objectives

The core objectives of this research are to:

1. Construct a new understanding of the concepts of sporting inclusion and sporting exclusion, drawing upon their impact in competitive sport.
2. Analyse current sport and legal approaches to inclusion and exclusion with reference to sex, gender, disability and race. Identify deficiencies and good practice in the current regulatory mechanisms.
3. Propose a regulatory framework for effectively managing inclusion and exclusion in sport and identify how this positions itself within the current models of sport regulation.

Competitive sport refers to activity which is carried out at an amateur, semi-professional or professional level. It is recognised and appreciated that sport is conducted for recreational purposes also, thus giving different meaning to the concepts of inclusion and exclusion. There is a great deal of literature which addresses inclusion and exclusion at a general social level, drawing upon the impact of economic status, welfare and class on our differences. Within this literature there are attempts to apply the resultant conceptual framework of social inclusion and social exclusion to the recreational sporting context, and the role of recreational sport within social inclusion and social exclusion political agendas (Houlihan and White, 2002; Thomas and Smith, 2009; Gratton and Henry, 2001; Coalter, 2007). However, whilst doing so is undoubtedly useful, it only presents a partial picture which does not necessarily account for the specificity of sport and the valuable role that certain forms of exclusion in sport can have in defending its essence. The purpose here is to shift the focus from political to sporting and gain a deeper understanding of the concepts and their operation in a competitive sporting environment.

It is accepted that inclusion and exclusion can take place because of a number of other human differences. The four categories of sex, gender, disability and race are chosen here because they broadly capture the essence of human differences and concern specific inherent human characteristics, which are the focus of this book. In addition, they represent major dimensions of the inclusion/exclusion debate in sport because they raise important matters about performance enhancement, the integrity of sport, matching ability, safety and the sporting culture. Some high-profile cases such as those involving Caster Semenya, Oscar Pistorius, Casey Martin and John Terry have tended to broadly fall into the categories of sex, gender, disability and race, which suggests that athletes are most often excluded on the basis of these differences.

There is a significant body of work concerned with specific forms of discrimination in sport in relation to sex, gender, disability and race. However, little specifically compares these areas (Schiek and Lawson, 2011), let alone expands into a broader consideration of inclusion and exclusion in competitive sport (Patel, 2009; Elling and Knoppers, 2005). Not only are sex, gender, disability and race explored in one place here but links are captured between them, to develop an overall understanding of factors concerning the balance between inclusion and exclusion in sport. Within sociology, this approach is referred to as intersectionality (Hargreaves and Anderson, 2014). That understanding is made more holistic by the fact that it eschews the tendency to take a specific disciplinary approach, in favour of one which interweaves all the main relevant disciplines. The value of a multi-disciplinary analysis is enhanced by the fact that it is used purposively to identify shortfalls in current practices and make recommendations for the balance between inclusion and exclusion.

Methodology

In order to satisfy the objectives outlined, the research exclusively employs a literature-based doctrinal approach. The research objects consulted here are a variety of computer- and paper-based sources. These include general sources of theoretical literature and empirical research located in text books and journal articles; sports governance and policy material, such as codes of practices and documents concerning the rules of sport and their enforcement; and domestic, regional and international legal material such as legislation, conventions, declarations and case law. Given the currency of the topics, newspaper materials have also been sourced. Since this book positions itself within the law and regulation literature, major research objects include primary and secondary legislation and case law. The main legal jurisdictions include the UK, EU, USA, Australia and Canada. These are primarily where the visible cases of inclusion and exclusion tend to be appearing and where they have been considerably addressed as sociopolitical matters. These parts of the world also have well-developed cultures around rule creation and rule enforcement. There are clear attempts by the legal authorities in these countries to deal with inclusion and exclusion and to explore the appropriate relationship between sport and law through legislation and policy.

The relationship between law and sport regulation in this particular field will be analysed. In doing so, the creation, interpretation and application of rules of sport that affect inclusion and exclusion will also be explored. These include rules laid down by the International Olympic Committee (IOC), the IAAF, Fédération Internationale de Natation (FINA) and Fédération Internationale de Football Association (FIFA). The compatibility of sport rules and actions with legal rules will be critiqued such as sports rules which restrict the fundamental freedoms of individuals but that are considered necessary for the greater good of sport. The extent to which sport should comply with the legal framework will also be considered.

One of the strengths of this research is its multi-disciplinary approach, drawing upon a range of other fields which extend beyond the confines of law and regulation. These include philosophy, psychology, science (including medicine and sport science), sociology and sport studies.

Organisation of the book

The book falls into three main parts and is presented sequentially:

Part I explores the significance of the main concepts of inclusion and exclusion, sex, gender, disability and race. It provides a sociological context for the sporting and legal matters which arise throughout. When understanding these concepts in general terms, the literature largely derives from social science disciplines such as philosophy and sociology as well as physical sciences including biology. This book evaluates the impact of our differences upon our interaction with the world. The origins of these differences and explanations for them need to be understood in biological and social contexts before we can consider how they operate in sport and law.

Part I seeks to distinguish these concepts in a competitive sporting environment and construct a new understanding of sporting inclusion and sporting exclusion. These proposed terms emphasise the effect that the essence of sport and the sporting culture has on inclusion and exclusion. Part I outlines the regulatory toolkit currently available to deal with sport-specific inclusion and exclusion, drawing upon policy and law measures, and sport regulation. In doing so, Part I highlights the current ways in which inclusion and exclusion are regulated, whilst also highlighting the potential gaps in this framework.

Part II follows with an application of this toolkit to inclusion and exclusion through an evaluation of a selection of legal and non-legal case studies of inclusion and exclusion in the areas of sex, gender, disability and race. The compatibility of the sport approach with domestic, regional and international legal mechanisms are critiqued, drawing upon primary and secondary sources of law, to pinpoint areas of good practice as well as deficiencies in the sport and legal regulatory approaches. The cases studies are compared and contrasted to explore how minority athletes are treated across the areas. Part II seeks to establish the legitimacy of the approaches to inclusion and exclusion, and the consistency of the treatment of minority athletes. It draws upon a range of disciplines in order to better understand what drives differential treatment between individuals.

Having distilled the legal and non-legal cases, Part III focuses on the future of the balance between inclusion and exclusion. It offers recommendations for reform of the framework which currently deals with inclusion and exclusion. Part III engages in a detailed comparative analysis of the four specified areas to identify the key themes which have emerged throughout Part II. The main regulatory approaches to inclusion and exclusion are identified, in addition to any sociocultural trends across the four areas which have played a significant role in the balance. In order to facilitate this analysis, a range of tables and figures graphically illustrate patterns and trends. These tools are evaluated to draw impressionistic conclusions about the consistency of the sport and legal approach across the four areas. They are used as a visual marker to identify the current balance between inclusion and exclusion in sport. Some basic trend analysis also accompanies this to ascertain where the problems of regulation in this field tend to be occurring.

The final chapters offer regulatory recommendations for striking the balance between inclusion and exclusion in sport. A multi-level template for reformative action is proposed for sports bodies to engage in and adapt within their sports in order to maintain a level of integrity. Underpinning this are recommendations for effectively regulating the balance through the existing spheres of law and regulation. These recommendations are also placed within the broader sociological context of sport to highlight their overall importance and significance in society.

References

Brackenridge, C., Howe, D. and Jordan, F. 2000. *Just Leisure: equity, social exclusion and identity.* Cheltenham & Gloucester College of Higher Education: Leisure Studies Association Publications.

Coakley, J. and Dunning, E. 2000. *Handbook of Sports Studies.* London: Sage Publications.

Coalter, F. 2007. *A Wider Social Role for Sport.* London: Routledge.

Elling, A. and Knoppers, A. 2005. Sport, Gender and Ethnicity: practices of symbolic in/exclusion. *Journal of Youth and Adolescence.* 34(3): 257–268.

Gratton, C. and Henry, I.P. 2001. *Sport in the City: the role of sport in economic and social regeneration.* London: Routledge.

Hargreaves, J. and Anderson, E. 2014. *Routledge Handbook of Sport, Gender and Sexuality*. London: Routledge.

Houlihan, B. and White, A. 2002. *The Politics of Sports Development: development of sport or development through sport?* London: Routledge.

Patel, S. 2009. *The level playing field: balancing inclusion and exclusion in sport.* Oral presentation given at the 'SRLA 22nd Annual Conference on Sport, Physical Activity, Recreation and Law' hosted by the Sport and Recreation Law Association in San Antonio, Texas, USA, March 2009.

Rojek, C. 2005. *Leisure Theory.* Basingstoke: Palgrave Macmillan.

Schiek, D. and Lawson, A. 2011. *European Union Non-Discrimination Law and Intersectionality.* Surrey: Ashgate Publishing.

Thomas, N. and Smith, A. 2009. *Disability, Sport and Society: an introduction.* London: Routledge.

Part I

Key concepts

1 Sport-specific inclusion and exclusion

This chapter introduces the main concepts of sport-specific inclusion and exclusion, which are integral to this discussion. Whereas references to sport within social inclusion and social exclusion are focused primarily on achieving political and social objectives, it will be proposed that we shift the focus of these definitions from social to sporting, in an attempt to uncover their meaning and behaviour in the context of competitive sport.

This chapter will draw upon existing sociological definitions and carve out a specific meaning of what shall be termed 'sporting exclusion' and 'sporting inclusion'. Since the heart of this discussion is concerned with managing physical and non-physical human differences, this chapter broadly explores these differences and engages in a sociological discussion of how these influence the processes of inclusion and exclusion. The social elements of these concepts will then be built upon in order to construct alternative definitions of inclusion and exclusion in the context of competitive sport, evaluating sport as a separate system within society. These definitions will underpin the following chapters and will be used as a benchmark for the identification of inclusionary and exclusionary practices in sport.

Inclusion and exclusion in human behaviour

At a human, basic level, we seek attachment and individual recognition through the formation of relationships and networks with other people or groups. Belonging to, and being with other people is essentially a 'fundamental human need' (Abrams *et al.*, 2004: 27). This is reinforced by the work of Maslow (1943) who theorises that humans have an entelechy or drive towards self-actualisation which entails progression through the satisfaction of a hierarchy of needs. He posits that once the psychological and safety needs of an 'organism' have been gratified, the person will strive for the fulfilment of belonging and love needs.

This is supportive of evolutionary literature which considers humans to be 'an intensely group-living species' (Buss, 1995: 22). The groups which we seek to join can either be the dominant social, economical or political group of a particular area, social circles within a community or group, or specific activities such as sport. The nature of the behaviour and activities which take place within those groups largely influences and affects the level of inclusion (Abrams *et al.*, 2004: 162).

There are a number of interconnected reasons why we may seek bonds, and why we attempt to obtain membership and access to groups. The central aim is to reap desired benefits, such as protection from perceived external dangers or from our own internal fears and insecurities. Another benefit is the feeling of recognition and acceptance of our differences. Throughout history, many individuals within diverse groups have sought acceptance and accommodation of their differences (Parekh, 2006: 1; Kymlicka, 1995: 3). We will explore these differences in detail shortly.

Human survival is considerably dependent upon our ability to collaborate with others around us. There are truly no activities which can be described as individual, and co-operation is almost a necessity. For example, it is suggested that, 'small, co-operative groups have been the primary survival strategy characteristics of the human species' (Brewer and Caporael, 1990: 240).

However, it is argued that actions such as co-operation, mutualism, altruism and self-sacrifice are overlooked within the evolutionary process, by competitive traits (Buss and Kendrick *in* Gilbert *et al.*, 1998: 984). Within group living exists an 'intensification of competition, risks of communicable diseases, and aggression from other group members' (Buss, 1995: 22). Therefore, another way of measuring inclusion is by exploring and assessing the value of exclusion instead (Hague, Thomas and Williams *in* Brackenridge, Howe and Jordan, 2000: 19). To exclude or to be excluded is a natural part of existence which is not exclusive to human beings. For example, ecologists have shown that exclusionary practices are common within or amongst species as a means of competing for survival and existence (Smith and Smith, 2008: 261; Shanahan, 2004: 23). In addition, many species, including human beings, live by some kind of social organisation or social hierarchy that can produce conflict (Smith and Smith, 2008: 232).

Charles Darwin's theory of natural selection refers to the 'preservation of favourable variations and the rejection of injurious variations' (Darwin, 2008: 63). Darwin advocates that those individuals who were best adapted to their particular environmental conditions would have a better chance of surviving and thriving. This theory has been used as a mechanism for evolution and alludes to the well-known phrase, 'survival of the fittest' whereby the fittest will survive and the weakest will not.

It is worth clarifying the phrase survival of the fittest since it has powerful meaning in a social and sporting context. The ideology of a struggle for existence was introduced by early writings of T. R. Malthus in 1859 (See Claeys, 2000). The formal term was first coined by Herbert Spencer, a philosopher and founder of sociology (Spencer, 1868). He used this to explore how intra-specific struggle has resulted in progress. In 1866, Darwin used the term as a synonym for 'natural selection' and a metaphor for the natural world, which appeared in the 1869 edition of his famous works *On the Origin of the Species* (Darwin, 2008). Spencer, Darwin and A. R Wallace (co-discoverer of natural selection) added that this struggle improved species as well as generating new ones. Striving for improvement and competing for survival is significant to this discussion since it essentially underpins the essence of competitive sport as we will see. The theory of natural selection assists in the understanding of our human differences and behaviours, which will become critical to the analysis of inclusion and exclusion in sport.

In addition to giving meaning to the natural world, the term has also been applied to human beings and human society, often being used to describe and promote sporting activity. For instance, Darwin redefined 'fitness' as 'intelligence' and accepted the application of natural selection to humanity by others (Claeys, 2000: 240). Spencer used the term to explain social and political processes, arguing that a process of natural selection was evident in society also (Heywood, 2003: 54). The application of this evolutionary process to society, has been controversially labelled, 'social Darwinism'. To be fit for purpose is to be self-actualised in Maslow's words (Maslow, 1943). There is debate surrounding this theory within the literature, given its connotations. It also prioritises self-interest over and above the human traits of mutual dependence, co-operation, collaboration and love (Midgley, 2002: 7; Darwin, 2008).

Despite this criticism, it is clear that human nature embodies elements of exclusion as a means of survival in society. It could be argued that the 'human landscape [is] a landscape of exclusion,' (Sibley, 1995: x) for it seems that 'there is a natural or socialised tendency for us to categorise objects into "good" or "bad" as a basic condition for survival' (Kitchen, 1998: 344). Exclusionary practices usually involve the isolation of an individual or group from a larger entity, whether in size, power or influence. The common theme throughout most references to exclusion is that it represents a barrier to inclusion because of a perceived judgement made about individual, socio-cultural or socio-economic differences (Hayes and Slater *in* Snape *et al.*, 2003: 74; Long and Welch *in* Snape *et al.*, 2003: 56). This can result in the exclusion of individuals from the desired benefits found within society, such as access to social groups, communities, the formation of personal relationships and engaging in leisure and sport.

Overall, it would be fair to say that both inclusion and exclusion are part of our natural instincts but are exercised in different ways and at different levels. Inclusion is concerned with membership into a group or community in order to seek acceptance of differences whereas exclusion is based upon a judgement made about a person or group's differences which is used to separate them and treat them in a different way. Human differences therefore play an important role in the processes of inclusion and exclusion.

Human differences

There are a range of human differences between people and it would be misleading to suggest that all of them can be explored here. Instead, there are three predominant, overarching categories of difference which tend to be consistent in the related literature. Differences can be understood as 'individual' based upon physical and non-physical appearance, ability and character; 'socio-cultural' based upon geographical and historical background and religious beliefs and values; and/or 'socio-economic' based upon status, wealth and class. Traditionally, formal and informal groups and communities have formed according to these differences or commonalities.

Individual differences

Individual differences tend to drive our categorisation in society, such as hair colour (Maslow, 1943: 390). Throughout this book references will be made to major individual differences based upon sex, gender, disability and race. These will be defined in detail in Chapter 2. These appear to be common markers for our personal or group identity and can encompass physical or non-physical attributes. A benefit to inclusion is that we are able to make sense of our own differences (Parekh, 2006: 142). Membership of groups provides a sense of fulfilment for an individual and can contribute towards defining one's personal identity (Rheker, 2000: 51).

Personal identity provides people with a 'moral anchor, a sense of direction and a body of ideals and values' (May *et al.*, 2004: 207). The anchor enables individuals to identify with a familiar space and contributes towards the establishment of a rooted sense of belonging. Inclusion promotes a sense of collaboration, and when achieved it can be a powerful tool for the promotion of self-identity and cohesion amongst groups and communities. If we are included into a group or community, this can lead to the validation of a human being as a 'person' both internally and externally. Spaemann (2006: 2) explores the status of an individual as a person and argues that this personal status is dependent upon a 'communicative event'. In other words, a person is not regarded as a person if they are debarred access to social recognition and interaction.

On the other hand, when we are excluded, this can lead to vulnerability, isolation and aggression (Abrams *et al.*, 2004: 48). The practice of exclusion can lead to a sense of empowerment and authority over others. This empowerment may be false depending on the nature of the exclusion being exercised.

Exclusion on the basis of individual differences is evidenced by the civil rights era in the USA where individuals of black origin were treated as inferior to white people. Skin colour was used to restrict individuals in all aspects of their lives, such as the right to vote, and resulted in segregation on buses, in schools and in most other spaces including sporting activity. This exclusion from society was premised upon the misguided stereotypical belief that black individuals were somehow less significant. Adolf Hitler's Nazi regime in Germany, the Apartheid era in South Africa and the slavery of Indians during the British rule also illustrate large-scale individual exclusion founded upon human differences.

There is a clear human obsession with the creation of divisions between differences as a means of managing inclusion and exclusion. Barriers can form a necessary part of one's life. In fact, they are needed as a 'point of reference with which to define ourselves and decide what differences to cultivate and why'

(Parekh, 2006: 150). Essentially, barriers, whether physical or perceptual, visible or hidden, exist to divide spaces between people and impose control or authority on upon a particular area. Perceptual barriers encompass social attitudes and behaviours which have developed over a period of time (Hayes and Slater *in* Snape *et al.*, 2003: 75). Barriers tend to influence the development of one's self-identity, not only through the boundaries that it can set, but also through the experience of being restricted.

Socio-cultural differences

Closely linked to individual differences is the influence of culture upon the processes of inclusion and exclusion. It is suggested that whilst 'every society must cater for individuals needs...culture also determines how individuals expressed their needs' (Loy and Booth *in* Coakley and Dunning, 2000: 9). Cultural values are therefore functional responses to the needs of an individual. Within the process of inclusion, culture plays an integral role in the formation of identity and in the influence over human activity and human differences. Culture can be described as a 'historically created system of meaning and significance...of which a group of human beings understand, regulate and structure their individual and collective lives' (Parekh, 2006: 143). Culture influences and impacts upon the way in which a society is governed and regulated as well as the values which it carries. It can open up and also close options for that cultural community. In other words it can create 'the conditions of choice but also demands conformity' (Parekh, 2006: 156).

Inclusion and culture share a reciprocal influential relationship. Inclusion can lead to a collaborative, co-operative culture and a diverse cultural population. Within most settings there exists a more dominant culture which individuals tend to live within. The dominant culture of a particular social setting can either support and develop personal identity, or seek to control us, particularly for minority individuals and groups. Human reaction to culture is to either conform to it in order to achieve inclusion, or challenge it and live outside of the normal societal trends. An inclusive 'kaleidoscope of culture' is one which embraces that expression and enables variations to co-exist naturally (Per Waldron *in* Kymlicka, 1995).

Conversely, there may be barriers between different cultures, which can lead to culture clashes. Space is used in society to express authority and division. Where barriers have created groups which are strong and well established, they are more difficult to access by those who do not usually conform to that space. Space becomes more rigid and structured, allowing for less movement and autonomy. Conversely, barriers which are more open and inviting are free and easily accessible to a wider range of individuals (Sibley, 1995: 80).

Goffman (1961: 15) speaks of 'total institutions' that are social establishments whether physical or spatial, which are restricted from the outside social intercourse through 'locked doors, high walls, barbed wire, cliffs, water, forests or moors.' Buildings, open spaces, roads and walkways are all 'cultural signifiers' which inform us whether we fit in (Kitchen, 1998: 349). Cultural norms force us to 'know our place' and know when we are out of place. The consequence of this obsession with division is often the social exclusion of individuals from society.

Socio-economic differences

Social inclusion and social exclusion are common political terms in the literature which are used to understand the relationship between people and the political, economical, legal and cultural functions of the State. Social inclusion is concerned with possessing the key to the political, economic and legal benefits as a citizen of a particular society, in other words, civil rights (McArdle and Giulianotti, 2006: 2). The feeling of belonging still exists but the focus is on the tangible benefits for an individual to survive and live under the same freedoms and restrictions as any other. Social inclusion is defined as 'extending civil rights and responsibilities to all members of society, by developing a framework of citizenship' (Rojek, 2005: 52; Coalter, 2007: 8). Social inclusion is also focused on ensuring that individuals within a society, share equality of opportunity.

Conversely, social exclusion has been coined as a political expression of the divisions and disparities within society as a whole. Originating from France to describe 'les exclus' who were deprived of social protection (Hills, 2002: 2), social exclusion describes the separation of the individual, from the 'political, economic and frequently socio-cultural processes of society' (Long and Welch *in* Snape *et al.*, 2003: 57). Social exclusion is a product of economic divisions that arguably form a necessary and inherent part of unequal capitalism. Poverty is in fact considered to be at the centre of social exclusion (Collins, 2014). Those with less disposable income are unable to engage with society as easily as richer individuals. The placement or displacement of economic groups in towns and cities leads to pockets of socially excluded communities.

Social exclusion may also be a product of a voluntary choice to disengage from the main activities of society. This implies that the nature and extent of exclusion and separation, varies according to who is being excluded, what they are being excluded from and why they may be excluded.

Categorisation and stereotypes

To include or to exclude on the basis of individual, socio-cultural and/or socio-economic differences is essentially a categorisation process. Categorisation of species and human groups has existed throughout history but has also raised serious scientific and sociological debate (Sibley, 1995: 26). For example, reliance on such taxonomic schemes has exaggerated the difference between the 'self' and 'other' and encouraged divisions between people based upon their individual differences which include a person's age, sex, social class, disability and ethnicity (Abrams *et al.*, 2004: 213). Excluded individuals are usually minorities who deviate from what is considered to be the norm of that society or activity.

Systems of categorisation which are based upon superficial differences to some extent reinforce stereotypical assumptions about individuals or groups. Stereotypes are essentially consequences of human attitude, which are made up of an 'intricate mixture of interest and fear, reverence and abhorrence, impulsion and repulsion' (Sibley, 1995: 15). Originally, stereotypes were understood as being prejudicial but are not necessarily negative and exist amongst all of us (Archer and Lloyd, 2002: 26). This is how we form bonds and relationships with particular people and how we make judgements about particular matters. Stereotypes are now understood 'in terms of the probability that a member of a particular group will behave in a particular way. These probabilities are useful because they simplify the complex social world we inhabit' (Archer and Lloyd, 2002: 26).

The danger with stereotyping is that the attributions of traits to categories can be exaggerated, misguided, and inaccurate or even false (Nugent and King *in* Miles and Phizacklea, 1979: 29). Stereotypes can distort our vision of the world by producing an over-simplified and unbalanced view (Midgley, 2002: 6). This may occur because a stereotype has evolved over a long period of time and may no longer apply in a modern setting or because it is based upon flawed non-evidential reasoning which can lead to harmful stereotyping. Standards of proof become lost within the process of stereotyping and conventional wisdom can often thrive.

For instance, deviance is a word that is associated with 'abnormality' and something which is far from the average or normal (Creswell, 1996: 24). The 'Object Relations Theory' explored by Sibley (1995: 5) explains the 'ways in which boundaries emerge, separating the good and the bad, the stereotypical representations of others which inform social practices of exclusion and inclusion but which, at the same time, define the self.' A person is considered normal when they possess the average ability relative to the expectation of their role in society – they are able to fit into the existing system of norms and values. Departures from what is considered the norm is usually regarded as inferior and thus treated in an exclusionary way (Rheker, 2000: 17). Stereotyping tends to 'emphasise the status quo and not allow for change' (DePauw and Gavron, 2005: 13). Through 'cultural practice' we are taught to 'pigeon-hole' similarities rather than accept difference (Kitchen, 1998: 344).

It is argued that 'from an evolutionary perspective, we humans have good reason to be wary of things which seem to be 'unnatural'' (Nature, 2008: 665). We are conditioned to be cautious of something if it is unknown to us because it may pose a danger or threat to us. However, such a reaction is considered to be borne out of emotion rather than by reason.

Because categories and stereotypes can evolve and develop, it often becomes the case that exclusion occurs naturally, without any thought or consideration. This is theoretically underpinned by the Pierre Bourdieu principle of the 'Doxa' (Bourdieu, 1977: 164; Hague, Thomas and Williams *in* Brackenridge, Howe and Jordan, 2000: 20). Doxa, as opposed to orthodoxy, refers to a societal realm that is never discussed or even contested, instead 'the tradition is silent, not least about itself as a tradition' (Bourdieu, 1977: 167). Individuals tend to unknowingly accept and take for granted, certain customs within this realm, even if they are repressive (Bourdieu and Eagleton, 1992: 114). When stereotypes become so embedded, even the stereotyped begin to believe it. For instance, the institutionalisation of disabled groups has led to them often accepting the inflicted image of themselves (Thomas and Smith, 2009: 8).

Bourdieu (1977: 169) mentions how 'the dominant classes have an interest in pushing back the limits of Doxa and exposing arbitrariness of the taken for granted; the dominant classes have an interest in defending the integrity of Doxa or…of establishing in its place the necessarily imperfect substitute, orthodoxy.' When Doxa is revealed, it can cause boundaries to be re-assessed. It is advocated that Bourdieu's theory is restrictive as it only relates to class (Creswell 1996: 21). However, there is potential to apply it to sport, which is a realm where the arbitrary treatment of minority athletes often becomes naturalised as we shall see (Bourdieu, 1977: 164).

In an attempt to form a framework of exclusion, Hague, Thomas and Williams (*in* Brackenridge, Howe and Jordan, 2000) propose that in addition to Doxa, or the 'embedded exclusions' which are never consciously identified, are the 'evident exclusions' which are openly recognised and debated, and the 'episodic exclusions' which essentially constitute a grey area and involve short-term exclusion which are produced by minor shifts. To simplify this view, exclusion may operate on two levels: the seen and the unseen. The latter more 'opaque' (Sibley, 1995: x) instances of exclusion are those which form a grey area because they are more difficult to identify and overcome where they are unjust. Similar distinctions are made by Elling and Knoppers (2005: 258) who identify a difference between a) structural inclusion and exclusion referring to (non) participation; b) cultural or symbolic inclusion and exclusion through social (normative) images; and, c) affective inclusion and exclusion through friendship networks.

From these theories it can be drawn that there 'are clear polarities of inclusion and exclusion which are either never challenged or are regularly contested' (Hague, Thomas and Williams *in* Brackenridge, Howe and Jordan, 2000: 20). Matters of difference, division, inclusion and exclusion, is therefore becoming much more pronounced in a world where immigration and globalisation are challenging traditional structures and belief systems (Rojek, 2005: 20).

Against this background of the nature and process of inclusion and exclusion, let us consider how human behaviour, difference and categories are exposed in the context of competitive sport. Currently the literature offers little in terms of the specific meaning of inclusion and exclusion in competitive sport, as distinct from recreational sport. Even sports research has tended to focus on sport and social inclusion/exclusion (DCMS, 2010: 35). Whilst recreational sport may be a field in which social inclusion values are more likely to evolve, competitive sport is predominantly based upon ability and performance. Tensions have existed between the use of sport to fulfil broader social policy goals and the demands of competitive sport (Houlihan and White, 2002: 80).

Sporting exclusion

The sociological definition of exclusion is the different or derogatory treatment of an individual or group on the basis of their individual, socio-cultural or socio-economic differences. Social exclusion focuses on the exclusion of an individual from the economic, political and legal benefits of society. Whilst sporting exclusion is not dissimilar to these definitions, it is a concept which gives credence to the nature and specificity of competitive sport, where athletes participate for the primary purpose of differentiating themselves from other competitors on the basis of their physical and non-physical attributes which can include sex, gender, disability and race.

Reasonable exclusion

Within the sporting arena, the criteria adopted to evaluate athletes is ideally and typically based upon sporting ability and performance. Reflected in the phrase survival of the fittest, sport has been created out of survival and war, with competition and winning at all odds, being a major motivating factor for sporting athletes and/or teams. The very nature of sport, as laid down by the inspirational Olympic slogan, is to be 'faster, higher, stronger' and strive to push the limit of human capacity. The potential risk of failure and exclusion comes hand in hand with success in sporting activity. In this sense, sport is one of the few areas where exclusion can almost be in the form of a necessity in order for human ability to progress and develop.

With this in mind, it could be said that exclusion forms part of the essence of sport itself and is embedded within the core values which sport holds. Sport demands and requires exclusive practice in order to be true to its specific nature and character. It is suggested that participation in sport is not 'based upon an ideology of "inclusion" or "sameness" ', but based upon differences in talent, classified on the basis of relevant inequalities' (Harris and Landeweerd, 2010: 4). Arguably, sport would be dull if there was absolute equality (Harris and Chan, 2008: 338). Whilst exclusion is not always a pleasant experience, it is nevertheless an accepted consequence of competing in a sport. Absence of this exclusionary element could leave sport without its integral purpose and function, particularly at an elite level, which is to further human capacity.

In order to protect this essence of sport, specific rules and regulations are imposed to manage our differences and match ability. These may include sex, gender, disability or race categories, age divisions, rules concerns advantage, the regulation of equipment and weight divisions. For instance, it is reasonable to exclude an athlete from wearing jewellery in a contact sport, since that may compromise the safety of other athletes. However, conflict arises when the athletes is wearing jewellery for religious purposes.

Unreasonable exclusion

At the other end of the scale there is unreasonable exclusion which can be overt or covert, seen or unseen (Brackenridge, Howe and Jordan, 2000; Sibley, 1995). Exclusion becomes unreasonable when the rules and regulations in place to manage our differences based upon sex, gender, disability and race, do not actually match ability or do not directly relate to the objective of protecting the essence of sport.

Sport is a realm which is held together by many of its own structures and frameworks and is soaked in traditional and long-standing values and belief systems. It possesses a degree of exclusivity and historical 'cultural distinctiveness' (Sudgen and Tomlinson *in* Houlihan, 2008: 70). Raitz (1995: 6) identifies how each sport carries with it, its own distinct space and emotional expression, which has evolved and developed to become its recognised heritage and culture. For instance, soccer was originally a sport which was associated with the working class, as opposed to rugby, which was attached to the middle class. This would have shaped the sporting space and affected who plays and accesses the sports.

In order to understand a particular sport, 'one must locate its position in the space of sports' (Bourdieu, 1988). Sporting spaces are produced by 'athletes, fans and many other stakeholders in the system of sport' and can be influenced by the 'event location, participant make-up and involvement, politics of sport and the policies that are an outgrowth of those politics' (Muller *in* Carmichael-Aitchison, 2007: 39; Roberts, 2009: 7). These influences impact upon the behaviour of those who consume sport by determining who can enter that space. This describes the 'sporting culture', which can have diverse effects on participation and access to sport. Messner (2002: 65), whilst describing the way in which US athletes, coaches and employees in sport may have experienced restrictions within their fields, highlights that 'they were bumping up against institutional structures-historically formed, entrenched systems of rules, conventions, allocations of resources and opportunities, and hierarchical authority and status systems'. Exclusionary practices in sport may instead be driven by traditional norms and sporting cultures which serve to maintain divisions between individuals and groups, based upon stereotypes which have formed and developed, as discussed above.

Where this takes place, it may do so overtly. This could be referred to as overt exclusion, or evidential exclusion (Hague, Thomas and Williams *in* Brackenridge, Howe and Jordan, 2000). It is widely documented that 'women, members of ethnic minorities, and persons with disabilities have been excluded or allowed limited access to sport' (DePauw and Gavron, 2005: 9). They have been marginalised as a result of 'culture, gender, ethnicity, class or disability affiliation' (DePauw and Gavron, 2005: 9). This can lead to potential conflicts with the principles set forth in international, regional and domestic equality legislation. As we shall see in Part II, an example of overtly unreasonable exclusion is the historical treatment of women in sport.

Sporting culture can also operate to exclude covertly or invisibly. Developing Bourdieu's theory (Bourdieu, 1977), a sport Doxa is created where certain existing beliefs are never contested or debated even though they no longer have a place in modern society and in fact act as barriers to participation. This unseen, more covert form of exclusion is largely under-researched because the explanations for exclusionary practices can only be speculated. In modern times, it would seem that society has moved away from traditional overtly exclusionary behaviour and instead adopt a more covert form of excluding, discriminating or ostracising minorities in given situations (Swim and Cohen, 1997: 104). This is due to the drive behind developing a more egalitarian society.

For instance, Swim and Cohen (1997) evaluate the scaling methods used to typically measure sexism, such as the Attitudes Towards Women Scale and also the Modern Sexism Scale. Drawing upon previous work (Benokraitis and Feagin, 1986) they identify three forms of sexism which exist: overt, covert and subtle. The last 'is characterised by openly unequal and harmful treatment of women that goes unnoticed because it is perceived to be customary or normal behaviour' (p. 104). Their findings suggest that there is a distinction between more traditional and modern forms of sexism. Further it is suggested that in cultures where sexism is recognised and officially disapproved, it is more likely to emerge in covert or subtle forms (Archer and Lloyd, 2002: 28).

To illustrate this, consider the participation of homosexual athletes in sport. Clearly there exist no formal rules or selection criteria which overtly exclude athletes who are homosexual. Any which have existed have been appropriately sanctioned by sports bodies or the law (Hardin and Whiteside *in* Hundley and Billings, 2010: 22). Instead sport is often regarded as having a 'homo-negative' climate which idealises masculinity (Brackenridge, Howe and Jordan *in* Carmichael-Atchison, 2007: 128). Gay men pose a threat to the hegemonic masculinity which breeds within sport (Anderson, 2002).

This exclusionary culture has prevented many sportsmen from publically announcing themselves as gay. Homosexuality is a concept which institutions such as sport would rather not confront and instead create environments which suppress it. It is suggested that the sexual orientation of gay men disturbs 'the unspoken rules of sexuality' within this heterosexual space (Creswell, 2006: 105). Despite inclusive measures by bodies such as the Football Association (FA) to combat homophobia in sport (The FA, 2012), a culture of exclusion continues to exist. In November 2010, for example, the head of the Croatian football federation, Vlatko Markovic, was criticised for expressing the view that there was no room for gay men in football (Connolly, 2010).

Indeed the sporting culture can be so dominant that this can have a destructive effect on one's identity. Trade-offs between personal and social inclusion often need to be made, in order to achieve inclusion within a group. The reluctance of athletes to reveal their sexuality maybe due to a fear of the severe social sanctions and negative impact on their career, given the climate of homophobia in sport (Anderson, 2002: 862). This leads to a false society instead of an equal or diverse one. However, the culture is shifting with athletes such as England cricket wicketkeeper Steven Davies, British diver Tom Daley and Australian swimmer Ian Thorpe recently publically announcing their sexuality, which is positive step for the future.

Sporting inclusion

Above, we identified that inclusion is part of a natural inherent need that, once satisfied, can provide us with a deep sense of fulfilment and satisfaction. Collaboration and co-operation is a necessary and unavoidable part of our social being. One of the common groups which individuals seek inclusion within is sport. This is because sport is said to possess a number of values which develop and enhance our sense of belonging such as fairness, team spirit, self-achievement, determination, knowing one's limits, appreciation of others, responsibility and solidarity to name a few (Rheker, 2000: 44–5). Sport can to lead to a 'common citizenship' which 'overrides divisions of class, gender, race, status, religion and associated distinctions of class' (Rojek, 2005: 50). Although these outcomes of sport are subject to debate, sport can 'confirm and/or construct part of people's social identity or image' (Elling, De Knop and Knoppers, 2003: 429).

Sporting inclusion can be distinguished from social inclusion. Social inclusion uses sport to overcome exclusionary barriers within society and it tends to focus more on inclusion and participation within recreational sport. Conversely, sporting inclusion is focused on ensuring that athletes have the access and opportunity to compete in competitive sport only where they are qualified to do so. They are qualified to do so when they meet the appropriate selection criteria. The athlete is not as central to this concept as meritocratic principles are. Sporting inclusion reflects a meritocratic society, which is one where any 'inequalities of wealth or social position solely reflect the unequal distribution of merit or skills amongst human being, or are based upon factors beyond human control, for example luck or chance' (Heywood, 2003: 35). This is deemed fair because individuals are not judged by their sex, gender, disability or race, but instead according to their talents and willingness to work. It is fair to say that sporting inclusion values equality of opportunity.

Those with the same level of talent and ability, with the same level of willingness, should have an equal chance of success (Mason, 1998: 73). Sport and equality is concerned with 'fairness in sport, equality of access, recognizing inequalities and taking steps to address them. It is about changing the structure and culture of sport to ensure that it becomes equally accessible to everyone in society, whatever their age, race, gender or level of ability' (Thomas and Smith, 2009: 54). As Weiler (2000: 24) describes it should be 'the quality of each candidate's talent, not the colour of his skin that determines who will secure the scarce and ever more lucrative positions both on the field and in the dugout.' Sporting inclusion is therefore concerned with challenging the stereotypical assumptions made about differences between individuals and groups. Those assumptions which are personally driven and based upon misguided predictions can lead to unequal processes and practices which restrict genuine integration in sport (Hylton and Bramham, 2008: 54).

Out of the sporting context, demands for equality of opportunity can be traced back to the ancient Greek times. For instance, Greek dramatist Euripedes considered equality of opportunity to mean impartial treatment for everyone (Capel and

Piotrowski, 2000: 29). The historical premise beneath 'equality of opportunity' is that if one works hard then one will succeed, otherwise, one deserves to fail (Mithaug, 1996: 17). Whilst this may appear to be extreme, it does highlight the fact that individuals need to recognise the distinction between their own capacity to be included and, being provided with the opportunity to be included (Mithaug, 1996: 69). It is about providing individuals with the opportunity to obtain these benefits and achieve their goals individually and deservedly.

Given this definition of inclusion, a very careful balance between the individual and the group interest is required, particularly in sport. If the 'boundary separating the rights of the individual and demands of the group drifts too far in one direction or the other, fairness is threatened' (Mithaug, 1996: 49). If we are to apply broad ethical and moral standards of sporting inclusion then it is likely that the preservation of the specific nature of sport and its own version of a level playing field is challenged (Weiler, 2000: 20). Inclusion should therefore be cautiously applied in sport. The law may play a critical role in ensuring that a balance is struck when applying equality legislation.

Sporting inclusion aims to ensure that athletes are judged according to their ability to compete in sport rather than being measured against extrinsic norms. An example of this is the participation of disabled athletes. As we shall see in Part II, the participation of disabled athletes such as Oscar Pistorius, into non-disabled categories has challenged the traditional structures of sporting activity. Integrating minority groups into sports where they are qualified to compete, would be a positive example of sporting inclusion. Ideally, through sport, there is potential to break down barriers of ignorance between people and groups, and instead embrace the diversities which exist amongst us.

Sporting inclusion advocates for the mitigation of human differences when athletes are qualified to compete in a particular sport. Sporting inclusion is not suggesting that 'all groups of people should be represented equally in all sports, but that participatory parity should be the norm' (Fraser, 2001; Elling and Claringbould, 2005: 511). The term participatory parity can 'justify claims for recognition as normatively binding on all who agree to abide by fair terms of interaction under conditions of value pluralism' (Fraser, 2001: 27). Sporting inclusion can be achieved by the transparent and consistent application of rules and criteria that govern sport.

Summary

The concepts of inclusion and exclusion appear to be natural human processes that exist as a means of managing and understanding the world in which we live and the many differences between us. Whilst sociologists disagree on whether collaboration or competition defines our purpose and behaviour, there is evidence of both attributes co-existing and operating. From this evaluation it can be drawn that whilst there are clear overlaps between inclusion and exclusion, there does appear to be a tension between the two concepts. Inclusion and exclusion operate individually and collectively, internally and externally, formally and informally, positively and negatively. They are forms of expression which are based upon categories and stereotypes. Minority groups tend to be caught in the middle of the tensions between the two concepts.

Sport-specific inclusion and exclusion are built around ensuring that the essence of sport, which includes differentiation upon the basis of sex, gender, disability and race, is balanced against the rights of the athlete to be included in sport where they are qualified to do so and where it is appropriate. These definitions highlight the unique ways in which inclusion and exclusion operate within sporting space, distinct from social inclusion and exclusion, which lean towards recreational sport. Consistent with the literature is the identification of both processes operating on a scale from reasonable to unreasonable and overt to covert.

References

Abrams, D., Marques, J.M. and Hogg, M. 2004. *The Social Psychology of Inclusion and Exclusion*. New York: Hove Psychology.

Anderson, E. 2002. Openly gay athletes: contesting hegemonic masculinity in a homophobic environment. *Gender and Society*, 16(6): 860–77.

Archer. J. and Lloyd. B. 2002. *Sex and Gender.* 2nd Edition. Cambridge: Cambridge University Press.

Benokraitis, N.V. and Feagin, J.R. 1986. *Modern Sexism: blatant, subtle and covert discrimination*. Englewood Cliffs, NJ: Prentice Hall.

Bourdieu, P. 1977. *Outline of a Theory of Practice*. Cambridge: Cambridge University Press.

Bourdieu, P. 1988. Program for a Sociology of Sport. *Sociology of Sport Journal*, 5: 153–161.

Bourdieu, P. and Eagleton, T. 1992. Doxa and Common Life. *New Left Review*, 191(I): 111–121.

Brackenridge, C., Howe, D. and Jordan, F. 2000. *Just Leisure: equity, social exclusion and identity.* Cheltenham and Gloucester College of Higher Education: Leisure Studies Association Publications.

Brewer, M.B and Caporael, L.R. 1990. Selfish Genes vs. Selfish People: Sociobiology as Origin Myth. *Motivation and Emotion*, 14(4): 237–243.

Buss, D.M. 1995. Evolutionary Psychology: A new paradigm for psychological science. *Psychological Inquiry*, 6(1): 1–30.

Capel, S. and Piotrowski, S. 2000. *Issues in Physical Education*. London: Routledge Falmer.

Carmichael-Aitchison, C. 2007. *Sport and Gender Identities: masculinities, femininities and sexualities*. London: Routledge.

Chan, I. and Landeweerd, L. 2010. Enhancing disabilities: transhumanism under the veil of inclusion? *Disability and Rehabilitation*, pp. 1–6.

Claeys, G. 2000. The "Survival of the Fittest" and the Origins of Social Darwinism. *Journal of the History of Ideas*, 61(2), April: 223–240.

Coakley, J. and Dunning, E. 2000. *Handbook of Sports Studies*. London: Sage Publications.

Coalter, F. 2007. *A Wider Social Role for Sport*. London: Routledge

Collins, M. 2014. Sport and Social Exclusion. London: Routledge.

Connolly, K. 2010. Croatia football chief Vlatko Markovic hit by gay group's backlash. *The Observer* [online], 14 November. Available at: www.guardian.co.uk/football/2010/nov/14/gay-backlash-croatia-football-chief [accessed 20/11/10].

Creswell, T. 1996. *In Place/Out of Place: geography, ideology and transgression*. London: University of Minnesota Press.

Darwin, C. 2008. *On the Origin of Species*. New York: Oxford University Press.

DCMS 2010. *Understanding the Impact of Engagement in Culture and Sport*. London: Cabinet Office. [online] July. Available at: www.culture.gov.uk/images/research/CASE-systematic-review-July10.pdf [accessed 12/07/11].

Depauw, K.P. and Gavron, S.J. 2005. *Disability Sport*. Illinois: Human Kinetics.

Elling, A. and Claringbould, I. 2005. Mechanisms of Inclusion and Exclusion in the Dutch Sports Landscape: Who Can and Wants to Belong? *Sociology of Sport Journal*, 22: 498–515.

Elling, A. and Knoppers, A. 2005. Sport, Gender and Ethnicity: practices of symbolic in/exclusion. *Journal of Youth and Adolescence*, 34(3): 257–268.

Elling, A., De Knop, P. and Knoppers, A. 2003. Gay/Lesbian sport clubs and events: places of homo social bonding and cultural resistance? *International Review for the Sociology of Sport*, 38(4): 441–56.

Fraser, N. 2001. Recognition without Ethics. *Theory, Culture and Society*, 18(2–3): 21–42.

Gilbert, D.T., Fiske, S.T. and Lindzey, G. 1998. *The Handbook of Social Psychology*. 4th Edition, Volume 2. New York: McGraw Hill.

Goffman, E. 1961. *Asylums: essays on the social situation of mental patients and other inmates*. Middlesex: Penguin Books.

Harris, J. and Chan, S. 2008. Understanding the Ethics of Genetic Enhancement. *Gene Therapy*, 15: 338–339.

Heywood, A. 2003. *Political Ideology: an introduction*. 3rd Edition. New York: Palgrave Macmillan.

Hills, J. 2002. *Understanding Social Exclusion*. New York: Oxford University Press.

Houlihan, B. 2008. *Sport and Society*: a student introduction. London: Sage Publications.

Houlihan, B. and White, A. 2002. *The Politics of Sports Development: development of sport or development through sport?* London: Routledge.

Hundley, H.L. and Billings, A.C. 2010. *Examining Identity in Sports Media*. London: Sage Publications.

Hylton, K. and Bramham, P. 2008. *Sports Development: policy, process and practice*. London: Routledge.

Kitchen, R. 1998. 'Out of Place,' 'Knowing One's Place:' space, power and the exclusion of disabled people. *Disability and Society*, 13(3): 343–356.

Kymlicka, W. 1995. *The Rights of Minority Cultures*. London: Oxford University Press.

Maslow, A.H. 1943. A Theory of Human Motivation. *Psychological Review*, 50: 370–396.

Mason, A. 1998. *Ideals of Equality*. Oxford: Blackwell.

May, S., Modood, T. and Squires, J. 2004. *Ethnicity, Nationalism and Minority Rights*. Cambridge: Cambridge University Press.

Mcardle, D. and Giulianotti, R. 2006. *Sport, Civil Liberties and Human Rights*. London: Routledge.

Messner, A. 2002. *Taking the Field: Women, Men and Sports*. University of Minnesota Press.

Midgley, M. 2002. *Evolution as a Religion*. London: Routledge

Miles, R. and Phizacklea, A. 1979. *Racism and Political Action in Britain*. London: Routledge and Kegan Paul.

Mithaug, D.E. 1996. *Equal Opportunity Theory*. London: Sage Publications.

Nature 2008. Defining Natural. *Nature*, 10 April, 452(7188): 665–666.

Parekh, B. 2006. *Rethinking Multiculturalism: cultural diversity and political theory*. Basingstoke: Palgrave Macmillan.

Raitz K. 1995. *The Theatre of Sport*. Maryland: The Johns Hopkins University Press.

Rheker, U. 2000. *Integration through Games and Sports*. Oxford: Meyer & Meyer Sport.

Roberts, K. 2009. Conflict and brinkmanship in sport form part of the narrative which fans find so fascinating and which has lawyers everywhere licking their lips. *Sport Business International*, 147, July, p. 7

Rojek, C. 2005. *Leisure Theory*. Basingstoke: Palgrave Macmillan.

Shanahan, T. 2004. *Evolution of Darwinism: Selection, Adaptation and Progress in Evolutionary Biology*. New York: Cambridge University Press.

Sibley, D. 1995. *Geographies of Exclusion*. London: Routledge.

Smith, T.M. and Smith, R.L. 2008. *Elements of Ecology*. Pearson International Edition; Benjamin Cummings.

Snape, R., Thwaites, E. and Ferguson, M. 2003. *Access and Inclusion in Leisure and Tourism*. Eastbourne: Leisure Studies Association.

Spaemann, R. 2006. *Persons: the difference between "someone" and "something."* Oxford: Oxford University Press.

Spencer, H. 1868. *The Principles of Biology*. Vol 1. New York: D Appleton and Company.

Swim, J.K. and Cohen, L.L. 1997. Overt, covert, and subtle sexism: A comparison between the Attitudes Towards Women and Modern Sexism scales. *Psychology of Women Quarterly* 21: 103–118.

The Football Association (FA) 2012. *Opening Doors and Joining In: the FA action plan for including LGBT people in football 2012–2016*. The FA. Available at: www.thefa.com/football-rules-governance/equality/lgbt-football [accessed 02/09/14].

Thomas, N. and Smith, A. 2009. *Disability, Sport and Society: an introduction*. London: Routledge.

Weiler, P. 2000. *Leveling the Playing Field: How the Law can Make Sports Better for Fans*. London: Harvard University Press.

2 Physical and non-physical human differences

Having introduced the main concepts of sporting inclusion and sporting exclusion, this chapter will define sex, gender, disability and race. As we shall see in Part II these human differences challenge the balance between inclusion and exclusion most frequently. In addition, they represent major dimensions of the inclusion/exclusion debate in sport because they raise important points about performance enhancement, the integrity of sport, matching ability, safety and the sporting culture.

Some athletes within the areas of sex, gender, disability and race are considered to be minorities in sport because they share the characteristics of being 'numerically inferior' and are in a 'non-dominant position' to the rest of the named population in sporting activity (Rehman, 2010: 434). This chapter will explore the reasoning behind this treatment and seek to provide a clearer sense of the terms.

Sex

The term 'sex' refers to the inherent biological characteristics which are determined at birth. Sex tends to be defined by a number of factors such as genetic or chromosomal sex, gonadal sex (reproductive glands), internal and external morphological sex (genitalia), hormonal sex, phenotypic sex (secondary sexual features) and sexual identity (Cooper, 2010: 238). Assigning an individual's sex is an important feature of the regulation and governance of populations, particularly recording procedures such as birth certificates.

An interchangeable term is 'gender', which derives from the ongoing social consequences for the individual. Gender was first used by Greek Sophists in the fifth century BC to describe the threefold classification of the names as masculine, feminine and intermediate (Archer and Lloyd, 2002: 17). Gender appears to have replaced the term sex in politically correct speech. It is suggested that this shift evolved to highlight that distinctions between men and women arise mostly from cultural rather than biological sources. It is debatable whether or not sex does imply a biological origin (Humberstone *in* Laker, 2002: 58).

Biological versus socio-cultural differences of the sexes

The binary categories of sex are reflected in some developed world views of creationism and premised upon the Old Testament, which posits that God created Eve from Adam's rib (Archer and Lloyd, 2002: 99; Buss and Kendrick *in* Gilbert *et al.*, 1998: 984). This model of interpretation is one where men and women were compared with a single perfect form (one-sex), with men being considered closer to that perfect form. Women were historically considered to be inferior to men (Laqueur, 1990: 4). This view has been influenced by religion, conventional wisdom (common sense as the literature refers) and scientific knowledge at the time.

There are clear differences between men and women and these can be traced back to evolutionary principles. A historic natural division of labour increased the inherent psychological differences between males and females during primeval times. Men and women are expected to differ in areas where they experienced adaptive problems over human evolutionary history, during their development or over different environments inhabited (Buss, 1995: 19; Buss and Kendrick *in* Gilbert *et al.*, 1998: 994). As they faced problems during their evolution (it must be noted here that both sexes have also faced similar adaptive problems such as both creating mechanisms to deal with changes in body temperature, skin friction and also long-term mating factors), the two sexes adopted varying strategies to ensure their survival and reproduction. For instance, the division of labour between male hunters and female gatherers of plant food presented a range of challenges which caused men and women to adapt. These roles act as a possible reason for men's greater upper body strength and spatial rotation ability, and women's greater spatial location memory (Buss, 1995: 19).

Darwin's evolutionary theory of sexual selection has frequently been applied to sex differences to explain the 'struggle between the males for possession of the females' (Darwin, 2008: 68). It is therefore opined that sex differences derive from differing fitness-related goals. Due to man's competition with other men for sexual access to women, as well as protective instincts, they developed dispositions such as violence, competition and risk taking (Eagly and Wood, 1999: 410). Women on the other hand favoured attributes more akin to nurture.

The evolutionary theory remains under scientific debate amongst anthropologists (Eagly and Wood, 1999: 411). It has been criticised for lacking an appreciation of the influence of culture upon adaptive mechanisms. Culture reflects both the 'biological endowment of humans', as well as the 'constraints of their social and physical environments' (Eagly and Wood, 1999: 414). It is argued that culture cannot be viewed separately from the individual as they are dynamic systems that operate beyond a context (Eckes and Trautner, 2000: 390). Feminist perspectives also conflict with this idea on the basis that male dominance within science has arguably influenced research in human sciences (Archer and Lloyd, 2002: 6).

On the other hand, therefore, the social structural theory asserts that the origins of sex behavioural differences are situated in the contrasting social positions of women and men (Eagly and Wood, 1999: 412; Eckes and Trautner, 2000: 160). Supporting this is the 'social roles theory' that 'emphasises the numerous ways in which the social behaviours that differ between the sexes are embedded in social roles – in gender roles as well as in many other roles pertaining to work and family life' (Eagley, 1987: 9). The division of labour between men and women affects not only societal expectations of the traits and behaviours of men and women, but also the perceptions that men and women have about their own capacities and skills (Deaux and LaFrance *in* Gilbert *et al.*, 1998: 790). These characteristics 'provide rich and well differentiated sets of concepts and terms to categorize and characterize boys and girls, men and women, to separate between female and male roles, rights and responsibilities' (Eckes and Trautner, 2000: 3).

Social structuralists accept that biological differences between men and women have influenced these roles, such as men's greater size and strength, which prioritises their positioning within manual jobs, compared with women's focus on children and caring for the young. In many societies it is often the case that women have been given less power and status than men. Women perform different employment functions from men and experience little representation in many senior levels of organisations. According to this theory, these differing roles are referred to as gender hierarchy and are considered to be the underlying cause for sex differences.

One of the criticisms of this theory is that culture and social structure are not a causal force of sex differences, only that they reflect an underlying logic of evolved dispositions (Eagly and Wood, 1999: 414). Whereas biologists have used Darwin's principles of sexual selection to explore sex differences, social scientists have used the perspective of gender roles (Geary, 1998: 3). Gender roles are defined as those shared expectations (about appropriate qualities and behaviours) which apply to individuals on the basis of their socially identified gender (Eagly, 1987: 12). Where men control a disproportionate share of power and resources, gender ideology is based upon what is referred to as a 'simple binary classification model' (Coakley and Pike, 2009: 258). According to this model, all people are classified into the categories of male or female. Such a model is central to the way people see the world. However, it is noted that it takes dedication to maintain these ideas because the model is inconsistent with biological evidence showing that anatomy, hormones, chromosomes and secondary sex characteristics vary in complex ways which cannot be divided into two distinct, overlapping sex categories (Coakley and Pike, 2009: 259).

That is not to say that categories are not important, as differences are clearly present between sex and gender. Both theories are not so opposed to each other since both agree that there are differences. Both models suggest that the sexes adjust to environmental conditions. The theories conflict in their evaluation of the timing and nature of these adjustments. A middle ground is the 'biosocial' model which proposes that biological and environmental influences are both important during the development of sex differences between boys and girls (Archer and Lloyd, 2002: 76). One of the most consistently found features of the social behaviour of children is the formation of same-sex play and social groups (Geary, 1998: 241).

For both of these theories, it is agreed that the future will reveal how accurate they are. There are notable changes in the inclusionary and exclusionary behaviours of men and women, with women, who have historically been the minority, increasingly taking up employment positions in formerly male-dominated areas. It is argued that changes in social structures and processes will assist in the elimination of gender differences (Lueptow *et al.*, 2001: 4). Societal shifts towards equal opportunities in work and leisure are much more prominent with attitudinal changes emerging. However, some research suggests that stereotypes are intensifying and even though we see social changes, these are not being followed by change in sex typing. Recent literature proposes that women in management are still under-represented and sex segregation is still overtly present in areas such as sport (Carter and Silva, 2010; Glaister, 1974: 48).

Gender

Gender is the societal dominant view on how a man or woman should aesthetically look and behave. The term gender also refers to a person's lived experiences which have come to form their identity. Whereas sex considers what is biologically male and female, gender considers what is masculine and what is feminine. Whereas biological sex appears to be fixed, the concepts of masculinity and femininity are 'constructs of a particular culture or society and may therefore be open to change' (Humberstone *in* Laker, 2002: 59). It seems to be agreed that 'gender is a complex construct with different dimensions ranging from genetic sex to sexual orientation, gender roles and images, and gendered display' (Hartmann-Tews and Pfister, 2003: 7). These concepts are 'continually created, recreated, delineated, acted out and policed through social interaction' (Shy, 2007: 110). Because sex and gender exist so closely together it may be that they are essentially the same thing (Cowan, 2005).

The paradigms of two genders founded on two biological sexes evolved in the early eighteenth century and is considered to be a western view (Herdt, 1994: 111). Minorities tend to be those who do not conform to the typical male/female structure, such as transgender and intersex individuals. Whereas western civilisation attempts to suppress and ignore any sexual contradictions and ambiguities within this binary, the divisions of men and women in other civilisations are not so distinct or important, with gender blending being a more accepted process elsewhere (Waldemar, 1988; Whittle, 2002: 4). For instance, many countries accept and recognise third gender categories and non-conformist behaviour such as the 'Xanith' in the Omani, the 'Fa'afafine' in Samoa, the 'two spirit people' in Native American tribes, the 'she males' in Singapore, the 'khusra' in Pakistan, the 'acaults' in Burma and the ancient 'hijras' of India. These non-exhaustive examples are a strong testimony for the proposition that western sex and gender categories are certainly not universal.

At the heart of this obsession with categorisation of sex and gender, or classification anxiety, is power (Pearlman, 1995: 844; Cowan, 2005: 71). This classification anxiety shapes the law relating to the identification of sex and gender. As with sex, classification provides structure to regulatory institutions and is a useful means of identification. However, it is argued that the western categorisation of individuals on the basis of their sex, gender or sexuality, influences our own views and perceptions of those individuals (Archer and Lloyd, 2002: 105). The law has traditionally viewed sex and gender as identified at birth upon the basis of anatomical features. This has impacted upon structures in sport where most sports are divided according to sex and gender. Gender differences have been a significant marker of our inclusion or exclusion into society and, in turn, sporting activity.

Disability

Humans differ in their physical and intellectual abilities. Historically, disability was linked to images of deviance and individuals who were hindered by impairment (Thomas and Smith, 2009: 8). Deviance is a word which is associated with 'abnormality' and something considered far from the average or normal (Creswell, 1996: 24). Originally, the definition of disability was based upon a medical approach as introduced by the World Health Organization (WHO) in 1980 (Thomas and Smith, 2009: 9). It was premised upon the concept of a 'broken body' (WHO, 1980). This model dominated discussion about disability for most of the twentieth century, with its roots in the historical discrimination of disabled people during the rise of industrialism. The model suggests that disability is a result of a loss or limitation of function or some other defect. It served to separate individuals with disabilities from society and prevented them from being a burden on the wider society (Thomas and Smith, 2009: 8). The treatment of disability has typically been that they 'ought' to be non-disabled and should be 'physically whole'. Research relating to the human body and sport has traditionally been found in the sciences, such as anatomy, kinesiology, biomechanics and physiology (Promis *et al.*, 2001: 39). Within these areas the general view has been that, 'any divergence resulting in negative cognitive, physical, or sensory abilities when compared to those of a mundane population norm results in a person who will necessarily be disadvantaged' (Koch, 2005: 123).

As a result of the growing dissatisfaction amongst political campaigners with the medical definition, the social model was introduced which argues that increasing societal barriers serve to exclude disabled people from mainstream society (Oliver, 2013). Professor Jacobus tenBroek made significant contributions to the early development of the social model of disability (Stein and Lord, 2007: 170). He argued that physical limitations of a disabled individual have far less to do with their ability to participate in society than did factors concerning public attitude, most of which were misconceived (Stein and Lord, 2007: 170). This shift aided the development of significant policy changes by governments as discussed in the next chapter.

The social model symbolises a prominent shift from the medical approach. Disability is now viewed as something which one may become as a result of the environmental concerns which surround them, rather than something which someone is by definition. It is now a 'socio-cultural construction rather than natural kinds or given states of being' (Van Hilvoorde and Landeweerd, 2010: 3). It is suggested that disability should be viewed on a spectrum rather than understood in the narrow and limited constraints of either model. This approach has also been criticised for its value and relevance in the context of the modern world (Oliver, 2013). An alternative model, which includes elements of both concepts, may be more suitable (Condry, 2008).

The conceptual tensions are reflected in the continual social problems of integration which disabled individuals face and there still remain disparities in areas of human activity. Human differences in ability can cause practical problems of integration, which has been accounted for by making reasonable accommodations or adjustments to society. What is consistent throughout these definitions of disability is the strength of focus on the concept of normality and a disabled individual's lack of ability to carry out 'normal' activities. Individuals with disabilities are evaluated in relation to their 'functional ability to carry out the routine tasks of everyday life' (Nixon, 2007: 419). It would appear that any individual with a perceived disability is forced to find their place within an overriding existing societal structure that is based upon traditional and evolved norms and expectations of how a human should appear and what they should be capable of achieving. It is fair to say that we live in a world which is 'primarily built around standards of normality' (Van Hilvoorde and Landeweerd, 2008: 98). Within that world, we typically design life for the average human being. Society and evolution is framed around the ideology of 'normalcy' (Koch, 2005: 128).

Normalcy is achieved through cultural hegemony, where 'a capitalist culture's most powerful economic groups obtain consent for their leadership through the use of ideological norms. Social structures and relationships which help the powerful but disadvantage those on margins are presented as "natural" ' (Hardin and Hardin *in* Gilbert and Schantz, 2008: 25). The concept of normalcy is further exaggerated in elite sports where the process of normalisation greatly differs from everyday life. For instance, in our daily lives, 'there is little reason to qualify people who integrate their prostheses into their lived bodies as impaired' (Van Hilvoorde and Landeweerd, 2010: 2). In sport, however, there is a clear demarcation, which has been brought about through the cultural evolution of segregated sporting competitions, such as the Olympic Games, the Paralympic Games and the Special Olympics.

Race

All human groups belong to the same species of *Homo sapiens*. That said there are undeniable physical and non-physical differences between our appearance and character such as physical appearance and colour of skin, geographical positions and environments, religion and culture, different belief systems and practices, language and behaviour. Some of these differences arise naturally out of mutations or random changes in genes that can alter a characteristic, which can then be inherited. Such differences occur in all species, such as bacteria, plants and animals, and they are all subject to change. Most mutations are not beneficial, since any change in the suitability of an organism to its environment that makes it less likely to survive is not likely to persist in the population. However, over time or distance, environmental conditions change which means that mutations which improve the survival of any animal, including humans, will be selected for if they are now beneficial. Since environmental changes are unlikely to be the same in all areas of a species' range, selection pressures will be different, leading to a gradual divergence in behaviour or appearance in semi-isolated populations.

Race has been conceptualised over time and through different cultures, as a means of explaining how these differences have been formed. The Darwinist biological position asserts that race is not fixed by these differences and instead species adapt to their surroundings through natural selection. For instance, our genetic make up, skeletal frame and skin colour has been determined by our evolutionary adaptation to the geographical environment, climate and various circumstances. This process of adaptation may have also influenced our cultural values. The biological position also stresses that our likeness is greater than our differences (Bois *in* Back and Solomos, 2000: 105).

Populations have lived together in a number of ways on earth, collectively or diversely. Differences between us are most pronounced by the examples of homogenous groups who live interdependently without breeding. Examples of such large homogenous groups are those referred to as gypsies who are located within Western Europe and the wild tribes located in India and South America (Park *in* Back and Solomos, 2000: 167).

Comparatively, other groups have lived more closely resulting in the dissipation of racial differences. Categories have become less distinct as the culture of inter-mixing has increased and developed. Particularly in the last 400 years the movement of individuals resulting from migration, colonisation, globalisation, industrialisation, commerce and slavery has increased racial amalgamation (Spracklen, 2008: 225).

In this sense, it could be more accurate to use to the concept 'population' rather than race, with race being used as a synonym for subspecies instead. The use of the word race in science is subject to continued debate because of the transient nature of our differences. Other propositions are offered to explain differences between us:

- Many religions attribute our existence as descent from a higher power or the Creator. In some cases physical differences between us as species were then explained as a by-product of an arbitrary action or punishment by the higher power. This created a sense of hierarchy amongst different people such as white supremacy and black inferiority.
- Species as typologies of people, fixed in common characteristics such as Europeans or Africans.
- Differences have been explained by the 'story of man's progress to superior modes of living' (Banton *in* Back and Solomos, 2000: 61), which has led to the inequality of treatment between different groups in society.

- Social scientists argue that difference is brought about by culture, consistent with sex and gender theories. A significant debate which surrounds the construction of race is whether it based upon biological or cultural meaning (Gunaratnam, 2003: 4; Chappell *in* Laker, 2002: 92). Social scientists are often reluctant to accept evolutionary theory as a means of interpreting human affairs and instead refer to it as 'racist' at times (Midgley, 2002: 8). It is evident that race can incorporate both when the actuality of the concept is considered.

Explanations for our racial differences are often entangled, which can lead to the use of the concept of race being confused at times. Race is particularly interesting here because it prompts a consideration of our physical characteristics, just as sport does. In addition, in modern times, race is used for understanding populations and demographics through a census and through gathering equal opportunities data for employment purposes. The accuracy of this analysis is contested since racial diversity in populations has arguably 'made racial categories impossible to sustain in any useful or meaningful sense' (Spracklen, 2008: 225). On this point, it was not until 2001 when the UK Census added the category of mixed race. The general grouping of mixed race identities reveals the complexities of the concept of race particularly as a typology. The suggestion that racial categories lack real meaning is true if this refers to the use of race as a fixed typology. However, when race is used to reflect population differences as explored above, it is a useful identification marker of our species.

The use of the concept becomes problematic when the differences between us are stretched and overgeneralised to apply unequally to entire civilisations. This leads to misguided or false assumptions about groups which can result in unequal treatment. As a result, many contend that 'race is a biological myth based on socially created ideas about variations in human potential and abilities that are assumed to be biological' (Coakley and Pike, 2009: 317). It would appear that biology and cultural explanations of our differences become blurred and prejudice leads to the creation of racial categories which are premised upon stretched biological notions. For instance, historically it was claimed that these categories were connected to varying levels of intellect and ability, thus suggesting that different races were superior (Bell, 2008: 8). The term was used to dictate class and order, usually through white supremacy (Long and McNamee, 2004: 407).

Problems emerge when people do not accept the changing nature of the term race and attempt to explain difference in a linear fashion, in the sense that physical differences explain cultural, value and behavioural differences (Todorov *in* Back and Solomos, 2000: 69). The result of this approach is negative at times and can lead to what is termed 'racism.' Racism as an act or behaviour uses physical and non-physical differences discussed as a reason for treating groups and individuals differently and usually derogatorily, rather than using them to understand and accept differences. It can exist individually, on an everyday level through use of language or behaviour between people, or institutionally, through structures and ideologies (Hylton, 2010: 350; Lusted, 2009: 735; Bell, 2008: 11).

Some argue that racism is an act of 'powerism' since it displays an exertion of power through prejudice (Hylton, 2010: 524; Marks, 2003). However, Long and McNamee (2004: 413) argue that racism exists on a spectrum. They play with the idea that someone may exhibit racist behaviour without being a racist. They create a 'race register' to attempt to chart behaviour which may or may not be considered racist and inexcusable. This portrays the individual nature of racism and highlights that there may be different instances relating to race which cannot necessarily be classed as purely racist. Furthermore, consider the term cultural ignorance where individuals may be unaware or uneducated about particular human differences. Whether ignorance is justifiable or, in the alternative, whether ignorance is classed as racism, is debatable. Behaviour may not itself be racist but may have racist consequences (Long, 2000: 125).

Overall, it is argued that, 'contemporary racism cannot be understood simply as prejudice against individuals on the grounds of their colour' (Fredman, 2002: 53) because the notion is filled with content from different fields such as the sciences, law, history and politics. If used to describe the process of evolutionary and cultural adaptation, then race is a valid construct. However it begins to lack a real objective basis when differences are explained using exaggerated misguided or even false assumptions about entire populations (Winant *in* Back and Solomos, 2000: 678).

Summary

This chapter has explored some of the primary human differences between us and has offered some explanation for the possible variations which exist. The common differences between our sex, gender, race and sometimes disability is attributed to biological and evolutionary processes such as adaptation. This is complemented by or is conflictive with the impact of culture and the environment. Consistent across the four areas is the debate surrounding whether biology or culture determines our human identity. It is rational to assume that a combination of both has shaped the way we are.

Understanding our differences better informs us of the practices of inclusion and exclusion. Differences between us are used as markers for differential treatment and behaviour, notably when our differences tend to move us outside of the usual 'norm.' Such treatment can be the product of stretched, misguided and sometimes false conceptual understandings of our differences.

In defining our sex, gender, disability and race, there is a tendency to understand people as either one thing or the other. Our world is constructed and regulated in this way. This is perhaps the only logical and consistent way of dealing with some activities. However, this chapter has revealed that differences between us are present but are hard to distinguish accurately in such a linear fashion. Instead differences 'actually span a spectrum of natural possibilities' (Cooper, 2010: 235). This creates a conflict between the realities of sex, gender disability and race, and the current linear structures in place in sport and society that serve important purposes for the majority but can lead to issues of inclusion and exclusion for the minorities who are more widely spread across the spectrum. The minorities identified tend to be women, disabled individuals, those who transgress from traditional gender norms and, particular racial groups.

Within sport, our differences are much more pronounced when they are considered in light of sport-specific inclusion and exclusion. Clear definitions of our differences become important when an athlete is being included or excluded on the basis of biological or cultural markers.

References

Archer, J. and Lloyd, B. 2002. *Sex and Gender.* 2nd Edition. Cambridge: Cambridge University Press.

Back, L. and Solomos, J. 2000. *Theories of Race and Racism: a reader.* London: Routledge.

Bell, M. 2008. *Racism and Equality in the European Union.* New York: Oxford University Press.

Buss, D.M. 1995. Evolutionary Psychology: A new paradigm for psychological science. *Psychological Inquiry*, 6(1): 1–30.

Carter, N.M. and Silva, C. 2010. Women in Management: Delusions of Progress. *Harvard Business Review*, March: 19–21.

Coakley, J. and Pike, E. 2009. *Sports in Society, Issues and Controversies.* Maidenhead: McGraw Hill.

Condry, S.N. 2008. *Disability, Sport and the Limits of Law.* M. Phil, University of Stirling, School of Law.

Cooper, E.J. 2010. Gender testing in athletic competitions-human rights violations: why Michael Phelps is praised and Caster Semenya is chastised. *Journal of Gender, Race and Justice*, 14: 233–264.

Cowan, S. 2005. "Gender is no substitute for sex:" A comparative human rights analysis of the legal regulation of sexual identity. *Feminist Legal Studies*, 13: 67–96.

Creswell, T. 1996. *In Place/Out of Place: geography, ideology and transgression.* London: University of Minnesota Press.

Darwin, C. 2008. *On the Origin of Species.* New York: Oxford University Press

Eagly, A.H. 1987. *Sex Differences in Social Behaviour: A social-role interpretation.* Hillsdale, NJ: Erlbaum Publishers.

Eagly, A.H. and Wood, W. 1999. The Origins of Sex Differences in Human Behaviour: evolved dispositions versus social roles. *American Psychologist*, 54(6), June: 408–423.

Eckes, T. and Trautner, H.N. 2000. *The Developmental Social Psychology of Gender*. New Jersey: Lawrence Erlbaum.

Fredman, S. 2002. *Discrimination Law.* Oxford: Oxford University Press.

Geary, D.C. 1998. *Male, Female: the evolution of human sex differences.* Washington, DC: American Psychological Association.

Gilbert, D.T., Fiske, S.T. and Lindzey, G. 1998. *The Handbook of Social Psychology.* 4th Edition, Volume 2. New York: McGraw Hill.

Gilbert, K. and Schantz, O.J. 2008. *The Paralympic Games: empowerment or side show?* Maidenhead: Meyer and Meyer Sport.

Glaister, I.K. 1974. Physical Education: an integrating force? *Report of the ATCDE Physical Education Section Conference.* Held at Chelsea College of Physical Education, Eastbourne.

Gunaratnam, Y. 2003. *Researching 'Race' and Ethnicity: methods, knowledge and power.* London: Sage Publications.

Hartmann-Tews, I. and Pfister, G. 2003. *Sport and Women: social issues in international perspective.* London: Routledge.

Herdt, G. 1994. *Third Sex, Third Gender: beyond sexual dimorphism in culture and history.* New York: Zone Books.

Hylton, K. 2010. How a turn to critical race theory can contribute to our understanding of 'race,' racism and anti-racism in sport. *International Review for the Sociology of Sport*, 45(3): 335–354.

Koch, T. 2005. The Ideology of Normalcy: the ethics of difference. *Journal of Disability Policy Studies*, 16(2): 123–129.

Laker, A. 2002. *The Sociology of Sport and Physical Education.* London: Routledge Falmer.

Laqueur, T.W. 1990. *Making Sex: body and gender from the Greeks to Freud.* Cambridge: Harvard University Press.

Long, J. 2000. No Racism Here: A preliminary examination of sporting innocence. *Managing Leisure* 5(3): 121–133

Long, J.A. and McNamee, M.J. 2004. On the moral economy of racism and racist rationalisations in sport. *International Review for the Sociology of Sport*, 39(4): 405–420.

Lueptow. L.B., Garovich-Szabo. L. and Lueptow, M.B. 2001. Social Change and the Persistence of Sex Typing: 1974-1997. *Social Forces*, September, 80(1): 1–35.

Lusted, J. 2009. Playing games with 'race': understanding resistance to 'race' equality initiatives in English local football governance. *Soccer and Society*, 10(6), November: 722–739.

Marks, J. 2003. *What it means to be 98% Chimpanzee.* London: University of California Press.

Midgley, M. 2002. *Evolution as a Religion.* London: Routledge.

Nixon, H.L. 2007. Constructing Diverse Sports Opportunities for People with Disabilities. *Journal of Sport and Social Issues*, 31(4), November: 417–433.

Oliver, M. 2013. The Social Model of Disability: thirty years on. *Disability and Society*, 28(7): 1024–1026.

Pearlman, L. 1995. Transsexualism as Metaphor: the collision of sex and gender. *Buffalo Law Review*, 43: 835–872.

Promis, D., Erevelles, N. and Matthews, J. 2001. Reconceptualising Inclusion: The Politics of University Sports and Recreations Programs for Students with Mobility Impairments. *Sociology of Sport Journal*, 18: 37–50.

Rehman, J. 2010. *International Human Rights Law.* Harlow, UK: Pearson Longman.

Shy, Y.L.A. 2007. "Like any other girl": male to female transsexuals and professional sports. *Sports Lawyers Journal*, 14: 95–110.

Spracklen, K. 2008. The Holy Blood and the Holy Grail: myths of scientific racism and the pursuit of excellence in sport. *Leisure Studies*, 27(2), April: 221–227.

Stein, M.A. and Lord, J.E. 2007. Jacobus tenBroek, Participatory Justice, and the UN Convention on the Rights of Persons with Disabilities. *Texas Journal on Civil Liberties and Civil Rights*, 167: 167–185.

Thomas, N. and Smith, A. 2009. *Disability, Sport and Society: an introduction.* London: Routledge.

Van Hilvoorde, I and Landeweerd, L. 2008. Disability or Extraordinary Talent – Francesco Lentini (three legs) Versus Oscar Pistorius (no legs). *Sport, Ethics and Philosophy*, 2(2): 97–111.

Van Hilvoorde, I and Landeweerd, L. 2010. Enhancing disabilities: transhumanism under the veil of inclusion? *Disability and Rehabilitation*, pp. 1–6.

Waldemar, B. 1988. *The spirit and the flesh; sexual diversity in American Indian culture* Boston, MA: Beacon Press.

Whittle, S. 2002. *Respect and Equality – Transsexual and Transgender Rights.* London: Cavendish Publishing.

World Health Organization (WHO) 1980. *The International Classification of Impairments, Disability and Handicap.* Geneva: WHO.

3 The regulation of inclusion and exclusion

This chapter aims to critically examine key policy, law and sport measures that operate to regulate inclusion and exclusion. The measures will be set against a background of distinct theoretical approaches which can be adapted to the regulation of equality and sport. In doing so, discussion will centre around 'mapping law' in order to better understand the nature of law in a broad sense, but more specifically in sport (Twining, 2000: 136; de Sousa Santos, 2002: 417).

The relationship between sport and the law is well documented by experts in the field of sports law particularly (Gardiner *et al.*, 2012). Sports governing bodies have a general tendency to regard the involvement of the law as a potential threat to the special essence of sport. Instead internal sports regulation is favoured, using a complex network of normative rules such as the rules of the game, administrative rules, unwritten customs, values and cultures that influence the rules of the sport and codes of ethics (Gardiner *et al.*, 2012: 73). These are not legally binding but have practical effects (Harlow and Rawlings, 2009: 192). This chapter will identify the impact of this autonomy on the regulation of inclusion and exclusion in sport and the protection of equality principles.

Policy measures

Persistent inequalities and patterns of social exclusion amongst minority and marginalised groups are being addressed through the enactment of legislation and implementation of government policies. These political strategies and agendas seek to achieve and promote social inclusion. For instance, in Britain social inclusion became significant within social policy following the election of the Labour government in 1997 (Thomas and Smith, 2009: 58).

Social exclusion agendas were firmly embedded within policies for sport, since sport has been widely used to assist in the delivery of important community, health, and welfare outcomes particularly for minority groups. It is believed that sport and leisure acts as a way of accessing and integrating poorer communities into British society through its contribution to social and community cohesion (Gratton and Henry, 2001: 189; SEU, 2001: 130). In terms of achieving social inclusion, sport is also perceived as a neutral ground in which individuals can compete equally.

The New Labour commitment to 'Sport for All' reinforced the promotion of sports participation to assist in social inclusion benefits (Department for Culture, Media and Sport [DCMS], 2002). The perception of sport as a solution to social concerns are considered part of a wider 'functionalist perspective' which contends that institutions, such as sport, have a special function in society (Elling *et al.*, 2003: 415). It is strongly contended that these are presumed outcomes of sport participation, which are not always achieved (Coalter, 2007: 9). Particularly at a competitive level, there are many undesirable consequences of such influential power, such as cheating, violence and discriminatory practices.

Equality policies within sport have been visible for a number of years, with formal documents emerging in the 1990s (Collins, 2014; Houlihan and Lindsey, 2013). The political agenda to use sport to deliver major government objectives, contributed towards this influx of equality promises within sport in the UK. Key changes in discrimination legislation (see below) also led to this development.

Sport governing bodies and organisations tend to demonstrate their commitment to equality and non-discrimination in the form of a plethora of documents outlining their position on sports equity (Lusted, 2014). It is suggested that sport policies in England have adopted a 'top-down' approach, which is dictated by the DCMS, Sport England, and UK Sport (Lusted 2014; Collins, 2014). For instance, the UK Sport commitment to equality is outlined in the Equality & Diversity Strategy, Policy and Action Plan 2010 (UK Sport, 2014). These policies are then transferred to governing bodies such as the FA who in 2012 introduced their Inclusion and Anti-Discrimination Action Plan for addressing discrimination in English football and achieving a better level of inclusion (The FA, 2012). A range of equality policies specific to sex and gender, disability and race, exist within each sport and will be explored in Part II.

However, the relevance and effectiveness of these initiatives are debated and criticised as being slow and rhetorical (Lusted, 2014). It is argued that they have achieved very little in terms of practical reform. Even for Nordic countries, who are considered to be leaders in gender equality in sport, it is argued that 'gender equality as a political endeavour in sport is sometimes ambiguous and contradictory' and has had limited impact upon the culturally rooted gender regime in sport (Larsson *in* Hargreaves and Anderson, 2014: 226). In the UK, whilst some progress has been made, resources for active change are restricted. It is suggested that without legal intervention, there has to be an acceptance that not all of these ideas will be implemented (Collins, 2014: 269).

Law measures

In everyday language, the idea of inclusion is a liberalistic concept, in which priority is given to the 'right' of an individual. A right is considered to be a 'moral or legal entitlement that others are duty bound to respect' (Donnelly and Kidd, 2006). In this context, social groups or collective bodies should give due consideration and respect to individual rights (Heywood, 2003: 30). In order to overcome disproportionate treatment on the basis of human differences, the law incorporates and embraces the idea that people should be treated equally and enjoy fundamental rights.

The level or type of equality which should be protected and encouraged by the law is surrounded by philosophical debate. For instance, formal equality, or 'symmetrical equality' (Fenwick, 1998: 507) is based upon the principle that like should be treated as like to uphold values of formal justice and individualism (Connolly, 2011: 5). This has been criticised on the basis that it serves to preserve the status quo within society, rather than taking into account the social contexts within which individuals and groups operate.

Substantive equality then, is a development or revision of this model. It is premised on the idea of equality of opportunity and equality of results and gives more specific meaning to equality by recognising the social context of imbalances, differences of situations between individuals and groups, differences of market situations and historical differences (Fenwick, 1998: 508). Substantive equality places responsibility upon the dominant group to bear the cost of discriminatory practices.

The principle of equality is found within the rule of law. This is a phrase commonly given to special virtues of a legal system (Finnis, 2011: 270). Whilst the rule of law is a globally accepted concept, definitions vary according to culture, geography and values (Heckman *et al.*, 2010). The rule of law assists in the promotion of fair decisions and restraining the abuse of power. The central tenets of the rule of law at least include that law must be transparent, clear, stable and applied to everyone according to its terms, and courts should be independent (Tamanaha *in* Palombella and Walker, 2009: 3). Those who have the authority to create and apply the rules should do so in an official capacity, are accountable for their compliance to the rules and administer the law consistently. Dicey (1959: 187) interpreted the British rule of law to include three concepts:

1 No man is above the law.
2 Equality before the law.
3 The principles of the constitution are the consequence of the rights of individuals as defined and enforced by the courts.

Given the importance of equality as a foundation of law, it is considered a protectable legal right. The principles of equality and non-discrimination form part of the emphasis on human dignity which underpins the entire structure of modern human rights regimes. Human rights refer to 'those inalienable rights that all individuals possess according to natural law, and which must not be removed through any kind of social exchange' (McArdle and Giulianotti, 2006: 2). Fundamental rights (human rights or natural rights) refer to rights that human beings hold, prior to their recognition by a legal system, or despite their denial by a legal system (Jackson and Leopold, 2001: 13). The rights of individuals are laid down in equality legislation.

The sources of human rights law and mechanisms for protection are commonly classified as international (universal non-discrimination principles introduced by the United Nations (UN) and developed through a regime of subsequent conventions, declarations and supporting instruments), regional (Europe, Central and South America, Africa and Asia who operate varying human rights regimes) and domestic (the interpretation of international and regional principles by individual governments and the enactment of human rights legislation by the law makers of each country). These levels broadly capture the diverse network and operation of equality law across the world (De Schutter, 2010).

International level

International law is distinct from other national legal systems because there is an absence of sovereign authority that enforces decisions (Rehman, 2010: 18). It possesses *sui generis* characteristics because it places obligations upon the States which binds them to respect the principles of the law and assume certain duties in order to fulfil the human rights provisions.

The Charter of the United Nations was adopted in 1945 and expressed the protection of human rights and fundamental freedoms as its central organisational objectives. The global human rights movement was strengthened by the adoption of the Universal Declaration of Human Rights 1948 (UDHR) by the UN General Assembly. As the foundation of international human rights law, it was the first instrument which set out internationally accepted basic civil, political, economic, social and cultural rights for all human beings. It serves as a framework for the enactment of a wide body of legally enforceable global human rights instruments which have translated the concepts of the document into law through the formation of treaties, principles, agreements or conventions at a domestic, regional and international level of governance.

The rights covered by the UDHR represent a common standard of achievement for encouraging and promoting respect of particular rights and freedoms which all people should be able to enjoy. The Declaration consists of 30 articles covering a range of civil, political, economic, social and cultural rights which apply universally to every person 'without distinction of any kind, such as race, colour, sex, language, religion, political or other opinion, national or social origin, property, birth or other status' (Article 2 UDHR).

At the time of its creation the UDHR was not intended to be a legally binding document. However, the preamble to the document clearly emphasises the need to protect human rights through the rule of law. An obvious obligation is to protect individuals and groups from human right breaches and to refrain from interfering in the enjoyment of human rights. Positive actions must be taken to facilitate the enjoyment of basic human rights (UN, 2011).

Some of the provisions contained in the instrument have been customarily included into international law and general principles of law. For instance, international courts have referred to, and applied the UDHR and domestic courts have relied on the provisions in a number of human rights cases (Baderin and Ssenyonjo, 2010: 9).

The objective of using the UDHR as a springboard to treaties was achieved by the introduction of the International Covenant on Civil and Political Rights

(ICCPR), and the International Covenant on Economic, Social and Cultural Rights (ICESCR), which came into force in 1976. As a three, these documents represent the International Bill of Rights. These have further developed the rights of the UDHR and have made them legally enforceable on the States who have ratified them. The body of provisions which stem from the UDHR reinforces the proposition that a 'transnational *jus commune* of human rights' has been built as a result of the cross references between international, regional and domestic courts who interpret the different provisions that share a common language with the UDHR (De Schutter, 2010: 31).

The United Nations Educational, Scientific and Cultural Organisation (UNESCO) is a special branch of the UN and promotes dialogue between civilisations, cultures and people to achieve global visions of sustainable development encompassing observance of human rights, mutual respect and the alleviation of poverty (UNESCO, 2014). They also conduct significant work in the fight against discrimination, using sport as a vehicle for change.

Many of the human rights articles contain limitation clauses indicating that a right is not absolute and should be adapted to meet a State's interest in protecting public safety, order, health or morals or national security. The exercise of human rights are sometimes subject to the 'common good' (Finnis, 2011: 218) as Article 29(2) UDHR indicates. Limitations serve to balance inclusion and exclusion in society and ensure that the application of human rights is reasonable and practicable.

The application of human rights legislation to sport is rather uncertain at an international level because specific references to sport are absent from the provisions. For instance, Article 24 UDHR recognises that everyone has the right to rest and leisure. This does not necessarily encompass competitive sport. Article 27(1) UDHR recognises the right to participate in the cultural life of the community which again implies recreational activity.

The UDHR has influenced the establishment of a range of human rights instruments in the areas of sex, gender, disability and race. A number of ancillary international instruments support the International Bill of Rights and provide specific protection for minorities within these groups.

For instance, the UN has demonstrated a strong commitment to the promotion of women and their empowerment and has become leading advocates for women and equality through its main legislative bodies (Kluka, 2008: 25). The Convention on the Elimination of All Forms of Discrimination Against Women 1979 (CEDAW) was adopted to establish an international bill of rights for women as well as an agenda for action by countries who guarantee equality between men and women. Article 10(g) CEDAW makes reference to the same opportunities for men and women to participate in sport.

States who have accepted this Convention are legally bound to undertake a series of measures to eliminate discrimination against women in all forms. They are also committed to submit national reports on measures taken to comply with their treaty obligations. Conventions are binding law and there will be a process of enforcement for those who violate the terms of the Convention.

Supplementing this, the Brighton Declaration on Women and Sport 1994 aimed to address how to accelerate the process of change which would redress the imbalances women face in their participation and involvement in sport. The Brighton Declaration 'enlarged and coordinated the global debate on women and sport' (Kluka, 2008: 50). However, declarations are moral commitments made by signatories, they are not binding law.

The Yogyakarta Principles 2006 are a set of principles protecting sexual orientation and gender identity. The principles aim to ensure that binding international legal standards apply to sex and gender. They affirm the primary obligation of States to implement human rights and provide guidance for each principle on how to achieve this. No specific reference is made to sport but Principle 25 confirms that every citizen has the right to 'have equal access to all levels of public service and employment in public functions…without discrimination on the basis of sexual orientation or gender identity.' Principle 26 supports the right to cultural participation as introduced in Article 27(1) UDHR.

The Convention on the Rights of Persons with Disabilities 2006 (CRPD) was the first to specifically protect the rights of persons with disabilities. It aims to promote, protect and ensure the full and equal enjoyment of all human rights and fundamental freedoms by all persons with disabilities, and to promote respect for their inherent dignity (Article 1). Section 30(5) specifically protects the rights of people with disabilities to actively participate in sport, recreation, play and leisure.

To reaffirm that discrimination between human beings on the grounds of race, colour or ethnic origin is inconsistent with the ideals of any human society, the UN adopted the International Convention on the Elimination of All Forms of Racial Discrimination (ICERD) in 1969. The Convention aims to encourage States to adopt all necessary measures for the elimination of racial discrimination in all its forms and manifestations, and to prevent and combat racist doctrines and practices in order to promote understanding between races and to build an international community free from all forms of racial segregation and racial discrimination. Although no specific reference to sport is made, Article 5(e) seeks to protect the enjoyment of economic, social and cultural rights, with specific reference to the rights to work and the right to equal participation in cultural activities.

Regional level

Regional structures for the protection of human rights have assisted in the development and realisation of human rights at a grassroots level. They seek to provide a middle ground between the State and domestic institutions and the international system which is unable to deal with individual victims of human rights breaches (Shelton, 2008). It therefore fills a gap in the global system of human rights and offers a better balance.

Members of the Council of Europe are required to be signatories to the ECHR and to abide by its rights and protective provisions. Where individual complaints have not been remedied at a domestic level, they may be referred to the European Court of Human Rights (ECtHR), who are ultimately the guardians of the ECHR provisions.

Substantive Convention rights which are relevant in the context of elite sports participation include the right to private life (Article 8) and the right to possessions (Article 1 of Protocol 1). Article 14 ECHR guarantees freedom from discrimination and can be used in conjunction with such substantive rights to turn what would not normally be a violation of rights into one in cases where unjustifiable discrimination of any kind has occurred.

Whilst some of the rights are protected absolutely, the State is able to restrict most in certain circumstances, provided that this restriction is 'necessary in a democratic society' for the protection of one of the aims laid out in the Article concerned. Applying the necessity test is very much a case of analysing proportionality (Kumm *in* Pavlakos, 2007: 132). The doctrine of proportionality demands that the restriction must not go beyond what is necessary. It is a case of balancing to what extent a limitation on one's personal rights cross the line from being a necessary action in pursuit of a legitimate aim, to that of a measure which disproportionately infringes one's right. Member States are afforded a margin of appreciation when interpreting that balance since the role of the Convention in protecting human rights, is considered as 'subsidiary' to the roles of national legal systems (Fenwick, 2007: 36; Harris *et al.*, 2009: 350). However, this margin will be relatively small in certain areas.

Complementing the ECHR is the Council of Europe European Social Charter 1961 (ESC). It is a tool which guarantees social and economic rights and establishes supervisory mechanisms guaranteeing their respect by the State parties. The European Committee of Social Rights guards the ESC and monitors how compliant countries have been (Council of Europe, 2012b).

In the European Union, human rights provisions were previously absent from Community treaties. However, the European Court of Justice (ECJ) has since elevated the status of the ECHR, which is reflected further by Article 6 of the Treaty of Lisbon 2009 (TEU) (Foster, 2011: 123). Article 6(2) and 6(3) TEU states that the EU shall accede to the ECHR and that the general principles of the ECHR shall constitute general principles of EU law. Article 6(1) TEU gives full legal status to the Charter of Fundamental Rights of the EU. Established in 2000, this is first formal EU document listing civil, political, economic and social rights to which EU citizens should be entitled to. The Charter enhances the visibility of these rights within the EU and has played a significant part in transforming the culture and practice of the European institutions (De Schutter, 2010: 26). Equality principles are also recognised in Article 2 and 8 TEU.

The principle of non-discrimination is broadly recognised by Article 19 of the Treaty of the Functioning of the European Union (TFEU), which states that the Council may take appropriate action to combat discrimination based on sex, racial or ethnic origin, religion or belief, disability, age or sexual orientation. A number of articles specifically cater for the prohibition of discrimination on the grounds of nationality (Article 18 TFEU), sex (Article 157 TFEU) and free movement of workers (Article 45(2) TFEU). A range of secondary legislation, such as the Equal Treatment Directive 2006/54, The Framework Employment Directive 2000/78, Equal Treatment Between Men and Women in Access to and the Supply of Goods and Services Directive 2004/113 and the Race Equality Directive 2000/43, support this (Foster, 2011: 397).

In other regions of the world such as the USA, the Organisation of American States (OAS) have adopted two similar human rights provisions, The American Declaration of the Rights and Duties of Man (1948) and the American Convention on Human Rights (1970). The Inter-American Commission on Human Rights has a quasi-judicial function and is the first to hear the cases concerning human rights violations. Cases can then be referred to the Inter-American Court of Human Rights for a legally binding judgement.

At the regional level, little human rights case law relating to sport exists. In a doping case in 2009 two Belgian tennis players challenged the legality of the World Anti-Doping Agency (WADA) whereabouts rule at the ECtHR and the European Commission (EC) (Anon, 2009a; Anon, 2009b; Court of Arbitration for Sport [CAS], 2009). The challenge was to be brought under Article 8 ECHR, which acknowledges the right to respect for private life. The case was however withdrawn on procedural grounds, leaving the relationship between sport and human rights at this level underdeveloped.

Domestic level

The international system of human rights tends to ensure that domestic States fulfil their obligations by 'observing national law (constitutional or statutory) that is consistent with the international norms, or making the international norms themselves part of the national legal and political order' (Steiner, Alston and Goodman, 2007: 1087). An example of the domestic internalisation of human rights treaties which seek to protect human rights is the UK Human Rights Act (HRA) 1998, which recognises the rights of the ECHR as an integral part of domestic law. The HRA gives effect to the ECHR by imposing an obligation on public authorities to comply with Convention rights. This is not necessarily the case in all domestic States and a number of factors influence how effectively international human rights are absorbed, such as the absence of a human rights culture.

The UK courts have also accepted the principle of proportionality when interpreting Convention rights, to ensure that a restriction or objective pursues a legitimate aim, the measure designed to meet the objective is rationally connected to it and the restriction does not go beyond what is necessary (*de Freitas v Permanent Secretary of Ministry of Agriculture* [1999] 1 AC 69).

The accountability of sports bodies under the UK HRA is narrow since s. 6(1) HRA confirms that it only applies to public authorities. Whilst the UK courts have considered that sports bodies may be quasi or hybrid public authorities, that is, private bodies which exercise public functions, the position remains limited and narrow (Boyes, 2000). No cases have concerned challenges to inclusion/exclusion practices in sport.

Domestic anti-discrimination laws are commonly organised by sex, gender, disability and race in countries such as Australia (Federal and State Laws) and previously in the UK. The enactment of the UK Equality Act 2010 (EA) consolidates and repeals previous legislation in specific areas including the Sex Discrimination Act 1975, the Race Relations Act 1976, the Disability Discrimination Act 1995 and the Gender Recognition Act 2004 (GRA). The protected characteristics under the EA include disability, gender reassignment, race, sex, age, marriage and civil partnership, pregnancy and maternity, religion or belief and sexual orientation. The provisions of the EA are largely the same as previous legislation and include direct and indirect discrimination, harassment and victimisation. In addition, the Act recognises the existence of combined discrimination for those with dual characteristics under s. 14 EA. However, the UK EA contains an exemption clause for sporting activities under s.195:

(1) A person does not contravene this Act, so far as relating to sex, only by doing anything in relation to the participation of another as a competitor in a gender-affected activity.
(2) A person does not contravene section 29, 33, 34 or 35, so far as relating to gender reassignment, only by doing anything in relation to the participation of a transsexual person as a competitor in a gender-affected activity if it is necessary to do so to secure in relation to the activity:
    (a) fair competition, or
    (b) the safety of competitors.
(3) A gender-affected activity is a sport, game or other activity of a competitive nature in circumstances in which the physical strength, stamina or physique of average persons of one sex would put them at a disadvantage compared to average persons of the other sex as competitors in events involving the activity.
(4) In considering whether a sport, game or other activity is gender-affected in relation to children, it is appropriate to take account of the age and stage of development of children who are likely to be competitors.

This is consistent with some of the exemption provisions under the Australian anti-discrimination laws contained in the Sex Discrimination Act 1984 (s. 42(1)) and the Equal Opportunities Act 1995 (s. 66(1)). The exemption attempts to balance the rights of the individual against the essence of sport.

In the USA the Civil Rights Act 1964 was a landmark piece of legislation which outlawed racial segregation for African Americans. It has been influential in promoting equality in the National Football League (NFL) in the USA. Title VIII of the Act prohibits employment discrimination in the work place and this extends to private employers. With the threat of legal action under Title VIII, in 2002 the NFL adopted an affirmative action programme and introduced the Rooney Rule. The policy requires all NFL teams to interview at least one ethnic minority candidate when recruiting for senior coaching positions. Failure to comply with the rule results in a severe financial penalty. The Rooney Rule has advanced racial equality in the league and positively altered the diversity of the management composition.

The Americans with Disabilities Act (ADA) 1990 covers equal access and inclusion for individuals with disabilities. Within Title III the prohibition of discrimination requires owners and operators of facilities of public accommodation, to 'make reasonable modifications in policies, practices, or procedures, when such modifications are necessary to afford such goods, services, facilities, privileges, advantages, or accommodations to individuals with disabilities' (s. 42). The US ADA has advanced the social rights of participation in sport and recreation, particularly in the context of opening up public accommodations to meaningful participation (Lord and Stein, 2009: 278). The ADA is liberally construed to accomplish its purpose of deconstructing discriminatory barriers to allow disabled individuals with equal access to society (Liguori, 2003: 217).

In relation to sex, the passing by Congress of the legislation known as section 901 of Title IX of the Education Amendments Act 1972 prohibits sex discrimination in educational institutions in the USA. The provision withdraws federal funding from educational institutions if they are found to violate Title IX. By tackling discrimination in education and by enabling boys and girls to compete together and equally in most sports, it has served as a vehicle for women to pursue equality and oppose institutionalised sexism. This law is considered to be the centrepiece of US legislation relating to women in sport and equal opportunities. The case law which has emanated from these provisions will be explored in Part II.

Sport regulation measures

Sports law, that is, the relationship between law and sport, is an area of distinct debate and interest (Foster *in* Greenfield and Osborn, 2000: 268). At the one end exists the interventionist model which is based upon the idea that 'sport is a public function that the State has the right and the responsibility to deliver' through the enforcement of legislation (Lewis and Taylor, 2008: 5). Edward Grayson argues that the 'rule of law in sport is as essential for civilisation as the rule of law in society generally. Without it generally anarchy reigns. Without it in sport, chaos exists' (Grayson *in* Gardiner *et al.*, 2012: 70).

By contrast, the model of non-intervention and autonomy is one where sport is considered to be a self-regulating private sphere, which is immune from government responsibility (Harlow and Rawlings, 2009: 235; 239). The sophistication of the internal regulation of sport has begun to blur the boundaries between formal law and normative rules of sport, leading to the suggestion in the literature that a distinct discipline of 'sports law' has emerged (Davis *in* Siekmann and Soek, 2012: 1).

The models of regulation offered in the literature vary across a spectrum and their justifications for autonomy and self-regulation in sport are diverse. Foster presents different models for regulating sport, ranging from a 'pure market model', which advocates for a 'laissez-faire minimum interference to protect commercial interests', to the 'Socio-Cultural Model', which argues for supervised autonomy with constitutional safeguards in place to protect sports values with due process (*in* Greenfield and Osborn, 2000: 268).

Within the debate, each theorist adopts different typologies to describe levels of regulation within sport. Considerable attention has been paid to whether sport is operating and behaving in a global and autonomous way, thus creating a *lex sportiva* (Boyes, 2012; James, 2010; Foster, 2003; Beloff *et al.*, 1999; Mitten and Opie, 2010; Foster, 2006: 2; Foster *in* Siekmann and Soek, 2012: 241; Erbsen *in* Siekmann and Soek, 2012: 108; Nafziger *in* Siekmann and Soek, 2012: 66; Foster, 2006). The models of sport regulation tend to be focused upon the autonomy of sports governing bodies and the notion of self-regulation particularly in the context of disciplinary processes and commercial issues. Within these models, due attention is not paid to values concerning inclusion, human rights and equality, as we are concerned with here.

Broadly speaking, whether there is a distinct body of sports law or whether it is instead the application of general legal principles to sport, is not of great importance, and yet not of no importance either (Beloff, 2005: 49; Gardiner *et al.*, 2012: 85). We are concerned with a slightly different matter, which is how inclusion and exclusion can be regulated by sport and the law in a way that protects sporting values whilst at the same time giving due respect to societal values and human rights. The position here is that the law can act in a complementary manner to sport regulation in order to promote these values and provide a balance between inclusion and exclusion. What follows is an overview of the current domestic, regional (EU) and international sport regulation tools available to address inclusion and exclusion factors, exploring their mechanics and relevance to inclusion and exclusion (also used by Smith, 2011).

Domestic sports regulation

At this level of regulation there are clear tensions surrounding the public or private nature of the decision-making processes of sports governing bodies and whether they are subject to national law (Ellson and Lohn, 2005). This problem is also raised above in the context of the application of human rights legislation to sport.

For instance, some southern and eastern European States operate a more interventionist role, where sporting activity is considered to be a public responsibility and therefore subject to the rule of law (Parrish and Miettinen, 2008: 11). In France, a legal framework of sports codes provide for the regulation of sporting activity (James, 2010: 8; Lewis and Taylor, 2008: 5). In Portugal, the Sports Act 30/2004 consigns the fundamental principles of the most significant aspects of sport (Meirim, 2004). In Canada, the Physical Activity and Sport Act 2003 illustrates the government involvement in the delivery of sport.

In comparison, a non-interventionist role is taken in the UK where sport is not regarded as a public service and instead considered to be 'private' in legal terms (Boyes, 2000). In the UK, if an individual wishes to challenge the decisions or actions of a sports governing body, such as those which effect the inclusion or exclusion of an individual, the courts have determined legal intervention on the basis of whether the sporting activity is considered public or private and whether the decision or action concerns a commercial or non-commercial right. It is fair to say that the legal avenues available in the UK are rather limited, particularly in relation to a non-commercial challenge relating to inclusion and exclusion.

Instead, the courts appear to adopt a common law supervisory role and are prepared to establish a contractual relationship between the national governing body and the participant (*Modahl v British Athletic Federation Ltd* (No 2) [2002] 1 WLR 1192). The courts in the UK are also willing to engage the doctrine of restraint of trade to examine the rules and regulations laid down by sports governing bodies (*Nordenfelt v Maxim Nordenfelt Guns and Ammunition Co Ltd* [1894] AC 535). This is applicable where the actions or decisions of a sports body have had the effect of restricting the individual's ability to earn a living. There are limits to these seemingly positive routes, however, since they do not tend to apply to equality and infringement of fundamental rights.

EU sports regulation

A widely recognised model of sport regulation is the application of EU law to sporting activity. At this level, the broader relationship between sport and the law has been given detailed consideration. Given sports commercial enterprise and contribution to EU revenue, its rules and regulations must be created and applied in accordance with Community rules, which involves a careful balance. The ECJ has previously held that 'sport is subject to Community law only in so far as it constitutes an economic activity' (*Walrave and Koch v Association Union Cycliste Internationale* (Case 36/74) [1974] ECR 1405, para. 4). This position places rules which are of 'purely sporting interest' (Case, para. 8) outside the scope of EC law. It led to the creation of what is regarded as the 'sporting exception' and implied that the Commission were very mindful of the 'special nature' of sport (Parrish *et al.*, 2010: 61). However, the ECJ position produced uncertainty about what constitutes a purely sporting rule (Weatherill, 2006: 645).

Consequently, in *Meca-Medina and Majcen v Commission* (Case C-519/04 P) [2006] ECR I-699, the ECJ rejected the notion that there is any such sporting exception which places the rules of sport outside law:

> "The mere fact that a rule is purely sporting in nature does not have the effect of removing from the scope of the Treaty the person engaging in the activity governed by that rule or the body which has laid it down.
>
> (Case, para. 27)

The ECJ highlighted that it is difficult to divide the sporting aspect and economic aspect of sporting rules (Weatherill, 2006: 647). That said, the court accepted the special nature of sport by placing the onus on sports governing bodies to prove that the rule in question is necessary to the organisation of the sport, pursued a legitimate aim proportionately and is inherent in the pursuit of that sports objectives (Miettinen and Parrish, 2007). This assessment will be made on a case-by-case basis and potentially leaves informal and more culturally justified rules subject to challenge (Rincon 2007: 236; Parrish *et al.*, 2010: 61).

Although the distinction between economic and non-economic activity may well continue, it is submitted that the sporting exception has evolved to describe a more-sensitive application of EC law to sport (Parrish and Mietinnen, 2008: 73). This approach is aligned with current EU provisions. Following the ratification of the Lisbon Treaty in 2009 and subsequent amendments to the TFEU, Article 6 and Article 165 TFEU provides the EU with soft law competence to act in support of, to coordinate and to supplement the actions of member States in the field of sport (James, 2010: 11). The EU will give due attention to whether EU law should apply to the operation of a rule in a particular context or whether, as a result of the specificity of sport, the rule should be exempted (James, 2010: 14).

This is reinforced by the EC publication of the White Paper on Sport in 2007, the most comprehensive and substantial statement to date of the sports policies of the EU. This is not a legally binding document but makes a significant contribution to the discussion of the applicability of law to sport. The White Paper addresses sport through its social, economic and organisational dimension. The Commission believes that it can play a role in encouraging the sharing of best practice in sport governance through the development of a common set of principles for good governance such as transparency, democracy, accountability and representation of stakeholders (EC, 2007: 12). The 2011 European Commission Communication Document entitled 'Developing the European Dimension in Sport' builds upon these visions further (EC, 2011).

Consistent with the socio-cultural approach taken by the EU, the White Paper and the Communications Document does make specific references to sex, gender, disability and race when discussing the social value of sport. However, these are largely tackled from a 'social inclusionary' level. The White Paper proposes that sport should be accessible to all at a recreational level at least.

The organisational dimension is focused on the concept of specificity. The White Paper offers a definition (EC, 2007: 13):

> The specificity of sporting activities and of sporting rules, such as separate competitions for men and women, limitations on the number of participants in competitions, or the need to ensure uncertainty concerning outcomes and to preserve a competitive balance between clubs taking part in the same competitions.

Broadly speaking, the definition provides recognition at the EU level that sporting activity possesses elements of distinctiveness. The Communications Document reinforces the importance of the specificity of sport when evaluating the compliance of sport with EU law (EC, 2011: 10). It is, however, clear on its position that 'good governance is a condition for the autonomy and self-regulation of sport organisations' (EC, 2011: 10). Any derogation from the requirements of EU law must be in the pursuit of legitimate objectives and that any restriction must also be proportionate.

The sport-specific definitions of inclusion and exclusion also recognise the special nature of sport particularly in relation to its essence, which is to separate athletes on the basis of their human capacities and differences in order to promote competition and match ability. How the EU view of specificity balances against the fundamental rights of athletes will be addressed in the forthcoming chapters. The White Paper offers a broader consideration of sports issues beyond economic activities, which may offer scope for inclusion and exclusion. It seeks to commit to better regulation in this area by attempting to balance the special features of sport with central legal principles (Weatherill *in* Gardiner, Parrish and Siekmann, 2009: 101).

International sports regulation

At the international level exists sport tribunals such as CAS and the FIFA Dispute Resolution Chamber, the global anti-doping body WADA and international sports federations (ISF) instruments such as the Olympic Charter, which each demonstrate the potential capacity to deal with aspects of inclusion and exclusion.

The Court of Arbitration for Sport

Most of the ISFs now allow appeals from their own disciplinary tribunals or dispute resolution chambers to CAS. Established in 1983 by the IOC, CAS is now an independent and impartial arbitral tribunal which conducts *de novo* reviews of the rules, interpretation and application of the IOC and other ISF which impact upon an athlete's eligibility to participate in the Olympics and other international sports competitions (Mitten and Davis, 2008: 74). Based in Lausanne, Switzerland, CAS 'ensures uniform procedural rules, provides a stable legal framework, and facilitates efficient dispute resolution in locations convenient for the parties' (Mitten and Opie, 2010: 287). CAS arguably balances the integrity of athletic competition against the protection of athletes' legitimate rights (Mitten and Davis, 2008: 79).

The CAS code offers broad jurisdiction to hear any dispute or activity related or connected to sport, although most of the disputes tend to be commercial and disciplinary in nature (CAS, 2012; James, 2010: 56). When examining rules of an ISF, CAS assess whether they are reasonably being applied, are lawfully interpreted and that any penalties imposed are necessary, reasonable and proportionate (James, 2010: 56).

CAS is not an international court of law but instead an arbitration tribunal whose broad jurisdiction and authority is based upon the agreement of the parties (Mitten and Opie, 2010: 285). Through the adoption of the Swiss Federal Code on Private International Law, CAS agree to resolve disputes pursuant to the rules of law chosen by the parties, or without this, according to the law with the closest connection to the dispute (Mitten and Opie, 2010: 287). CAS, in their decision-making, have upheld and applied general legal principles and emphasised the responsibility of governing bodies to act in accordance with the general principles of law which are drawn from the legal systems of all nations. These principles include the legality of rules and application, legal certainty and retrospective application, legitimate expectation and acquisition of rights, good faith (not in bad faith, arbitrarily or capriciously), fairness, non-discrimination, proportionality and fundamental rules (rules must be construed in accordance with the fundamental rights protected under the ECHR) (Lewis and Taylor, 2008: 344).

The awards are considered to be foreign arbitration awards except in Switzerland and therefore need to be globally recognised by national courts in order to be legally enforceable. Those signed up to the Convention on the Recognition and Enforcement of Foreign Arbitral Awards (1958) are obliged to legally recognise and enforce an arbitration award, which makes CAS a successful regulatory process for managing sport disputes (Mitten and Opie, 2010). In doing so it is also developing the meaning of the special nature or specificity of sport.

Their function and role in dealing with matters concerning inclusion and exclusion will become more apparent in Part III and is dependent upon what type of sport rules or practices tend to be challenged in this area and to what extent CAS could offer a resolution.

World Anti-Doping Agency

The universal agreement to engage with CAS is also reflected in the agreement to collectively tackle doping in sport. This has led to the enforcement of a range of anti-doping policies and legislation which are legally enforced, which signifies a private but global system of regulation that is arguably contributing to this international/global system of law (Mestre, 2009: 105; Mitten and Opie, 2010: 281). Supporting this system is a range of public law instruments such as domestic and regional legislation.

In 1999, WADA was established as an independent body tasked with creating and maintaining unified standards for anti-doping testing and the imposition of sanctions for doping violations. In addition, its objectives were to co-ordinate efforts for sports organisations, anti-doping organisations and governments to combat doping in sport (David, 2009: 2). The List of Prohibited Substances and the Code collectively form part of the World Anti-Doping Program, which seeks to achieve the main objective of developing harmonised rules, disciplinary procedures and sanctions which are globally accepted. It is designed to protect the 'spirit of sport' (WADA, 2015).

The WADA Code is a fundamental and universal document upon which the anti-doping programme is based (Anderson, 2010: 120). It aims to produce international harmony by agreement with organisations who are signatories to it (David, 2009: 2). WADA provides a series of documents or models of best practice, to assist organisations with the adoption of the Code.

Around 570 sports organisations have accepted the Code, mainly comprising all the international federations of Olympic sports. Full compliance is required, which means that they must not only amend their rules and policies to include the mandatory articles of the Code but also that those articles are enforced in accordance with the Codes principles. This implementation is monitored by WADA. Under the EU White Paper 2007 additional legal enforcement is given to the Code. For athletes, the WADA code rules are a condition of participation.

Those who may have committed violations can be investigated, which can lead to the bringing of allegations and ultimately the imposition of sanctions against the athlete. CAS plays a central role in ensuring that there is a consistent process for investigating and hearing doping violations throughout the world of sport.

WADA is a private international organisation, which was initially led and influenced by the IOC. Governments cannot be signatories to the Code but have declared their support for it (David, 2009: 3). Since it has, strictly speaking, no regulatory powers, and little legal enforcement by itself, the International Convention against Doping in Sport was adopted by the 33rd UNESCO General Conference in 2005, which came into force on 1 February 2007. It aimed to commit States at both domestic and international levels to combat doping in sport. The Convention has been ratified by 130 countries and is designed to support WADA-led initiatives by underpinning them with the force of international law. UNESCO's recognition and support for WADA implies that this is an example of global administrative law, given WADA's hybrid public/private status.

The legal enforceability of the Code essentially derives from the universal agreement of sports bodies and their member and athletes in the sports to adhere to and apply the Code. In the context of inclusion and exclusion, this model of regulation, by agreement, is very persuasive.

The Olympic Movement

The IOC is an international, non-governmental not-for-profit organisation, serving as a protector of the Olympic Movement and holding responsibility for the interpretation and enforcement of the Olympic Charter (Brown and Connolly, 2010: 5). The IOC is the guardian of the Olympic Charter, to which all bodies involved in the Olympic Movement must comply with. The Olympic Charter is akin to a constitution because it is a fundamental document upon which the Olympic movement is based. The concept of Olympism tells us that 'the practice of sport is a human right' that should be free from discrimination (IOC, 2011: 10). One of the fundamental principles of Olympism is the 'preservation of human dignity' (IOC Principle 2). Those who submit to the Olympic Movement are obliged to adhere to these principles and have a legal duty to ensure that no athlete is excluded on grounds of discrimination. The IOC also displays an explicit commitment to WADA (Rule 43) and CAS (Rule 61) through the Charter (IOC, 2011; Osborn and James, 2012: 82).

The Charter does not derive from any legal authority but is often perceived as a treaty (Mestre, 2009: 14). Most nations have ratified the Olympic Charter in the international legal system and have acknowledged the supremacy of the IOC rules through the enactment of legislation or case law (Forgues, 2000; Mestre, 2009: 21). The treatment of the IOC and its Charter suggests that there is a 'general acceptance of the legal primacy of the Olympic Charter, not because it has any actual entrenched force, but rather by virtue of custom and transcendent socio-economic quality the Olympic Games possess' (Mestre, 2009: 15). The legal endorsement of these sporting values demonstrates an example of regulation which receives global recognition. It is suggested that the Charter is a source of 'Olympic Law' in sport regulation (Osborn and James, 2012).

Principles of the Charter are reflective of the UDHR. However, upon closer inspection, there is no legal right to participate in athletic competition and, in fact, this right is a conditional right to participate in sport on the proviso that an athlete complies with several eligibility requirements specified in the Charters Eligibility Code (Mitten and Davis, 2008). Nevertheless, the Olympic Charter is certainly a persuasive and powerful document that courts are reluctant to challenge as will be shown in Part II.

Summary

This chapter has provided a detailed evaluation of the current 'toolkit' available for managing and dealing with inclusion and exclusion in sport.

In the UK, key political and legal agendas have driven the enactment of equality measures in sport. The political focus is to deliver wider social objectives through the promotion of recreational sport. Sport equity policies have the potential to manage inclusion and exclusion but are currently criticised for their effectiveness.

There exists an extensive body of domestic, regional and international equality legislation, which aims to protect human rights by ensuring that citizens are treated equally without distinction of their differences. The compatibility of sport-specific inclusion and exclusion with the existing legal framework is not entirely clear because of the absence of explicit references to competitive sport and because of the treatment of sports bodies as private entities who are often exempt from equality provisions.

The regulation of sport forms part of a wide area of academic debate, focused upon the degree of intervention by the law and the models of regulation for sport. At the heart of this, lies the tension between the protection of the fundamental rights of athletes, and the protection of the specificity of sport. No explicit sport regulation measures exist to deal with inclusion and exclusion on the basis of sex, gender, disability and race although there are a number of tools and approaches within sport regulation which are potentially transferable as we have seen.

Part II seeks to analyse the current practices of inclusion and exclusion by documenting a selection of legal and non-legal cases concerning sex, gender, disability and race. It will highlight how these cases are approached by sport and by the law. The compatibility of the sport approach with domestic, regional and international legal mechanisms will be critiqued, drawing upon primary and secondary sources of law. An evaluation of the cases in these four areas will identify instances of best practices as well as inconsistencies of approach by sport and the law. Through an analysis of these cases it is possible to chart and critically analyse the current balance between inclusion and exclusion.

References

Anderson, J. 2010. *Modern Sports Law: A Textbook.* Portland: Hart Publishing.

Anon. 2009a. *CAS may not hear Wickmayer case for year.* Tennis.com [online], 15 March. Available at: www.tennis.com/articles/templates/news.aspx?articleid=4597 [accessed 05/06/09].

Anon. 2009b. Yanina Wickmayar and Xavier Malisse have doping ban suspended by Belgian court. *The Telegraph* [online], 14 December. Available at: www.telegraph.co.uk/sport/tennis/wtatour/6812193/Yanina-Wickmayer-and-Xavier-Malisse-have-doping-ban-suspended-by-Belgian-court.html [accessed 05/01/10].

Baderin, M.A. and Ssenyonjo, M. 2010. *International Human Rights Law: Six Decades After the UDHR and Beyond.* Aldershot: Ashgate Publishing.

Beloff, M. 2005. Is There a Lex Sportiva? *International Sports Law Review*, 3: 49–60.

Beloff, M., Kerr, T. and Demetriou, M. 1999. *Sports Law.* Oxford: Hart Publishing.

Boyes, S. 2000. The Regulation of Sport and the Impact of the Human Rights Act 1998. *European Public Law*, 6(4): 517–530.

Boyes, S. 2012. Sports Law: its history and growth and the development of key sources. *Legal Information Management*, 12: 86–91.

Brown, K.J. and Connolly, C. 2010. The role of law in promoting women in elite athletics: an examination of four nations. *International Review for the Sociology of Sport*, 45(3): 3–21

Coalter, F. 2007. *A Wider Social Role for Sport.* London: Routledge.

Collins, M. 2014. Contemporary Policy Debate. *Journal of Policy Research in Tourism, Leisure and Events*, 6:3: 268–271.

Connolly, M. 2011. *Discrimination Law.* 2nd Edition. London: Sweet and Maxwell.

Council of Europe 2012. European Committee of Social Rights. [online], Available at: www.coe.int/t/dghl/monitoring/socialcharter/ecsr/ecsrdefault_EN.asp [accessed 02/08/12].

Court of Arbitration for Sport (CAS) 2009. Press Release Tennis: Yanina Wickmayar and Xavier Malisse file appeals at the Court of Arbitration for Sport. *Court of Arbitration for Sport* [online], 18 November. Available at: www.tas-cas.org/d2wfiles/document/3758/5048/0/2009.11.18%20PR%20Eng.pdf [accessed 20/11/09].

Court of Arbitration for Sport (CAS) 2012. *The Code 2012 Edition* [online], Available at: www.tas-cas.org/d2wfiles/document/4962/5048/0/Code20201220_en_2001.01.pdf [accessed 01/08/12].

David, P. 2009. *Guide to the World Anti-Doping Code: A Fight for the Spirit of Sport.* Cambridge University Press.

DCMS. 2002. *Game Plan: a strategy for delivering governments sports and physical activity objectives.* London: Cabinet Office.

De Schutter, O. 2010. *International Human Rights Law.* Oxford: Oxford University Press.

De Sousa Santos, B. 2002. *Toward a New Legal Common Sense.* London: Butterworths.

Dicey, A.V. 1959. *An Introduction to the Study of the Law of the Constitution.* 10th Edition. London: The Macmillan Press.

Donnelly, P. and Kidd, B. 2006. Achieving Human Rights in and through Sport. *The Bulletin of the International Council of Sport Science and Physical Education* [online] September, 48. Available at: www.icsspe.org/bulletin/drucken_a4b0b689.php.html [accessed 10/11/11].

Elling, A., De Knop, P. and Knoppers, A. 2003. Gay/Lesbian sport clubs and events: places of homo social bonding and cultural resistance? *International Review for the Sociology of Sport*, 38(4): 441–56.

Ellson, S. and Lohn, M. 2006. Whose Rules are we Playing By? *Entertainment and Sports Law Journal*, [online], 3(2). Available at: www2.warwick.ac.uk/fac/soc/law/elj/eslj/issues/volume3/number2/ellson_lohn/ [accessed 01/08/12].

European Commission 2007. *White Paper on Sport* [online], Available at: http://ec.europa.eu/sport/documents/wp_on_sport_en.pdf [accessed 01/04/12].

European Commission 2011. *Developing the European Dimension in Sport.* [online], Available at: http://ec.europa.eu/sport/news/doc/communication/communication_en.pdf [accessed 07/06/11].

FA The 2012. *FA Agree Inclusion Plan*, [online] Available at: www.thefa.com/News/thefa/2012/dec/david-bernstein-anti-discrimination.aspx [accessed 27/08/14].

Fenwick, H. 1998. From Formal to Substantive Equality: the place of affirmative action in European Union sex equality law. *European Public Law*, 4(4): 507–516.

Fenwick, H. 2007. *Civil Liberties and Human Rights*, 4th Edition. London: Routledge.

Finnis, J. 2011. *Natural Law and Natural Rights*, 2nd Edition. New York: Oxford University Press.

Forgues, C. 2000. A Global hurdle: the implementation of an international non-discrimination norm protecting women from gender discrimination in international sports. *Boston University International Law Journal*, 18: 247–272.

Foster, K. 2003. Is There a Global Sports Law? *Entertainment Law*, 2(1): 1–18.

Foster, K. 2006. Lex Sportiva and Lex Ludica: the Court of Arbitration for Sport jurisprudence. *Entertainment and Sports Law Journal* [online], 3(2). Available at: www2.warwick.ac.uk/fac/soc/law/elj/eslj/issues/volume3/number2/foster/foster.pdf [accessed 01/08/12].

Foster, N. 2011. *Foster on EU Law*. Oxford: Oxford University Press.

Gardiner, S., Boyes, S., Naidoo, U., O'Leary J. and Welch, R. 2012. *Sports Law*, 4th Edition. London: Routledge.

Gardiner, S., Parrish, R. and Siekmann, R.C.R. 2009. *EU, Sport, Law and Policy.* The Netherlands: TMC Asser Press.

Gratton, C. and Henry, I.P. 2001. *Sport in the City: the role of sport in economic and social regeneration.* London: Routledge.

Greenfield, S. and Osborn, G. 2000. *Law and Sport in Contemporary Society.* London: Routledge.

Hargreaves, J. and Anderson, E. 2014. *Routledge Handbook of Sport, Gender and Sexuality.* London: Routledge.

Harlow, C. and Rawlings, R. 2009. *Law and Administration.* Cambridge: Cambridge University Press.

Harris, D.J., O'Boyle, M., Bates, E. and Buckley C. 2009. *Harris, O'Boyle and Warbrick: Law of the European Convention on Human Rights.* New York: Oxford University Press.

Heckman, J.J., Nelson, R.L. and Cabatingan, L. 2010. *Global Perspectives on the Rule of Law*. London: Routledge.

Heywood, A. 2003. *Political Ideology: an introduction.* 3rd Edition. New York: Palgrave Macmillan.

Houlihan, B. and Lindsey, I. 2013. *Sports Policy in Britain*. London: Routledge.

International Olympic Committee (IOC) 2011. *The Olympic Charter.* IOC.

Jackson, P. and Leopold P. 2001. *Constitutional and Administrative Law*. New York: Sweet and Maxwell.

James, M. 2010. *Sports Law.* Basingstoke: Palgrave Macmillan.

Kluka, D.A. 2008. *The Brighton Declaration on Women and Sport: A management audit of process quality.* Ph.D thesis, University of Pretoria, South Africa.

Lewis, A. and Taylor, J. 2008. *Sport: Law and Practice*, 2nd Edition. Sussex: Tottel Publishing.

Liguori, D.J. 2003. Fore! The supreme court tees off a standard to apply the Americans with Disabilities Act to professional sports in PGA Tour, INC, v Martin. *Widener Law Journal*, 12: 185–219.

Lord, J.E. and Stein, M.A. 2009. Social Rights and the Relational Value of the Rights to Participate in Sport, Recreation and Play. *Boston University International Law Journal*, 27: 249–281.

Lusted, J. 2014. Equality Policies in Sport: carrots, sticks and a retreat from the radical. *Journal of Policy Research in Tourism, Leisure and Events*, 6:1: 85–90.

McArdle, D. and Giulianotti, R. 2006. *Sport, Civil Liberties and Human Rights.* London: Routledge.

Meirim, J.M. 2004. Portugal: There is a new law in town. *International Sports Law Review*, 4, November: 97–99.

Mestre, A.M. 2009. *The Law of the Olympic Games.* Den Haag: TMC Asser Instituut.

Miettinen, S. and Parrish R. 2007. Nationality Discrimination in Community Law: An Assessment of UEFA Regulations Governing Player Eligibility for European Club Competitions (the home grown player rule). *The Entertainment and Sports Law Journal* [online], 5(5). Available at: www2.warwick.ac.uk/fac/soc/law/elj/eslj/issues/volume5/number2/miettinen_parrish/ [accessed 08/02/08].

Mitten, M.J. and Davis, T. 2008. Athlete Eligibility Requirements and Legal Protection of Sports Participation Opportunities. *Virginia Sports and Entertainment Law Journal*, 8: 71–146.

Mitten, M.J. and Opie, H. 2010. "Sports Law:" Implications for the development of International, Comparative and National Law and Global Dispute Resolution. *Tulane Law Review*, 85(2): 269–322.

Osborn, G. and James, M. 2012. The Sources and Interpretation of Olympic Law. *Legal Information Management*, 12: 80–86.

Palombella, G. and Walker, N. 2009. *Relocating the Rule of Law.* Portland: Hart Publishing.

Parrish, R. and Miettinen, S. 2008. *The Sporting Exception in European Union Law.* International Sports Law Series, Den Haag: TMC Asser Press.

Parrish, R., García García, B., Miettinen S. and Siekmann R. 2010. *The Lisbon Treaty and EU Sports Policy.* European Parliament: Directorate Central for Internal Policies.

Pavlakos, G. 2007. *Law, Rights and Discourse: the legal philosophy of Robert Alexy.* Oregon: Hart Publishing.

Rehman, J. 2010. *International Human Rights Law.* Harlow: Pearson Longman.

Rincon, A. 2007. EC Competition and Internal Market Law: On the existence of a sporting exemption and its withdrawal. *Journal of Contemporary European Research*, 3(3): 224–237.

Shelton, D. 2008. *Regional Protection of Human Rights.* New York: Oxford University Press.

Siekmann, R.C.R. and Soek, J. 2012. *Lex Sportiva: What is sports law?* The Netherlands: TMC Asser Press.

Smith, A. 2011. All Bets Are Off: match fixing in sport- some recent developments. *Entertainment and Sports Law Journal* [online], 9(1). Available at: www2.warwick.ac.uk/fac/soc/law/elj/eslj/issues/volume9/number1/smith/ [accessed 02/08/12].

Social Exclusion Unit (SEU). 2001. *National Strategy for Neighbourhood Renewal: Policy Action Team Audit.* London: Cabinet Office.

Steiner, H.J., Alston, P. and Goodman, R. 2007. *International Human Rights in Context.* Third Edition. Oxford University Press.

Thomas, N. and Smith, A. 2009. *Disability, Sport and Society: an introduction.* London: Routledge.

Twining, W. 2000. *Globalisation and Legal Theory.* London: Butterworths.

UK Sport 2014. *Equality* [online]. Available at: www.uksport.gov.uk/pages/policies-and-strategies/ [accessed 27/08/14].

UNESCO 2014. Introducing UNESCO: what we are [online] UNESCO. Available at: www.unesco.org/new/en/unesco/about-us/who-we-are/introducing-unesco/ [accessed 14/08/14]

United Nations 2011. The Universal Declaration of Human Rights [online]. United Nations. Available at: www.un.org/en/documents/udhr/ [accessed 11/12/2011].

Weatherill, S. 2006. Anti-doping Revisited – the demise of the rule of 'purely sporting interest'? *European Competition Law Review*, 27(12): 645–657.

World Anti-Doping Agency (WADA). 2015. *The World Anti-Doping Code* [online]. Available at: www.wada-ama.org/en/resources/the-code/world-anti-doping-code [accessed 18/02/15].

Part II

Cases of inclusion and exclusion in sport

4 Sex

The world of sport has traditionally been regarded as a male space. The Ancient Olympic Games restricted women from participating or watching sport on the basis that their very presence would reduce the strength of the warriors (Wackwitz, 2003). Women were previously excluded from competing in sport because of various social and medical assumptions held about their unsuitability to sporting activity (Archer and Lloyd, 2002: 4).

In modern times, the landscape of sport is quite different, with women's sport expanding and arguably growing at a faster pace than men's sport (Anon, 2011: 48). It is becoming a lucrative product in an evolving market of commercial opportunity. This shift in the 'gender regime' has prompted an evaluation of sporting boundaries.

In 2014, Helena Costa became the first female professional football manager to be appointed by a men's club, namely Clermont Foot 63. Later that year, former Arsenal Ladies football manager Shelley Kerr was appointed manager at a men's Scottish football club, becoming the first female manager in Scottish senior football. This marked a significant milestone for women in the sports industry, and reflected the changing dimension of sport and business (Patel, 2014).

On the field, the England women's rugby team won the Rugby World Cup in August 2014, training in their spare time and with no pay. Following their success, the Rugby Football Union announced that full-time contracts will be offered to 20 female players. Similarly, following their Ashes win, the England women's cricket team became full-time professional cricketers after the England and Wales Cricket Board announced significant pay rises and dedicated investment in the sport.

However, perhaps because of the delay in the creation and development of women's sports, participation rates between men and women continue to vary considerably and typically favour men in competitive and non-competitive positions. Whilst some studies suggest that the gender gap between male and female adult participation in sport is narrowing (White *in* Hartmann-Tews and Pfister, 2003: 40), there remain unavoidable disparities in funding, media coverage, sponsorship and employment opportunities.

Within months of being appointed, Helena Costa resigned from her post after claiming to have been ignored and sidelined in her role (Cohen, 2014). She was replaced by another woman, Corinne Diacre. Despite overt developments to overcome unnecessary barriers for women in competitive and non-competitive positions, covert practices continue to impact upon female engagement in sport.

For instance, casual sexism tends to contribute towards under-representation. Casual sexism relates to the 'relentless, nihilistic meanness that characterises contemporary discourse, which is aimed disproportionately at women' (Turner, 2009). This has become a permanent feature of the sport Doxa as earlier described. The focus on sexy images of women in sport and the expectation of femininity illustrates this. For example, in 2004, FIFA president Sepp Blatter who, overtly claimed to treat women's football as a serious priority, publically urged women footballers to wear skimpier kits in order to increase the popularity of the women's game (Anon, 2004a). This culture can have a damaging effect on the presence and success of women in sport. Conversely, it could be suggested that coverage of women has promoted female sport and the athletes are simply answering to market driven forces. The 'sexy' female athlete image sits in contrast to the masculine representation of the female body by the media. Athletes such as Serena Williams are demonised for their athletic arms, which challenges the feminine notion. The media play a vital role in creating a moral panic about the unnatural bodies of athletic females (Lafferty and McKay, 2004).

Upon this background, the presence of mixed-sex sports is rare since this would presumably challenge the biological and social understandings of the differences between men and women. As introduced in Part I, sport remains segregated along the lines of sex since this is considered to be part of the essence of sport and is based upon the presumption that men are more physically advantaged. This chapter will explore cases which have challenged the current practices of inclusion and exclusion in relation to sex, drawing upon instances when the divisionary lines between men and women in sport have been brought to challenge by women. Through this analysis an indication of the current balance between inclusion and exclusion can be made.

Ski jumping

In the case of *Sagen v Vancouver Organizing Committee for the 2010 Olympic and Paralympic Winter Games [2009] BCSC 942 (Sup Ct (BC))* (Patel 2010: 11), a group of 15 highly ranked female ski jumpers from five countries brought a claim against the Vancouver Organising Committee for the 2010 Winter Games (VANOC) arguing that a female ski jumping event should be included into the Games, just as it is for men. They argued that because VANOC plan, organise, finance and stage the ski jumping events for men, failure to offer an equal event for women violates women's equality rights as guaranteed under s. 15(1) of the Canadian Charter of Rights and Freedoms (1982).

Did VANOC breach the Charter?

Justice Fenlon needed to determine whether the Charter applied to VANOC and whether they had breached their obligations under it (Case, para. 9). In order for

VANOC to be captured under his Charter, the claimants were required to demonstrate that they were either controlled by government or performing a governmental function.

It was held in the case that there was no 'government control' over VANOC and instead they were 'like a franchisee of the IOC, than a purchaser of a product' (Case, para. 39). However a private entity that is not controlled by government can still be subject to the Charter if they carry out a 'government activity' (Case, para. 49). In this regard, the court held that whilst the IOC owns the Olympic Games, they do not actually stage the Games. It was found that the staging of the Games is a 'rare but uniquely governmental activity' that VANOC carry out in their role and are therefore subject to the Charter (Case, para. 63).

Despite this finding, VANOC were not found to be in breach of the Charter as they may have been carrying out a government activity by staging the Games but 'designating events as "Olympic events" is neither part of that government activity nor within VANOC's control' (Case, para. 123). Essentially they have no control over event selection since this power lies with the IOC. The IOC is a Swiss-based organisation which is not bound by the Canadian Charter for jurisdictional reasons (Case, para. 104). Interestingly, the claimants did not pursue the IOC, who owns the Games, or the Federation Internationale de Ski (FIS) who are the international governing body responsible for proposing new events.

In any case, any direct challenge against the IOC event selection criteria has historically been unsuccessful as demonstrated in the US case of *Martin v International Olympic Committee (1984) 740 F. 2d 67* detailed below. A number of IOC policies escape the legal fishing net and continue to exist to restrict individuals or groups from participation. Using the indirect approach of suing VANOC seems to solve 'the inherent jurisdictional problem involved in suing the IOC while avoiding the need to challenge the mechanics of how the IOC and or FIS reached their decision' (Lines and Heshka, 2009: 94). However, it is fair to assume that VANOC were not directly responsible for the exclusion of the female athletes, because they have no authority within the IOC event selection process. VANOC argued that the claimants named the wrong defendant (Case, para. 4). The only way in which VANOC could comply with the court's decision if the claimants were successful would be to refuse to host the men's ski jumping event (Case, para. 5).

Is the IOC selection criteria discriminatory?

In May 2006, the FIS voted to recommend women's ski jumping 'normal hill' (the 90m jump) be included in the 2010 Winter Games. However, upon recommendation to the IOC, in November 2006 they vetoed this proposal (Chan, 2009). The IOC asserted that this decision was based upon 'technical merit'. According to Rule 47 (3.2) of the Olympic Charter, events must have a recognised international reputation and must have two world championships to be included in the Games. In addition, only events practiced by men in at least 50 countries and on three continents, and by women in at least 35 countries and on three continents, can be included into the Games (Case, para. 81). Justice Fenlon deposed that both men's and women's ski jumping fall short of the required 'universality' (Case, para. 87) under this criteria. However, under rule 47 (4.4) it seems that men's ski jumping remains justified:

> Rule 47 (4.4): Sports, disciplines or events included in the programme of the Olympic Games which no longer satisfy the criteria of this rule may nevertheless, in certain exception cases, be maintained therein by decision of the IOC for the sake of the Olympic tradition.
>
> (Case, para. 84)

Justice Fenlon agreed that this exception rule *was* discriminatory as it amounted to historical stereotyping and prejudice which serves to exclude women and include marginalised men's events in order to maintain Olympic traditions (Case, para. 90). Because ski jumping has been a Winter Olympic sport since 1924, it is exempt from an Olympic gender equity policy which requires that since 1991 all new sports wishing to be included on the Olympic programme must include competitions for both men and women (Chan, 2009; IOC, 2014). Fenlon found that the maintenance of a men's event with no female equivalent on the basis of what constitutes a grandfather Olympic tradition, constitutes sex discrimination under the Canadian Charter (Ellison, 2009).

The application of these rules is inconsistent with the true 'technical merit' of women's ski jumping. Many of the women ski jumpers have competed against, and succeeded, over their male counterparts in mixed international competitions (Ellison, 2009). American Skier Lindsey Van held the record for the Whistler K95 ski jump having beaten her male competitors in an earlier competition at the facility (Case, para. 66). Interestingly her record is 'silent' and not recorded as 'official' perhaps because she completed this jump at the Canadian Championships in 2010, which is not an FIS-sanctioned event (Burton, 2010: 20).

Whilst Justice Fenlon accepted these achievements and sympathised that 'societal headwinds' have compromised the inclusion of female ski jumpers in the Olympics, at the same time, she appeared to be protecting the IOC by commending their policy initiatives aimed at including women in sport (Case, para. 100). She subsequently held that any discrimination suffered by the claimants derived from Rule 47 (4.4) and nothing else.

The decision was made that the claimants were successful in proving the inconsistent application of the selection criteria, but not that the selection criteria itself was discriminatory. On both issues, therefore, the claimants were unsuccessful. The Supreme Court later added that it will not hear an appeal by the female ski jumpers. However the athletes argue 'this is about human rights and discrimination and it's a wrong that must be righted' (Anon, 2009a).

Case summary

Justice Fenlon delivered a host of contradictory messages which represented a clear legal struggle to intervene in Olympic matters, even though there was an identification of discriminatory practice (Patel, 2010). Irrespective of who the defendant may be, international commitments to universal policies such as the UDHR, CEDAW and the Brighton Declaration place positive obligations upon the State to avoid and regulate discriminatory behaviour. These mechanisms as introduced in Part I require positive enforcement if they are to effectively manage the balance. The judgment in this case is difficult to reconcile with these obligations.

The reluctance to hold VANOC accountable may have been economically driven. Justice Fenlon could have been concerned that a decision against VANOC may prejudice any future Olympic opportunities for Canada. This places significant political and economic power with the IOC who has the autonomy to exercise a regulatory function as a private entity, and essentially apply whichever rules they wish. However, they are operating in a manner which is not accountable to fundamental norms such as human rights and equality. To justify this exemption on an economic basis is unacceptable.

Following public pressure, the IOC introduced female ski-jumping at the 2014 Sochi Winter Olympic Games (normal-hill competition), with German athlete Carina Vogt winning the gold medal at the event (Williams, 2013: 18).

Running

Prior to *Sagen* in *Martin v International Olympic Committee (1984) 740 F. 2d 67* the IOC refused to include the 5,000m and the 10,000m parallel women's races at the Los Angeles 1984 Summer Olympics in accordance with Rule 32 of the 1970 Olympic Charter. The claimant athletes argued that this amounted to discrimination on the basis of sex and violated their equal protection rights under California State legislation.

The US Court of Appeals (9th Circuit) held that the Act did not apply here since it was not intended to protect the creation of separate but equal events. Neither did the 'facially gender-neutral' IOC Rule 32 constitute 'arbitrary discrimination' since it was perceived to apply equally to all events. The judges accepted that such an exclusion was likely to cause 'irreparable harm' to the runners (Case, para. 675). However, they concluded that discrimination legislation was not intended to apply to competition of this nature (Case, para. 680).

The claimants in *Sagen* similarly argued that 'the historical hurdles and barriers have been so strong that the number of ski jumpers is likely to decline if the sport is not included in the 2010 Games' (Sagen: 96). In *Martin* the court was reluctant to get involved in the Olympic process and alter the terms of the agreement under the Olympic Charter (Case, para. 677). Pregerson J offered a dissenting opinion arguing that the historical attitude towards women in sport by the IOC has resulted in disparities between male and female opportunities at the Olympic Games. The IOC refusal to include a female event may have a long-term negative effect upon equality and human rights (Case, para. 679).

The approach of both the Canadian and American courts appears to prioritise Olympic traditions over principles of equality. The dialogue which emerged from the *Sagen* and *Martin* cases reveals the dangers of the covert operation of selection criteria and rules that threaten the inclusion of minorities in sport. These cases serve as an example of unreasonable exclusion by the sports body and by the law.

Canoeing

In recent times, the Olympic Programme has become more inclusive as evidenced by the success of women's boxing at the London 2012 Olympics, and the women's ski jumping event in Sochi. Despite significant progress for gender equality at the 2012 Games, disparities in the Olympic programme continue to be unresolved (Donnelly and Donnelly, 2013).

In 2012, a British female canoeist, Samantha Rippington, launched a legal challenge against the organisers of the London Olympics, LOCOG, because of the absence of women's canoe racing events in the programme (Ebner, 2012). In comparison, men have five canoe events, which was considered discriminatory. Since they refused to carry out an equality impact assessment, she brought judicial review proceedings in the English courts on the grounds that they had breached the public sector equality duty under s. 149 EA 2010, which requires a public authority to have due regard for the elimination of discrimination, the advancement of equality of opportunity and the fostering of good relations between men and women.

Similar to *Sagen*, the case raised the question of whether LOCOG performs public functions under the EA, and, if so, what their duties involve. LOCOG claimed to be exempt from the EA since they are a private organisation, with no government functions.

Despite the significant implications of this case on inclusion and exclusion in sport, permission to apply for judicial review was refused. With the support of Canadian lobby group WomenCAN, Rippington sought to fight for women's inclusion in the 2016 Rio Games (Ebner 2012). However, this will not happen since the International Canoe Federation (ICF) are pushing for inclusion in the 2020 Toyko Games.

There are inherent contradictions within the policies and practices of the IOC, an organisation which is tainted by internal bribery and corruption scandals (Miller *et al.*, 2001: 24). The principles of non-discrimination and human rights, contained in the Articles 4 and 5 of the Olympic Charter, sit in opposition to the outcome of these cases. Instead, the cases demonstrate that there is still a long way to go to achieve full gender equality (Donnelly and Donnelly, 2013).

Golf

Golf is a sport rich in history and is rooted in traditions and customs. Considered a private male space, women's inclusion has been slow despite their progress and success in recent times. They continue to experience barriers to membership and access to clubs. The age of these traditions conflicts with modern society and has placed pressure on clubs such as Augusta National Golf Club, the Royal and Ancient Club and the Marylebone Cricket Club, to change their exclusive policies. It could be argued that the reasons for this are largely financial, since in cricket, for example, clubs who refuse to alter their membership policies and constitution are denied Lottery funds for capital development in the UK. This may explain why a number of village teams have introduced women's cricket teams into their structure. The regulation of private clubs and their exclusive practices have been the subject of legal debate for a number of years.

In the Ireland case of *Equal Authority v Portmarnock Golf Club & Others [2005] IEHC 235 (H. Ct. June 10 2005)*, Portmarnock was registered as a golf club under licensing legislation which allowed it to sell alcohol to members. Section 8 Equal Status Act 2000 (ESA) provided a general rule that a club who had a drinks licence could not discriminate if it wished to keep its licence. Section 9 ESA provided an exemption to this rule where discrimination was permitted if 'its principle purpose is to cater only for the needs of persons of a particular gender, marital status, family status, sexual orientation, religious belief, age, disability, nationality or ethnic or national origin to the exclusion of other persons.' The club confined its membership to 'gentlemen' only and women were not permitted to become members even though they were permitted to play with or without a male member on identical terms applicable to non-male members. Women were not sold alcohol since they were not members (Fenelon, 2009).

The Equal Authority successfully won a ruling in the District Court that the club was a 'discriminating club' under s. 8 ESA and the court prohibited the club from being registered as a club, and in turn suspended from selling alcohol. The Court held that the purpose of the club was to play golf, and a literal approach was taken in the case. The club appealed to the High Court arguing that s. 9 (1) ESA protected them since they were catering to the needs of men only. This was upheld by the court.

The Equal Authority appealed the decision to the Irish Supreme Court who had to determine whether the club could rely on s. 9 (1) ESA. The case centred on the statutory construction of the exemption clause. The Equal Authority argued that the club are not exempt under s. 9(1) since 'the purpose of the club is to play golf or (more correctly) to provide facilities for the playing of golf, which cannot be described as catering for the needs of one gender only, or as a "need" at all' (Case, para. 13). They argued that the word 'needs' relates solely to 'absolute necessities, like air, food and water and not to social, cultural or recreational preferences' (Case, para. 6).

The decision of the Supreme Court was split. The overall outcome was to dismiss the appeal and uphold the High Court decision of no discrimination. Hardiman and Geoghegan JJ held that the principal purpose of the club is to cater for the 'golfing needs of persons of a particular gender only' specifically gentlemen (Case, para. 39). Conversely, Denham and Fennelly JJ dissented, departing from the High Court decision on the grounds that the principal purpose of the club is the playing of golf. To argue that the principal purpose of a golf club was something other than golf would be considered 'preposterous' (Case, para. 66).

The divided outcome of this case is similar to *Sagen* and *Martin* where the courts demonstrated a general reluctance to capture sports bodies within equality legislation. The dissent in *Portmarnock* and *Martin* highlight the difficulty often faced when balancing inclusion and exclusion in sport.

Boxing

In the UK case of *Couch v BBBC (1997 unreported, IT no. 2304231/97)*, Jane Couch, holder of the World Women's Welterweight title, was refused by the British Boxing Board of Control (BBBC) an application for a professional boxers licence which would grant her the right to box against females in Britain (the case transcript is unobtainable, for commentary see Felix, 1998; McArdle, 2008). Couch, known as the 'Fleetwood Assassin' applied to the industrial tribunal on the grounds that her application had not been given proper consideration by the qualifying body and had therefore contravened s. 13(1) Sex Discrimination Act 1975 (SDA).

In the case, the BBBC justified their decision on essentially three arguments. First, there appeared to be a notion that boxing posed particular dangers to the health of females if they pursued it. The BBBC presented numerous medical arguments to support the contention that special dangers were open to women in boxing (Felix, 1998). They included, trauma to the breasts, hormonal changes, premenstrual tension, painful periods (dysmenorrhoea), an increased tendency to bruise, problems with fatty necrosis during pregnancy and, finally, since drugs and medication is prohibited in the sport, contraceptive pills would not be permitted. There is legitimacy in the medical arguments if it is the case that the sport creates female specific risks. Whilst boxing rules seek to protect women and men from injuries, there may be reasonable grounds to exclude a female when gender-specific injuries cannot be guarded against.

Second, but rather unconsciously, that society does not wish to see women engage in acts of brutality. For instance, the secretary general of the BBBC, John Morris confirmed that the Board were not willing to take any steps to encourage the spread of women's boxing (Felix, 1998). This is an example of misguided paternalism (James, 2010: 234; Lafferty and McKay, 2004). The decision to consent to any risk involved in any sport is primarily the competitor's and the dangers that may occur during the game are at the risk of that individual. It is arbitrary to presume that because Couch was female, she lost her right to consent to such dangers.

Finally, the Board argued that female boxing would result in dramatic rule changes to boxing that would presumably alter the essence of the sport. If changes in the rules concerning weight categories and clothing lead to the essence of the sport being threatened then this may be a justifiable matter to consider.

The tribunal rejected each of these arguments and viewed the medical evidence to be a 'smokescreen' for the Board to hide its double standards behind (Felix, 1998). Even if there were any truth in the arguments, 'a desire to protect women from the consequences of making an informed choice about consent to injury and the voluntary assumption of risk, provided no defence to a sex discrimination claim' (Felix, 1998). The tribunal concluded that the BBBC lacked evidence for their arguments and held that the primary reason to deny her a licence was on the ground of her sex (Case, para. 12 cited *in* McArdle, 2008: 54). Rule change concerns were unanimously rejected as these concerns have already been successfully dealt with in countries where women's boxing is widely accepted (USA, Germany, Belgium, Holland, Hungary.)

Overall, it was held to be 'incontrovertible' that 'but for' her sex, Couch would have been treated more favourably. Subsequently, three months after the judgement she was granted a licence to box in Britain. The BBBC adapted its regulations to provide for women's boxing in light of this. British boxer Nicola Adams MBE became the first female gold medal winner in boxing at the London Games 2012, which demonstrates the success of women in the sport.

This case is located in a sport which is subject to popular debate. The legality of boxing is contentious because of its inherent dangers and risks to the physical and non-physical health of men and women. The British Medical Association perceives boxing, regardless of gender, to be a dangerous sport which should not be encouraged further (Anon, 2009b). Sport should not be so dangerous so as to cause a competitor *unlawful* injury and there should be sufficient regulations in place to reduce these risks. The broader arguments presented in the case about health risks and societal attitudes to brutality are equally applicable to men also. It follows that if there are suggestions that a sport such as boxing is too dangerous for anyone, regardless of sex, then the legality of boxing should be challenged. The decision of the tribunal implicitly reflects this.

In a very similar Australian case, the opposite decision to *Couch* was reached. In *Ferneley v Boxing Authority of New South Wales [2001] FCA 1740*, an adult 18-year-old female professional boxer applied to the Boxing Authority of NSW for registration as a boxer. It is a criminal offence under s. 15 of the Boxing and Wrestling Control Act 1986 (NSW Act) for a person to engage in a boxing contest without registration as a boxer. However, her application was denied because according to s. 8(1) of the NSW Act, only a male person over the age of 18-years-old can submit an application to the Boxing Authority of NSW to be registered as a boxer. Therefore, it is always a criminal offence for a female to box since there is no provision for female registration. This exclusion appears to be deliberate as is reflected in the parliamentary debates prior to its enactment which emphasised that 'current community standards' do not accept the risk of women 'becoming freaks in some sort of Roman circus disguised as a sporting contest' (per Mr MA Cleary MP Case, para. 6).

As a result of this restriction, Ferneley brought a claim to the Federal Court of Australia against the Boxing Authority for its handling of her application, and against the State of NSW in relation to the terms of the NSW Act. She relied on the Sex Discrimination Act 1984 (Aus. SDA) to argue that both respondents had unlawfully discriminated against her on the basis of her sex.

The Court held that the Boxing Authority has not breached the Aus. SDA in their handling of the application because they did not fall within the type of authorities or applications covered by the Act. Justice Wilcox stated that his decision does not turn on the desirability or undesirability of permitting female boxing contests, but instead the proper interpretation of the Aus. SDA (Case, para. 99). In supporting the Boxing Authority the case appears to uphold Mr Cleary's paternalistic comments (Burke, 2004: 178). The court failed to hold the sports governing body responsible under equality legislation and interpreted it in a way which exempted them.

Sport exemption clauses

A subsidiary aspect of *Couch* and *Ferneley* was the reliance by the BBBC and the Boxing Authority on sport exclusion clauses in sex discrimination legislation, to render their actions completely lawful. In the UK, s. 44 Sex Discrimination Act 1975 (SDA) previously read;

> Nothing in Parts II-IV shall in relation to any sport, game or other activity of a competitive nature where the physical strength, stamina or physique of the average woman puts her at a disadvantage to the average man, render unlawful any act related to the participation of a person as a competitor in events involving that activity which are confined to competitors of one sex.

The SDA has now been replaced by the EA but continues to include an identical clause under s. 195. At the time of its passing through Parliament, s. 44 was given little deliberation about its purpose or impact (Pannick, 1983: 9). During the parliamentary debates, Lord Somers stated that 'men and women should be equal, most certainly, but I sincerely hope that they will always remain different' (HL Deb 15 July 1975).

It would appear that s. 44 existed to maintain knowledge and attitudes towards women that were reflective of the 1970s. The opinion was that men's sporting space demanded protection and separation from female activity because of the physiological differences in strength, speed and stamina that would create unequal competition. The courts and tribunals tended to apply the provision only to mixed-sex competitions where women seek to compete in male teams or events. It would seem that the objective of the exemption was not to encompass female-only sports or non-competitive aspects of sport. When sports governing bodies or organisations have attempted to rely on it to support exclusion on the basis of sex, it has been rejected by the courts in areas such as officiating (*British Judo Association v Petty* [1981] ICR 660, CA) and coaching (*Hardwick v FA* IT case, unreported. Case no. 2200651/96, *Saunders v Richmond Borough Council* (1977) IRLR 362, [1978] ICR 75, EAT, *Moore v The Squash Rackets Association Ltd* IT case, case no. 50482/94, May 9 1995).

Lending support to this is the Employment Appeal Tribunal case of *Greater London Council v Farrar [1980] 1 W.L.R 608.* This case concerned a professional female wrestler who challenged a local authority for prohibiting the issuing of licences of premises for boxing or wrestling to women. In the first instance, the tribunal held in favour of *Farrar* and found that the condition which prohibited women's wrestling was unlawful under the SDA. In addition, they held that s. 44 did not operate to exempt women's wrestling from the SDA because it did not include sports where women were matched against other women (Case, para. 609). On appeal, the prohibitive condition was allowed on procedural grounds concerning the local authority's obligation to comply with a previous requirement (p. 611). However, Slynn J agreed that s. 44 is 'dealing with a situation in which men and women might both be playing in the same game or taking part in the same event' (Case, para. 613).

A similar situation has taken place under s. 42(1) Aus. SDA which reads:

> Nothing in Division 1 or 2 renders it unlawful to exclude persons of one sex from participation in any competitive sporting activity in which the strength, stamina or physique of competitors is relevant.

This is reproduced in legislation for the different States of Australia. The clause justifies exclusion on the basis of 'average anatomical characteristics' relating to sex, rather than on the basis of 'individual sporting performance' (Burke, 2004: 169). Its exact meaning and intentions are also very vague and has caused problems of interpretation in the Australian courts.

The Boxing Authority relied on this in *Ferneley* and its interpretation was a subsidiary issue of the case. However, since it was the first time that it had been argued in a court, it was viewed as desirable to address by Justice Wilcox who expressed that the wording was unfortunate since it might be construed to apply to same sex activities. However, it seemed clear to him that the provision was intended to only apply to mixed-sex participation (Case, para. 89). He justified this on the basis that if the provision was not intended to apply to mixed-sex participation then it would lead to strange results.

Clearly then such exemption clauses are only intended to apply to mixed-sex sports. The balance between inclusion and exclusion in sport on the basis of sex appears to be most precarious in the areas of mixed-sex sports since this directly challenges an integral structure of sports, which is sex segregation. Exemption clauses that support the segregation of men and women raise important points about the biological and social construction of men and women in the context of inclusion and exclusion in sport. It is not clear from the wording which sports strength, stamina and physique are relevant to. For instance, are they contact or non-contact, team or individual? This uncertainty forces an evaluation of the necessary skills and attributes of particular sports. The scientific truth behind such a proposition also requires clarification for it to be supported. The difficulty continues to be not so much the individual words of these exemptions but the clarification of what Parliament meant by the inclusion of these words (*Taylor v Moorabbin Saints Football League & Football Victoria [2004] VCAT 158).*

In the case of *Robertson v Australian Ice Hockey Federation [1998] VADT 112 (26 March 1998)* the Australian Ice Hockey Federation (AIHF) stipulated that females are not permitted to play in contact leagues with males over 12-years-old.

Victorian Ice Hockey competitions are organised into senior grades and junior grades. Robertson was a 15-year-old female ice hockey player. She began playing in the lower junior level ranks where non-contact ice hockey is played by children of both sexes under the age of 13. She secured a non-contact position as a goalkeeper in a higher contact junior grade club. However, because of the AIHF rules concerning mixed-sex competition she was restricted from playing with the club. Her only alternative would be to play in a female higher-level junior grade club. There were no such clubs in close proximity to Robertson for her to compete in. Robertson therefore brought a claim against the Federation arguing that they had discriminated against her on the basis of her sex. The Federation relied upon an equivalent provision under the Aus. Equal Opportunity Act 1995 (EOA), s. 66(1) which permits discrimination of one sex in competitive sport when the strength, stamina or physique of competitors is relevant. President McKenzie confirmed that whilst s. 66(1) EOA does apply to contact ice hockey since strength, stamina and physique is relevant, it cannot be sustainable for the exclusion of a female in the non-contact position of a goalkeeper (Case, para. 11).

This interpretation was upheld in the case of *Emily South v Royal Victorian Bowls Association* [2001] VCAT 207 (28 February 2001). South was a 19-year-old keen player of lawn bowls who was denied the opportunity to become an affiliated member of the Royal Victorian Bowls Association (RVBA) in order to compete in competitions, because she was female (Case, para. 4). South brought tribunal proceedings against the RVBA arguing that the decision to refuse her membership constituted sex discrimination under the EOA. The RVBA relied on s. 66 (1) EOA and were responsible for proving the establishment of this exception. The case turned on whether strength, stamina or physique is *relevant* to lawn bowls, which is not made clear in the statute. Deputy President of the tribunal, Coghlan agreed with the interpretation in *Robertson* because it cannot be interpreted to mean any sporting activity which involves strength, stamina and physique since this would 'strip the section of any meaning' and stretch it beyond its primary objective.

Having outlined the intended aims of s. 66(1) Coghlan turned to the objectives and rules of lawn bowls, which appeared to be the same for men and women. The RVBA led evidence of a scientific test showing that amongst a range of shots available in lawn bowls, a male bowler would have a distinct advantage over female bowlers executing a drive shot (an attacking or defensive shot) (Case, para. 44). The RVBA employed a second investigation to show males to be more accurate at lawn bowls than females (Case, para. 56).

Upon cross examination these tests were criticised and revealed to be flawed. Coghlan held that the RVBA had failed to prove that 'women cannot or do not use the drive shot' (Case, para. 74). Whilst there may have been evidence to show that men employ the drive shot more often than women and that it does require more strength than another shot such as a draw shot, the RVBA did not sufficiently prove that 'this is related to the difference in strength between men and women or that if it is related to differences in strength, that employing the drive makes competition uneven' (Case, para. 74). The RVBA were forced to delete the requirement that only men can be affiliated members thus allowing South to re-apply for membership.

In *Taylor v Moorabbin Saints Football League & Football Victoria* Justice Morrris interpreted s. 66(1) to hinge upon the meaning of the word relevant. He used three criteria to determine whether such a provision applies:

1 the relative differences between the sexes in strength, stamina and physique;
2 the nature of the competitive sporting activity (not just the sport, but also the age group); and
3 whether the differences between the sexes are significant (in the sense that they matter) in participating in the competitive sporting activity (Case, para. 29).

The decision in *Robertson* and *South* can be contrasted with the approach taken by the UK courts to s.44 SDA in *Bennett v. Football Association Ltd.,* 28 July 1978; Court of Appeal (CA) (Civil Division) Transcript No. 591 of 1978, C.A. Only once has s. 44 been successfully applied in the context of a girl wishing to compete in a boy's soccer team. Theresa Bennett was an 11-year-old female footballer who applied to be registered at a male club. The FA prohibited mixed teams and matches between men and women. The local FA claimed that they were bound by the FA and the European Football Union, which restricted female players. Bennett, was therefore debarred the chance to compete on grounds of her sex.

Bennett took her case to court and was supported by the Equal Opportunities Commission (EOC). The court ruled in favour of Bennett stating that s. 44 failed in light of evidence which suggests that boys and girls under the age of 12 are not dissimilar.

However, on appeal Lord Denning reversed this decision. He contended that in the absence of the s. 44 exception, the defendants would have had no justification for their actions and would have clearly been in breach of the SDA. Denning held that 'football is a game which is excepted from this statute' (Case, para. 4). He went on to express that if the law included football within the SDA then it would expose itself to 'absurdity' and would be 'an ass – a idiot if it tried to make girls into boys so that they could play in a football league' (Case, para. 5). He rejected medical evidence which used 'graphs and all sorts of things' to show that, below the age of puberty, the strength, stamina and physique of girls and boys is not markedly different (Case, para. 4).

Eveleigh LJ also rejected this evidence and dismissed the proposal to divide games for under 12s and over 12s. He interpreted s. 44 to refer to activities of a competitive nature where the physical attributes of '*womankind'* put them at a disadvantage. The judgment was predicated on the fixed notion that football was somehow a genetically determined male sport.

The age of the Bennett case is reflective of the previous overall ban on women of all ages playing football. In 1921 the FA announced that football was unsuitable for women, denying teams such as the famous Dick Kerr Ladies Football

Club from competing (Newsham, 1997: 49). Whilst football has come a long way since then, women continue to be faced with restrictions. For instance, at the time of writing, a group of leading female footballers began legal proceedings against the Canadian Soccer Association and FIFA, after it was announced that the 2015 Women's World Cup in Canada was to be played on synthetic pitches, which is considered inferior to grass pitches and also poses specific safety risks to the athletes.

In 2007, 11-year-old Minnie Crutwell secured the right to continue to play for two boys' soccer clubs instead of having to switch to move to a single sex team under the FA rules, which restrict participation at the age of 12. After lobbying with the support of the British sports minister Tessa Jowell, Crutwell forced the FA to reconsider its age limit for mixed-sex teams (Tozer, 2007). In 2010, the FA agreed to extend its age limit to under 13 from the 2010–11 season. This followed an FA-commissioned report by Brunel University in 2008 which found that if girls play with boys they will benefit from opportunities for skill development, challenge and enjoyment, social interaction and, finally, the report found that there is considerable overlap between boys and girls in relation to size, motor skill development and ability between 11–13-year-olds (The FA, 2010).

The approach of the law to prevent *Bennett* can be largely dismissed in light of the FA changes. The age bracket varies in different countries. In the Netherlands, mixed teams are permitted in youth football up until the age of 19 at all levels. Until the age of 12, mixed teams are enforced as a rule. Above 12, girls have the choice to play in a mixed team or join all-girls teams (Brink *et al.*, 2010: 121). As scientific knowledge progresses, it seems that the age limit is increasing but there is not a universal approach.

Contrary to s. 44 SDA, the exemption provisions s. 42(1) Aus. SDA and s. 66(1) Aus. EOA include a statement which makes such clauses inapplicable to children under the age of 12, thus acknowledging that physiological differences between children overlap. In *Ferneley* it was noted that this age boundary existed to eradicate myths relating to strength, stamina and physique in sport (Case, para. 78). Mckenzie in *Robertson* also agreed that it does not and cannot logically apply to children under 12 (Case, para. 9).

Justice Morris in the Australian case of *Taylor v Moorabbin Saints Football League & Football Victoria [2004] VCAT 158* offered detailed scientific evidence of the differences in strength, stamina and physique between the age groups of 12–16, focusing on the contact sport of Australian Rules Football. In which case, it was held that 14-year-old girls cannot lawfully be excluded from the sport, but that it is lawful to exclude girls over 15-years-old since relative differences in strength, stamina and physique were sufficiently significant (Case, para. 82). The decision appeared very balanced as Justice Morris went onto highlight that sport governing bodies should be lawfully allowed to adopt such rules, but at the same time the girls themselves should have the right to free choice. It was also noted that children who engage in such sports at a young age, boy or girl, are likely to be stronger and fitter than those in that average age group. It was therefore recommended that a wise policy would take self-selection into account when making such decisions (Case, para. 84). This proposition basically means that age is not necessarily the best form of categorisation.

These cases demonstrate that the sex-segregated structure of sport is continually challenged and exposed for its inadequacy. Social shifts in the gender regime weaken the previous attitudes of sports bodies and Parliament. Following increasing scrutiny, s. 44 SDA was eventually treated as 'dead law' (McArdle, 2008: 48; Patel, 2007). However a version of it continues to exist under the UK EA.

Based on the discussion thus far, it seems unreasonable, and potentially discriminatory, to exclude girls or women from competing in sports 1) against each other when health risks specific to women can be reasonably guarded against and 2) against boys, when they are below the approximate age of 13.

The position of mixed-sex adult sports is less certain and has fuelled a number of debates. Examples of men and women competing together have historically been a novelty, such as in 1973 when female tennis player Billie Jean King beat former world champion player Bobby Riggs.

In contrast to the triumph of King, in 1992 Martina Navratilova was beaten by Jimmy Connors in a tennis match battle of the champions. Similarly in 1998, German tennis player Karsten Braash, who was ranked 203 at the time, beat both Venus and Serena Williams, after the sisters claimed that they could beat any male player ranked around 200 in the world.

In December 2004 FIFA refused to allow Mexican female soccer star Maribel 'Marigoal' Dominguez to sign a two-year contract with second division club Celaya, a men's team who were reportedly looking for some publicity (Tuckman, 2005). Whilst the national football association accepted this move, it was referred to FIFA who confirmed that men and women must remain separate. Previous attempts to sign female players were made by Italian club Perugia but were aborted before the FIFA ruling (Anon, 2003). In 2004, at the Athens Olympics, Dominguez led the Mexico women's team to the quarter finals. However, FIFA went on to ban her further from competing in an exhibition match outside the league with men.

The lack of support for mixed-sex sports is overtly and covertly expressed in sport and society. For instance, in cricket in 2005, the newly appointed president of the Marylebone Cricket Club (MCC), Robin Marlar, openly conveyed that it was 'absolutely outrageous' that girls played cricket with boys (Harrison, 2005). More covertly, the surrounding culture of sport is expressed as male (Malcolm and Velija *in* Atkinson and Young, 2008: 225).

The current segregation of adult sports informs us that men and women would remain separated if a female adult wished to compete alongside adult males. The rationale behind this segregation in sport seems to rest on two interconnected arguments that are influenced by a range of moral, medical and aesthetic factors and reflected in the sport exemption clauses (Hartmann-Tews and Pfister, 2003: 267).

The strength argument

Female exclusion from sport has been justified on the basis of the physiological differences between men and women which make competition between them imbalanced and therefore contrary to the essence of sport. Section 44 SDA (now s. 195 EA), s. 42 (1) Aus. SDA and s. 66(1) Aus. EOA adopts this approach by positing that average strength, speed and stamina typically favour the average man and will put him at an advantage over the average woman in sports. The inherent problem with this assertion is its overly broad application.

Part I highlights the fact that men are inherently stronger and more aggressive than women as a result of evolutionary and social adaptive problems and roles throughout history. From a physiology perspective, VO_2 max (oxygen uptake) is closely associated with success in endurance events. A high VO_2 max will be associated with high endurance and someone with a high VO_2 max will therefore (typically) be able to exercise at higher intensities. It is accepted that women achieve a lower VO_2 max score than men, which can be due to body composition and haemoglobin concentration (McArdle *et al.*, 2007: 244). In terms of body composition, men tend to possess less body fat and more muscle mass than women and therefore are able to generate more total anaerobic energy than women. Although trained athletes possess less body fat, women still possess more than their male counterparts. A greater haemoglobin concentration in men means that they are able to circulate more oxygen during exercise, which increases their aerobic capabilities.

When evaluating differences in muscle strength, it is important to look at the cross-sectional muscle area as well as the absolute muscle strength. In terms of the muscles cross-sectional area, those with the largest muscle cross-sections generate the greatest absolute force (McArdle *et al.*, 2007: 515). There seems to be little difference when testing the same size muscle of men and women. In terms of absolute muscular strength however, men appear to possess much greater strength (Epstein, 2013: 65). If we consider the sport of weight lifting, where men and women participate in the same categories on the basis of identical body mass, it is found that lighter weight categories produce smaller sex differences whereas larger body mass women tend to lift about 60 per cent of the maximal weight lifted by their male counterparts (McArdle *et al.*, 2007: 516).

It has been suggested that the way in which muscle strength is scientifically calculated can have an effect on the differences rated between men and women (p. 516). In sports which require exceptional muscular strength, power and anaerobic capacity, it is argued that gender equality may emerge one day in middle distance swimming events, where there has been closer male and female times recorded (McArdle *et al.*, 2007: 819). From a social perspective, traditional gender roles and differences in absolute strength have resulted in misconceived approaches to strength training for women (Ebben and Lenson, 1998). Had it not been for the unenlightened medical knowledge and years of being debarred from competitive sport, studies propose that women would be on a more level footing with men (Anon, 1999). Physiology perspectives do not ignore the fact that social factors can also account for body fat and haemoglobin differences in men and women (McArdle *et al.*, 2007: 244).

Physiological differences between men and women in sport are more exposed in activities such as running. In recent times, the 'gender gap' between male and female running times has caused huge scientific and academic debate (Tatem *et al,* 2004; Anon, 2004b; Constance, 2004; Seiler and Sailer, 1997; Whipp and Ward, 1992). Studies suggesting that women may one day run faster than men have been heavily criticised (Anon, 2004b: 147; Constance, 2004). Those who believe that the gender gap will remain, do so on the basis that the 'hormonal gap' between men and women can never be closed (Seiler and Sailor, 1997). Suggestions that gender differences decrease as the race distance increases have also been criticised (McArdle *et al.*, 2007: 245).

With this brief evaluation of the physiological differences between men and women it is clear that physical strength will favour men on average. In order to provide some level of consistency within sport, it seems reasonable to some extent to organise sports along the lines of sex since strength is a dominant factor of many sports which determines the outcome of success or failure in a competition. From a regulatory perspective, there does require some demarcation of physical differences to ensure competitive balance and maintain safety. However, to prohibit the practice of all mixed-sex sports because of strength differences ignores the significant variations between sports, since different sports require different skills and abilities which do not always include strength.

Non-contact sports such as golf are a good illustration of this. Men's strength allows them to hit the ball further and for this reason the sport adheres to these biological differences by placing the tees further away for men. However, once within 125 yards of the pin, strength is less important and instead style and technique impact upon performance. Consequently, although strength may make a female less able to hit the ball further, she is still capable of competing due to other factors and attributes which a sportsperson may excel in. Historically, many successful women have played in the men's PGA tour events. More recently, Hawaiian golfer Wie exceeded women in tournaments early on in her career, and won the Hawaii State Open in 2002 against a host of scratch players and former male professionals, from a set of tees only 10 per cent shorter in yardage. At the Sony Open in Hawaii 2004, although she may have missed the cut by a single shot, upon qualification she finished tied 47th against 96 men and from championship tees. Her early success exposed some of the traditional structures of golf.

In team sports, different positions exist which require varied levels of strengths. The decision in *Robertson* emphasises this. In boat racing, for example, whilst the average woman would naturally be at a disadvantage to a male in rowing, the role of coxing a crew has no advantage for a male. Furthermore, every sport does not require strength as a leading factor. The strength argument may therefore fail in certain circumstances.

The restriction of mixed-sex sports on the basis of strength also disregards the significant differences between each individual human being and within the sexes. It appears to ignore the fact that there is considerable overlap between men and women's anatomical and physiological characteristics which impact upon sporting performance (Burke, 2004: 173). Whilst it is certain the men are naturally stronger than women, so too are individuals naturally stronger than each other within one sex. Such broad application reflects a misguided use of stereotypes which have led to the enforcement of regulatory mechanisms such as the exclusion clauses, reflecting those inaccuracies at times. Whilst it is accepted that men are generally stronger than women, this should only be used to exclude them where strength is a dominant factor of that sport. Where it is not, then this can lead to unreasonable exclusion. What underpins this strength argument is the idea that because women are not as strong as men, mixed participation could lead to possible health and safety risks for women.

The safety argument

Secondly, the safety of athletes is a common argument which presents itself when challenges to sports bodies are made. It is argued that females would be at a greater risk of physical harm and injury if they were to compete in sports with men because of the physiological differences between the sexes. Ability would not be matched because of this, which would threaten the safety of the athletes. In order to guard against this, sport has created rules and selection criteria which aim to match ability and ensure safety. This can be termed the precautionary principle.

The focus on the protection of women is reflective of their wider treatment in society. The historic exclusion of women from physical activity has usually been connected to their perceived role as mother and wife. Although there has been a shift in the medical opinion of women in sport, the misguided paternalistic protection of women still continues to surface.

From a practical perspective, it could be argued that where strength is a determinant factor and where safety may be threatened as a result of the physical make-up of a woman, most likely in sports which involve physical contact between men and women, then it is a reasonable justification to exclude women from those activities, unless appropriate modifications could be made to the sport to include them. The US courts have been faced with clarifying the correct application of the precautionary principle when determining the applicability of equality legislation to sport.

Title IX specifically excludes contact sports from its application on the basis of safety, since females are considered to be at risk from bodily contact with males. Contact sport included ‘boxing, wrestling, rugby, ice hockey, football, basketball and other contact sports the purpose or major activity of which involved bodily contact’ (Title IX). This exemption permits the existence of all-male contact teams in educational establishments in the USA and they are only required to provide all-female equivalent teams if a sufficient standard of interest and ability exists to sustain such a team (Sangree, 2000: 391). Governing bodies have relied on this to exclude females from competing in sports on the basis that it would be dangerous for them.

The workability of this approach has been difficult because of the lack of clarity between contact and non-contact sports. Some sports are difficult to classify as contact or non-contact. For instance, soccer and basketball are strictly speaking non-contact sports, with rules in place to expressly prohibit contact (Sangree,

2000: 396). However when properly played, 'incidental' contact is inherent and inevitable in the sport. The court has ruled on the contact sport exemption that girls should be judged by their ability instead (*Mercer v Duke University* 181 F. Supp 2d. 525, 531 (MDNC 2001); *Lantz by Lantz v Ambach* 620 F. Supp 663 (1985)).

Despite the contrasting opinions of the courts on what constitutes a contact sport, it appears that contact sports may be defined by the rules and the culture of the sport. Incidental contact can take place in the heat of the moment of a sport, or as part of the nature of the sport. Such sports would therefore fall under the 'catch all' element of the exemption 'and other sports the purpose or major activity of which involves bodily contact.' Perhaps the driver behind this could be economic, that is, exempting the sports which produce the highest revenue (Sangree, 2000). A more suitable question to ask is whether bodily contact forms the purpose or essence of the sport, which would create particular risks to females if they were to compete with males.

In purely contact sports, it is undisputable that bodily contact forms the essence of the sport. It is here where the precautionary principle has some legitimacy because of the differences in strength between men and women. However, for female children competing in mixed-sex sports, the US legal approach has largely been to support them because of the effect of puberty on physiological differences as discussed earlier.

In *Clinton v Nagy,* 411 F. Supp. 1396 (N.D. Ohio 1974), a 12-year-old girl was refused permission by the US Football Association to compete in an American football team simply because it 'was the law' and because of safety concerns (Case, para. 1397). Clinton therefore brought a sex discrimination claim against the defendants. The District Judge Lambros held that the defendants had failed to prove that Clinton did not possess the relevant qualifications or physical ability required of male members to compete in the league. Neither did they prove that she is more susceptible to injury than other members because she is female. He also stated that safety equipment given to boys in the league is adequate for the protection of a female in the league also.

On the general point of contact sports, Lambros held that football by its nature is a dangerous game, which is a wider societal concern. Regardless, it continues to be played and encouraged even though there are potential dangers (Case, para. 1400). Overcoming these potential dangers arguably develops particular characters in boys such as leadership, which should also extend to girls. Overall, he asserted that 'it is necessary that we begin to focus on the individual rather than thinking in broad generalities which have oftentimes resulted in the imposition of irrational barriers, against one class or another' (Case, para. 1400).

The defendants failed to justify why safety arguments only applied to girls and not boys as in the case of *Darrin v Gould, 540 P.2d 882 (Wash. 1975).* Two sisters aged 16 and 14, wished to play contact American football but there were no contact football teams for girls. The high school football team coach viewed that they were qualified and eligible to practice with the boys' team. However, the Washington Interscholastic Activities Association (WIAA) regulations prohibited girls from participating with boys. The Darrin family brought a claim against this decision which was rejected by the court and an appeal followed. The appeal was upheld by Judge Hamilton who expressed that boys as well as girls run the risk of physical injury in contact football games (Case, para. 892). Yet on the same day as the WIAA restricted the girls from competing, they permitted the inclusion of an unqualified boy to play on a high school football team. This privilege was not given to the girls who met the requirements, thus highlighting the inconsistent application of the precautionary principle.

Judge Roberts in the case of *Force by Force v. Pierce City R-VI School District, 570 F. Supp. 1020 (S.W. Mo, 1983)* offered poignant commentary on the trend towards what was regarded as gender-based classification. A 13-year-old student attempted to compete in the boys' school football team because there was no female equivalent. However, she was refused by the school board on the grounds that since male athletes will outperform female athletes in most athletic endeavours, sports need to be segregated in order to maximise participation and opportunity for each sex. On this point Judge Roberts agreed with the importance of encouraging participation of both sexes but did not accept gender-based classification was the way to achieve this. He remarked that each sport is different, 'volleyball is not football; baseball is not hockey; and swimming is not tennis' to emphasise the lack of logic behind denying all persons of one sex the opportunity to test their skills at a particular sport (Case, para. 1028). The board also contended that the segregation of females and males in a football team maintains safety standards but failed to provide supporting evidence. This was considered overly paternalistic by the judge (Case, para. 1029).

In *Adams by Adams v Baker* 919 F. Supp 1496 (1996) a school restricted a 15-year-old girl from wrestling in the high school team with boys. The school board relied on the Title IX exemption to support their actions since this was a contact sport (Case, para. 1501). In addition they referred to moral objections from parents, the possibility of sexual harassment lawsuits, the safety of the athlete and the disruption to the school setting. The athlete claimed that the school district had violated her right to equal protection by refusing to let her try out for the team because of her gender. The court upheld the Title IX exemption (Case, para. 1503) and agreed that safety and sexual harassment were important objectives to pursue. However, they held that the policy prohibiting females from wrestling was not substantially related to those objectives. Instead, the defendants evidence that females are at a greater risk was based upon 'generalized assumptions' which reflect an overpaternalistic attitude as raised above (Case, para. 1504). The court made the point that it is 'improper to subject boys to greater danger than girls' (Case, para. 1504).

The judgments in these cases reveal that whilst the precautionary principle is a legitimate objective to pursue, there needs to be a direct relationship between the objective and the imposition of sex segregation in sport. It can certainly not just apply to one sex when both are exposed to the same risks. In addition, the scientific evidence presented by the defendants in the cases, to show that girls are more susceptible to serious injury than boys in particular sport, was consistently rejected as unsupported and insufficient by the courts. The court rationale behind these decisions appear to be based upon the evidence that girls and boys share little physiological differences before puberty, as concluded in the FA-commissioned Brunel study.

In the case of *Fortin v Darlington Little League 514 F.2d 344 (1975)* a 10-year-old girl was restricted from playing baseball. The District Court denied the girl inclusion on the grounds of 'rational' exclusion (Case, para. 346). The court felt that there would be a serious risk if girls played a technically non-contact sport such as baseball because of the physical differences between men and women. The CA reversed this decision in the absence of any substantial evidence supporting a claim that there were relevant physical differences between boys and girls (Case, para. 349). Instead, the exclusion was based upon 'archaic and over broad generalisations about the difference in roles of men and women' (Case, para. 348). The CA found that the previous court decision was unsupported.

Where strength is a determinant factor of the sport, and where strength is measurable, it is important to maintain segregation of men and women in order to match ability for safety and entertainment reasons and to be true to the fundamental essence of the sport. Mixed-sex boxing is a good example of the legitimate application of the precautionary principle. Little coverage of this sport appears in the media or the literature, but there are examples of athletes such as Laila Ali, Jackie Frazier Lyde, Irichelle Duran and Freeda Foreman who practice the sport. In the US case of *Lafler v Athletic Board of Control 536 F. Supp. 104 (WD Mich. 1982)* the court held that the inclusion of a 19-year-old female novice into a male boxing competition would fundamentally alter the essence of boxing. The rationale is reasonable since safety and anatomy does matter in boxing. It was accepted that the real differences between men and women are relevant in this sport (Case, para. 106). Boxing has developed rules and procedures designed for men. It was therefore highlighted in the case that it is unrealistic for women to operate under the same rules since their specific safety needs would be compromised. The claimant admitted to wearing a breast protector to safeguard against gender-specific injuries. However, wearing a breast protector would conflict with Rule 6, Article 9 of the Amateur Boxing Federations (US ABF) rules since blows to the chest are permitted in men's boxing and women would be more prone to injury since they have sensitive mammary glands, which men do not have. These rule differences could therefore alter the essence of boxing if it is confirmed that punches to the chest are an essential feature of the sport. The ABF rule also requires men to wear a protective cup to safeguard against their unique anatomical characteristics, but this does not conflict with the rules.

Similar rule change concerns were also raised in *Couch* but they were rejected by the courts possibly because the case involved same-sex boxing. *Lafler* implies that separate competitions are more appropriate because 'where the sexes are not situated equally with respect to a particular activity, the state may deal with the sexes differently in regulating the activity' (Case, para. 107).

It was also accepted that although in previous cases involving other contact sports, arguments relating to injury to females were rejected, boxing was differentiated because it used 'body weight as a proxy for strength in an attempt to equalize the relative physical capabilities of opposing boxers. The general dissimilarity in body make up between men as a class and women as a class would jeopardize the use of body weight for this equalising purpose in a unified male and female competition. Therefore, these general class characteristics are relevant to a decision regarding the status of women in boxing, even though they might not be relevant in other sports' (Case, para. 107).

Summary

Whilst divisions between men and women are an integral part of the essence of sport, this chapter has examined whether there is any truth behind the rationale, and the legitimacy of the sport and regulatory approach to sex segregation.

Many decisions were positive resulting in justifiable inclusion. The courts have tended to reject arguments by sports bodies or authorities that girls are at risk from physical harm if they compete with boys and they have favoured young female athletes when they have been unreasonably excluded from competing in mixed-sex contact or non-contact competitions. One exception to this is *Bennett*, which can largely be discounted given current social shifts towards increasing the age restrictions on mixed-sex participation. The *Taylor* decision establishes reasonable age limits to mixed-sex participation but also suggested that such categorisation may not be the most appropriate form of managing inclusion and exclusion. In these cases the courts have interpreted exemption clauses in a way which seeks to identify the most rational meaning.

The *Lafler* case reveals that exclusion can be justifiable in certain situations where the physiological differences will unavoidably impact upon strength and safety. It is necessary to uphold the segregation of the sexes where strength is a determinant factor of the sport and where female safety may be compromised as a result of the imbalance of strength differences between men and women.

Areas of most contention have been female only sports and there have been mixed approaches by the courts. A number of sex cases have resulted in unjustified exclusion. Consistent throughout these cases is the reluctance of the law courts to intervene in sporting issues and to apply non-discrimination laws. In many of the cases the matters were heard by different courts who have reached contrasting decisions. The inconsistency produced in these cases arguably reflects the difficulties that the courts face in balancing inclusion and exclusion in sporting activity.

References

Anon. 1999. Sporty women held back by sexist myths. *BBCi Website* [online], 31 March. Available at: http://news.bbc.co.uk/1/hi/health/307769.stm [accessed 14/03/01].

Anon. 2003. Perugia Pursue Female Star. *BBCi Website* [online], 10 December. Available at: http://news.bbc.co.uk/sport1/hi/football/europe/3093147.stm [accessed 11/12/03].

Anon. 2004. Women footballers blast Blatter. *BBCi Website* [online], 16 January. Available at: http://news.bbc.co.uk/sport1/hi/football/3402519.stm [accessed 18/01/04].

Anon. 2004b. Linear models cant keep up with sport gender gap. *Nature*, 432, 11 November.: 147.

Anon. 2009a. Women fail in ski jump appeal. *BBCi Website* [online], 22 December. Available at http://news.bbc.co.uk/sport1/hi/olympic_games/vancouver_2010/8427216.stm [accessed 23/12/09].

Anon. 2009b. Women's boxing gains Olympic spot. *BBCi Website* [online], 13 August. Available at http://news.bbc.co.uk/sport1/hi/olympic_games/8196879.stm [accessed 01/03/10].

Anon. 2011. Closing the Gap. *Sport Business International*, 168, June: 48–54.

Archer. J. and Lloyd. B. 2002. *Sex and Gender*, 2nd Edition. Cambridge: Cambridge University Press.

Atkinson, M. and Young, K. 2008. *Tribal Play: subcultural journeys through sport.* Bingley: Emerald Group Publishing.

Brink, M., Loenen, T. and Tignchelaar, J. 2010. Sex segregation and equality in a multicultural society: inferiority as a standard for legal acceptability. *Utrecht Law Review.* 6(2): 115–144.

Burke, M. 2004. Radicalising Liberal Feminism by Playing the Games that Men Play. *Australian Feminist Studies*, 19(44), pp.169–184.

Burton, R. 2010. A Divisive Strategy. *Sport Business International*, 155, April: 20.

Chan, C. 2009. Female ski jumpers seek Olympic inclusion. *Epoch Times* [online], 1 May. Available at: www.theepochtimes.com/n2/content/view/16139/ [accessed 20/04/10]

Cohen, C. 2014. Why this female football manager quitting should matter to you. *The Telegraph.* 28 June [online] Available at: www.telegraph.co.uk/women/10931749/Why-this-female-football-manager-quitting-should-matter-to-you.html [accessed 11/08/14].

Constance, H. 2004. An Everlasting Gender Gap? *Science*. 305(5684), 30 July: 639–640.

Donnelly, P. and Donnelly, M. 2013. *The London 2012 Olympics: A gender equality audit.* Centre for Sport Policy Studies Research Reports. University of Toronto.

Ebben, P.W. and Lenson, R.L. 1998. Debunking Myths that Block Opportunity. *The Physician and Sports Medicine*, 26(5): 86–89.

Ebner, D. 2012. Female canoe racer takes Olympic inequality to court. *The Globe and Mail* [online] 18 July. Available at: www.theglobeandmail.com/sports/olympics/female-canoe-racer-takes-olympic-inequality-to-court/article4426727/ [accessed 09/09/14].

Ellison, J.G. 2009. Women Can't Jump: Canadian court outsources sexual discrimination in Winter Olympics. *The Faster Times – International Law and Society* [online]. Available at: http://thefastertimes.com/internationallaw-society/2009/07/27/female-ski-jumpers-vancouver-olympics-canadian-court-allows-sexual-discrimination/ [accessed 10/04/10].

Epstein, D. 2013. *The Sports Gene: Talent, practice and the truth about success.* London: Yellow Jersey Press. FA., The., 2010. *Mixed football announcement.* [online] TheFA.com. Available at: http://nav.thefa.com/sitecore/content/TheFA/Home/GetIntoFootball/NewsAndFeatures/2010/mixed-football-announcement-180310 [accessed 30/12/14].

Felix, A. 1998. The Fleetwood Assassin Strikes another Blow for Female Boxing. *Sports Law Bulletin*, 1(3), May/June.

Fenelon, L. 2009. Discriminating Tastes. *Law Society Gazette*, December: 16–19.

Harrison, D. 2005. Absurd, old fashioned and patronising. *The Daily Telegraph* [online], 2 October. Available at: www.telegraph.co.uk/news/uknews/1499705/Absurd-old-fashioned-and-patronising.html [accessed 04/10/05].

Hartmann-Tews, I. and Pfister, G. 2003. *Sport and Women: social issues in international perspective.* London: Routledge.

HL Deb 15 July 1975 vol 362 cc 1113-221 [online]. Available at: http://hansard.millbanksystems.com/lords/1975/jul/15/sex-discrimination-bill [accessed 10 July 2011].

International Olympic Committee (IOC). 2009. *Factsheet: women in the Olympic Movement.* Olympic.org [online], December. Available at: www.olympic.org/Documents/Reference_documents_Factsheets/Women_in_Olympic_Movement.pdf [accessed 30/12/14].

James, M. 2010. *Sports Law.* Basingstoke: Palgrave Macmillan.

Lafferty, Y. and McKay, J. 2004. Suffragettes in Satin Shorts? Gender and Competitive Boxing. *Qualitative Sociology*, 27(3): 249–276.

Lines, K. and Heshka, J. 2009. Ski jumping through Olympic sized hoops: an analysis of Sagen & Others v Vancouver Organising Committee (VANOC) for the 2010 Olympic and Paralympic Winter Games. *International Sports Law Review*, 4: 92–99.

McArdle, D. 2008. Swallows and amazons, or the sporting exception to the Gender Recognition Act. *Social and Legal Studies*, 17(1): 39–57.

Mcardle, W.D., Katch, F.I. and Katch. V.L. 2007. *Exercise Physiology.* Lippincott: Williams & Wilkins.

Miller, T., Lawrence, G.A., McKay, J. and Rowe, D. 2001. *Globalisation and Sport.* London: Sage Publications.

Newsham, G. J. 1997. *In a league of their own! The Dick Kerr Ladies Football Team.* Chorley: Pride of Publishing.

Pannick, D. 1983. *Sex Discrimination in Sport.* London: Equal Opportunities Commission.

Patel, S. 2007. *Women in Sport: an Anglo-American Comparison.* Oral presentation given at the "Girls and Women Rock: Celebrating 35 Years of Sport and Title IX" Academic and Legal Conference hosted by Cleveland University, Cleveland, USA in March 2007.

Patel, S. 2010. Women's Ski Jumping and Olympic Programme Inclusion. *World Sports Law Report*, 8(7) July: 11–14.

Patel, S. 2014. The Legal View. *SportsPro Magazine*, September, 69.: 58.

Sangree, S. 2000. Title IX and the Contact Sports Exemption: gender stereotypes in a civil rights statute. *Connecticut Law Review*, 32(2): 381–449.

Seiler, S. and Sailer, S. 1997. The Gender Gap: Elite women are running further behind. *SportScience News* [online] May–June. Available at: www.sportsci.org/news/news9705/gengap.html [accessed 30/12/14].

Tatem, A.J., Guerra, C.A., Atkinson, P.M. and Hay, S.I. 2004. Momentous sprint at the 2156 Olympics? *Nature*, 431, 30 September: 525.

Tozer, J. 2007. 11-year-old girl wins landmark right to play football with the big boys. *Mail Online* [online]. Available at: www.dailymail.co.uk/news/article-458021/11-year-old-girl-wins-landmark-right-play-football-big-boys.html [accessed 1/03/10].

Tuckman, J. 2005. It's a Man's Game. *The Guardian* [online], 5 January. Available at: www.guardian.co.uk/football/2005/jan/05/womensfootball.sport [accessed 06/01/05].

Turner, J. 2009. It's Time to Challenge Casual Sexism. *The Times Online.* [online]. Available at: www.thetimes.co.uk/tto/life/article1750638.ece [accessed 28/12/14].

Wackwitz, L.A. 2003. Verifying the Myth: Olympic Sex Testing and the Category "Woman". *Women's Studies International Forum*, 26(6): 553–560.

Whipp, B.J. and Ward, S.A. 1992. Will women soon outrun men? *Nature*, 335(6355), 2 January: 25.

Williams, M. 2013. A pragmatic solution for gender equity in Canadian elite sport. *International Sports Law Journal*, 13: 18–34.

5 Gender

In Part I we established the overlap between the concepts of sex and gender, with sex being the biological identification of a man and woman, and gender as the social identity attached to masculinity and femininity. Against the background of the previous chapter, this chapter will investigate the participation of intersex individuals and transgender individuals who do not conform to the traditional gender notions of male or female. Their inclusion into sport conflicts with the current categorisation of sporting activity and raises important concerns about the impact of performance advantage upon the balance between inclusion and exclusion in sport.

The regulatory mechanisms in place to manage the balance, tends to draw the line according to the level of advantage that an athlete possesses. With this in mind, the concept of fair/unfair advantage in sport will be evaluated to assess how consistently cases concerning advantage in sport are managed (Patel, 2008; Patel 2009a; Patel 2009b). This chapter continues to uncover the truth about human differences, which have over time been misinterpreted particularly in competitive sport.

Sex testing in sport

As we have seen, the participation of women in sport has generally challenged the expected gender roles. On the one hand, they are celebrated for their strength, power and stamina but at the same time viewed with suspicion because these are traits which still remain associated with masculinity and, in turn, advantage in sport (Olsen-Acre, 2007: 210). This was particularly pertinent at the time of the Cold War when sex testing was introduced to regulate advantage and restore the 'natural' order between men and women.

Sex testing began as a way of deterring deliberate cheats in the Eastern Bloc. The Cold War brought about increased competition which created many opportunities for female athletes but also began to scrutinise those who did not look feminine (Wamsley, 2008: 11). Suspicions around this time were high, with drugs and 'uncertain women' threatening the purity of sport. Indeed sports bodies were keen to prevent the re-occurrence of men such as German athlete Hermann Ratjen (or Dora Ratjen) in 1936, masquerading as women in order to triumph in female competitions (Doig *et al.,* 1997: 2).

Attempts to enter female competition were premised upon the idea that men possessed inherent physical characteristics which were superior to women, making them more suited to sport. Upon this, participation would lead to unfair outcomes if men competed in women's events. In addition, it was considered that only normal feminine looking women should compete in sport and the rules of sport should reflect that.

In order to prevent gender fraud and scandal, sex testing was a method of regulating advantage (Menon, 2010). Such testing has been central to a number of conflicting ethical and practical arguments within sport, regulation and society because the methods were not necessarily based upon accurate markers. They led to the exclusion of individuals whose gender was naturally uncertain and could not be strictly categorised.

For example, sprinter Stella Walsh nicknamed 'stella the fella' (Ritchie *et al.*, 2008: 395) was a Polish emigrant who lived in the USA and won the 100 metre gold medal in 1932. She was later killed in a shooting and in her autopsy it was found that she possessed both male and female genitalia. In 1934, Czechoslovakian Zdenka Koubkova twice broke the women's world 800 metre record but was later discovered to have ambiguous genitalia and underwent reassignment to become male. These examples began to threaten the typical male and female dyad which existed in sporting competitions as it was increasingly thought that if these individuals possessed male genitalia also, then they were cheating as they had an advantage over other women.

The first method of sex testing was a 'peek and poke' examination based upon outward appearance only. Female ambiguity prompted the requirement at the 1966 European Track and Field Championships in Budapest, of female athletes to parade naked in front of a panel of gynaecologists to confirm their identity (Heggie *in* Hargreaves and Anderson, 2014: 342). All passed the test but it proved to be very humiliating. Women themselves, however, felt it important to prove their true identity. Irina and Tamara Press from the former Soviet Union dominated a number of track and field events during the 1950s and 1960s. However, they never attended the examinations which sparked controversy over their identity. This test was concerned only with the athlete's outward appearance to determine sex, which is inaccurate and misleading.

As technology advanced, genetic and hormonal checks such as the 'Barr body test' was introduced at the 1968 Summer and Winter Games. This was concurrent with the introduction of drugs testing by the IOC. Testing moved away from outward appearance and was instead based upon the chromosomal definition of sex which typically constitutes an XX configuration with a female and an XY configuration with a male. Spectators and competitors in sport feared that if we allow women who naturally possess the chromosomal XY pattern then they will begin to dominate. This reinforced the belief that the possession of a male Y chromosome produces superior athletic ability.

Such testing forced many top athletes quietly out of competition. The confidential nature of the information regarding these tests makes it difficult to confirm exactly how many athletes quietly withdrew. One study found that one in

504 athletes competing in selected events during 1972 and 1990 were disqualified for failing a sex test (Olsen-Acre, 2007: 219). In 1964 Polish sprinter Ewa Klubukowska was the first female athlete not to pass the test upon discovery of an irregular XXY chromosome pattern (Shy, 2007: 99). She was disqualified from competing and her 100 metre sprint record was removed from the record books.

In 1991, the inaccuracy and illegality of this procedure prompted the IAAF to abolish mandatory chromosomal and genetic testing on the grounds that women with 'birth defects of the sex chromosomes' have no unfair advantage and should be permitted to compete. In addition, they expressed that chromosomal make-up needs to be considered alongside legal and psychological recognition of sex. The primary reason of preventing gender fraud was not necessarily sustainable and instead a case-by-case approach should be adopted (Ljungqvist *et al.,* 2006). However, the IAAF council continued to give discretionary authority to medical delegates to test the sex of an athlete.

The IOC on the other hand, continued with testing and introduced a new test, the polymerase chain reaction (PCR) test in Albertville 1992. It was another type of chromosome detector which also failed to consider the wider range of factors which determine sex such as self-identification. The PCR analysis was solely based upon the technically preferable SRY gene test, which identified ambiguous female athletes upon discovery of a Y male chromosome (Nau, 1992). At that time it was thought that this accurately distinguished men and women. If a woman possessed this chromosome then it was argued that she had an unfair advantage in the field as she possessed more strength. Genetic anomalies and other considerations in relation to the determination of sex were simply not considered. In 1996, eight of over 3,000 female athletes at the Atlanta Olympic Games tested positive for evidence of a Y chromosome but were permitted to compete because they were found to have a condition that inhibits the masculinising function of the hormone testosterone. Over five Olympic Games, approximately one in every 421 female athletes were found to have a Y chromosome (Foddy and Savulescu, 2010: 2).

The IOC abandoned the SRY test and they banned mass sex testing at the Sydney Games in 2000. The previous inconsistencies with the tests demonstrate the unreliability of the method. In fact, chromosomes remotely affect performance and biology is certainly against such chromosome sex determination (Gooren and Bunck, 2004: 425; Samuels, 2004: 151).

In modern terminology, gender verification has replaced sex testing, and the process has moved to a 'suspicion-based' model where testing can still take place on an individual basis. In the 2008 Beijing Olympics the organising committee released a state-of-the-art sex verification laboratory to be available throughout the game to run blood tests on 'suspicious looking women' (Buzuvis, 2011: 37).

The history of sex testing informs us that the underlying rationale was to prevent gender fraud, eliminate scandal, ensure fairness and fair performance advantage, and maintain the natural order of masculinity and femininity (Cooper, 2010: 251). Today, this rationale is not entirely relevant since the existence of men disguising themselves as women seems unrealistic in modern sport. The literature documents no more than two reported instances of this taking place in history (Menon, 2010: 409; Patino *et al.*, 2010: 314). Ensuring fair advantage in sport is a legitimate aim. Sport is categorised along sex and gender lines in order to uphold competition and safety. However, the consequences of testing and dividing sport along only some of the factors which determine sex can lead to the unreasonable exclusion of innocent women who may naturally vary.

Intersex

The term intersex refers to a subset of variations of sexual differentiation, which can stem from ambiguity in one of the factors which typically determine sex, such as genetics, hormones or genitalia. Intersex is rare but refers to a spectrum of conditions as we shall see below (Tucker and Collins, 2009: 148). Such conditions have the potential to threaten the life of the individual and can also result in difficulties during puberty. Previously these individuals were referred to as hermaphrodite, but the term has been criticised as it tends to place such individuals in the 'realm of mythology' rather than within society (Aaronson and Aaronson, 2010: 1). Some experts use the collective name of 'disorders of sex development' (DSD) (Aaronson and Aaronson, 2010: 2) but this is not necessarily satisfactory because the term 'disorder' suggests something which is dysfunctional. For now, the term intersex will be adopted here.

In sport, some forms of intersex conflict with sex testing because individuals may possess characteristics which are presumed to provide an unfair advantage. The current assumption upon which sex testing methods and sex segregation in sport is based, supposes that the long-term androgen exposure of men after puberty, coupled with the male-specific Y chromosome widens the physiological gap between men and women (Ballantyne *et al.*, 2011: 2). The DNA of humans is made up of 22 pairs of autosomes and one pair of sex chromosomes in most cell types in our bodies (Tucker and Collins, 2009: 148). Normally speaking, a female possesses an XX pattern and a male possesses an XY pattern. However, it is possible for different cells in an individual to naturally contain different sex chromosomes. This diversity is referred to as mosaicism.

Little is actually known about the relationship between intersex and an unfair advantage in sport (Tucker and Collins, 2009: 150). It may be impossible to know whether an unfair advantage exists due to the rarity of these conditions as well as the ethical implications of confidentiality. Individuals may live their lives assuming that they are one sex/gender. It is suggested that there is a high rate of women in sport who, possibly unknowingly, have an intersex condition (Foddy and Savulescu, 2010: 2). The results of sex tests may produce a range of psychological concerns for an athlete. Men and women claiming to be 'natural' have a naïve view, as elite sports are thought to be filled with women and men who have genetic or congenital conditions. One person in every 100 possesses a body that differs to that of a typical male or female (Middle Sex, 2005).

For instance, partial or complete androgen insensitivity syndrome (AIS) occurs in females who possess a Y chromosome resulting in the individual's chromosomal, gonadal and hormonal sex being male but their secondary characteristics, such as musculature, being female. As a result, their external genitalia are female and so they develop into, and identify with, a woman. This can be a result of androgen synthesis or action. Androgens can have a range of effects on the primary and secondary sex characteristics of humans, through the development stage and throughout adulthood. They importantly develop the growth of body hair and male sex organs and also restrict the development of female characteristics, such as breasts. In relation to sport, they assist in the growth of skeletal muscle, bones and red blood cells, all of which play an important part in athletic ability (Foddy and Savulescu, 2010: 1).

A similar syndrome is known as congenital virilising adrenal hyperplasia (CVAH) where XX subjects produce an abnormal amount of androgen, which results in an affected XX foetus with ovaries but also with external male genitalia. They are therefore raised as boys. In some of these cases the condition produces salt wasting in the body which can hinder growth but can also result in the development of high muscle strength. Under a sex test such women would pass but would possess naturally producing steroids.

Those who are known to have Turner's Syndrome are found to be missing an X chromosome. They are subsequently represented as XO instead of XX. It has been reported that even this has prevented female athletes from enjoying life-long careers in sports. Some individuals may be neither XX nor XY or some may have both XX and XY cells (For more detail see Patino *et al.*, 2010: 310). Sex tests fail to consider men who also possess variations such as 'super men' who carry the YY chromosomal pattern. Ironically, certain types of genetically abnormal males would pass a verification test and could participate as a female under the chromosome method (Fastiff, 1992: 944). A male with XXY chromosomes (Klinefelter Syndrome) would pass the test, even though the Y chromosome identifies him as male. The same would apply to a male with XX chromosomes. Both of these variations continue to have a normal male body build, male muscle strength and a male psychological and social orientation. Of course, the likelihood of this is very remote yet it reflects the impracticality of only considering one aspect which determines sex.

Maria Patino and Santhi Soundarajin

A widely reported case study concerns Spanish hurdler Maria Martinez Patino who, in 1985, failed a test at the World University Games in Kobe after it was found that she possessed a Y chromosome and male genitalia. She ignored all advice to fake an injury and quietly retire. Instead, she triumphantly won the competition, despite losing her sports scholarship and being erased from sporting history (Epstein, 2013: 59). She was the first woman to protest about her disqualification and was eventually reinstated. In fact, her legacy challenged the concept of who is male or female for the purposes of sport and whether the chromosome tests were an appropriate method for determining this (Greenberg, 1999; O'Reilly, 2010). Patino was raised as a girl despite her ambiguous genitalia and never personally doubted her femininity as there were many other factors which determined her sexuality.

Patino suffered from AIS. Although she had a Y chromosome, testes and testosterone secretion at puberty, her body developed as a female and she had no competitive advantage (Patino *et al.,* 2010: 311). It would be 'illogical' to disqualify an individual with AIS from competitions because the typical female in fact has a competitive advantage over them (Dreger, 2010: 23).

Such cases have continued to surface and at the Asian Games in 2006, an Indian female athlete Santhi Soundarajin, was stripped of her 800 metre silver medal after failing an IOC sex test. She was found to possess 'abnormal chromosomes' and was diagnosed with a more complex version of AIS. She claimed to be treated as a 'social outcast' and was forced to become a labourer in India. She was so psychologically traumatised by the experience that she stopped competing and allegedly attempted suicide (Mitra *in* Hargreaves and Anderson, 2014: 384). Soundarajin later applied for an athletics coaching course but was again forced to undergo a sex test. In 2012, the Indian government agreed to remove this requirement and she was eventually permitted onto the course.

These examples illustrate human variation that challenges the rigid and inaccurate binary categories of sex. Their ridicule and ostracisation is inconsistent with principles of equality. The cases of Caster Semenya and Park Eun-Seon have forced governing bodies to pay closer attention to these human variations in the context of balancing inclusion and exclusion in sport.

Caster Semenya and Park Eun-Seon

In August 2009, 19-year-old South African middle distance runner, Caster Semenya won the women's gold medal and set a world record in the 800 metre track event at the World Championships in Berlin. Prior to this, controversy surrounding her gender had already begun and following the findings of initial tests, the IAAF asked South Africa to withdraw her from their team for Berlin, but Athletics South Africa (ASA) insisted that she run. Following her victory, debate continued on the basis of her improved performance times. She was subject to derogatory treatment from spectators and fellow competitors who expressed their concerns about her identity (Kimmel, 2009). It was also suggested that a member of the competing team accompanied Semenya to the bathroom (Levy, 2009).

Upon this controversy, the IAAF ordered her to undergo a gender-verification test. The test required a physical medical evaluation, including reports from a gynaecologist, endocrinologist, psychologist, an internal medicine specialist and an expert on gender (Smith, 2009). Semenya did not consent to have her sex tested, which further raises a number of ethical and legal questions about the legality of sex testing (Cooper, 2010: 254).

There were unconfirmed media reports in 2009 that her sex test revealed both male and female characteristics, with a presence of internal testes and testosterone levels which were considered higher than those of the average woman

(Buzuvis, 2011: 36). In July 2010 she was cleared to compete and returned with a win at an athletic event in Finland (Kessel, 2010).

The IAAF, the South African government and the legal representative for Semenya agreed that the test results remained confidential and that she retained her world title (O'Reilly 2010; Longman 2009; IAAF, 2010). It is speculated that Semenya underwent medical treatment to 'resolve her gender issues' (Anon, 2010a; Hart, 2010). This may have involved lowering her levels of testosterone.

A similar case emerged in football, involving Park Eun-Seon, a 27-year-old female footballer who plays for a South Korean team. Following her improved performance, in November 2013 six rival teams ordered that she underwent a gender test in order to prove her identity. They threatened to boycott league matches if this was not carried out (CNN, 2013). Having competed in the Olympic Games and World Cup tournaments, she has been subject to many sex tests upon selection. Although she passed the tests, the details have never been released. Park claims to have been humiliated by this ordeal. The threat has been met with resistance by the Seoul City Sports Council who argued that this was a serious infringement of her basic human rights. They do not intend to impose the test upon Park but state that if FIFA require such testing for international games then this will have to be considered (The Guardian, 2013).

In February 2014, the National Human Rights Commission of Korea filed a complaint to the Korean FA (KFA) against the coaches of the club who forced Park to undergo testing. The Commission claimed that this constituted sexual harassment and an infringement of human dignity. The KFA punished the coaches with a warning, which was criticised, and they will continue to be challenged by the Commission despite Park's transfer to a Russian team in July 2014.

In contrast to Semenya, Patino and Soundarajin, Park received support from the relevant authorities who recognised that there was a violation of human rights. Whilst this demonstrates a positive approach to regulation, all intersex cases raise significant concerns about the internal regulation of sex categories in sport and the external legal regulation of protecting human rights.

Sport regulatory mechanisms

In January 2010, the IOC met with medical professionals to revise gender-verification policies. The previous policy was not entirely clear on the issue of what the legitimate circumstances are to challenge a competitor's gender (Macaulay *et al.*, 2010: 26; Simpson *et al.*, 2000: 1569). Whilst Semenya was not explicitly on the agenda, she was at the centre of this discussion.

In May 2011, the IAAF adopted the revised IOC rules. The policy states that all references to 'gender verification' and 'gender policy' terminology have been abandoned (Rule 1.4 IAAF, 2011b). The new rules concern female athletes with hyperandrogenism, a term used to describe those females who produce excessive levels of androgen hormones (IAAF, 2011a; IAAF, 2011b). The rules seek to balance the essence of sporting activity with the inclusion of athletes with hyperandrogenism, subject to compliance (IAAF, 2011b).

The female with the condition, who is legally recognised as a female, is eligible to compete in female competition provided that, 'she has androgen levels below the male range (measured by reference to testosterone levels in serum) or, if she has androgen levels within the male range she also has an androgen resistance which means that she derives no competitive advantage from such levels' (IAAF, 2011b). A panel of international medical experts will independently review cases and make recommendations to the IAAF over eligibility (Anon 2011a). To test for eligibility, a multi-level medical process has been introduced for the full examination and diagnosis of the athlete, upon referral from the panel. The levels include an initial clinical examination, a preliminary endocrine assessment and a full examination and diagnosis (Rule 5.1 IAAF, 2011b). This process will be strictly confidential and there appears to be flexibility in the adoption of these procedures for each individual. Athletes who refuse to comply with this process, or who do not pass the evaluation, will be banned from competition (IAAF, 2011b).

The new clear-cut rules may not be perfect but could present a reasonable compromise, recognising the interests of the athlete as well as the protection of the essence of sport. The new policies move away from 'sex tests' and instead adopt a hormone-based approach, which is considered an important performance factor in the determination of eligibility (Marchant, 2011).

However, at the time of writing, Indian teenage sprinter Dutee Chand fell short of these rules and was banned from international competition after being diagnosed with hyperandrogenism. She can only return if she undergoes surgery to lower her testosterone levels to an acceptable female level. In October 2014, she filed an appeal to CAS against the IAAF rules (CAS, 2014).

Experts have raised a number of criticisms about the implications of the policy. Primarily, the rules assume that high levels of testosterone in women confer an unfair advantage. This has evolved to become conventional wisdom in sport and society. It is therefore difficult to accept the truth, which is that 'there is no evidence showing that successful athletes have higher testosterone levels than less successful athletes' (Karkazis *et al.,* 2012: 8). Furthermore, no evidence confirms whether conditions such as AIS, provide athletes with an unfair advantage in sport (Marchant, 2011; Glazer, 2012).

The policy prioritises testosterone over a range of other biological factors which impact upon sport performance, yet are not regulated at all and are an acceptable part of sport (Karkazis *et al.,* 2012: 3). Isolating hyperandrogrenism as a sole determinate of advantage is considered an impossible task. It is also impossible to quantify a 'normal' range of androgens in women.

Some suggest that this suspicion model is exclusionary and discriminatory because it breeds dangerous stereotypes about appearance and excludes athletes until their condition is treated (Mitra *in* Hargreaves and Anderson, 2014: 390). Furthermore, the rules do not apply to, or exclude male athletes who may, for example, have the intersex condition Diplo, which causes them to produce higher levels of testosterone than other men (Buzuvis *in* Sartore-Baldwin, 2013: 63; Glazer, 2012: 565).

Instead, it is suggested that restrictions on natural variations in hormone levels should be relaxed since other physiological variances including height and oxygen capacity are accepted in sport (Marchant, 2011). Women with high testosterone levels are not necessarily different from women who are naturally taller or stronger. There are also calls for self-declarations of sex and gender to determination eligibility (Mitra *in* Hargreaves and Anderson, 2014: 390). Ultimately, it is argued that the policing of 'biologically natural bodies' is not entirely fair (Karkazis *et al.,* 2012: 14).

Legal mechanisms

It was reported that Semenya might have launched a legal challenge against the IAAF, claiming that they infringed her fundamental human rights relating to dignity and privacy (Anon, 2010b). The law has a duty to protect individuals from infringements of their basic human rights. However, the integration of intersex individuals in equality legislation depends on the interpretation of the word 'sex' (Zaccone, 2010: 430). Legislation is not generally worded to encompass intersex individuals. Upon this, recognition of intersex individuals has largely escaped legal attention with basic human rights failing to extend to them (Larson, 2011). Recognition would require legal instruments to specify men, women and others. For instance, some developments have been made in Australia where in March 2010 they became the first country in the world to introduce a 'Sex Not Specified Recognised Details Certificate' as a substitute for a traditional birth certificate, as well as recognition of intersex in other areas of law (Larson, 2011: 228). In Australia, Bangladesh and India, a third gender option X is added to passports, which reflects acceptance and accommodation (Anon, 2011b).

It is assumed that human rights legislation would be interpreted to encompass intersex individuals because to exclude them would go against the overall objectives of such instruments. Assuming legislation is interpreted correctly, there may be a legal responsibility to protect the rights of athletes to participate when they are qualified to compete (Larson, 2011: 230). Gender policies specifically challenge legal human rights standards concerning privacy and dignity since it could be argued that they are invasive and intrude on the lives of females.

The female-only approach to sex testing may be also susceptible to challenge on the grounds that it discriminates on the basis of sex (Glazer, 2012). They 'treat men and women differently from one another without demonstrating an acceptable rationale supporting the regulation of androgens in women, but not men' (Crincoli, 2011). As we have seen in the previous chapter, equality legislation places the onus on the regulating body to justify the differential treatment.

In Semenya's case the South African government reportedly issued a complaint to the United Nations Division for the Advancement of Women (DAW) over the treatment of the case (Anon 2009). The African National Congress claimed that sex testing violated Article 13 CEDAW and since it is a binding instrument, it could be used by States to pressure the IOC and the IAAF to enforce it and change their policies at the cost of refusing to host events.

Secondly, it was claimed that her treatment violated the Brighton Declaration and the Beijing Platform for Action 1995 to which the IOC and the IAAF are signatories. The Platform for Action calls for gender-sensitive programmes for girls and women of all ages and support in all areas of athletics including coaching and administration at the national, regional and international levels (Cooper, 2010: 244). Both of these declarations are not binding law but place a duty on international communities to pressure organisations such as the IOC and the IAAF to adhere to their commitments under these principles. Subjecting intersex individuals to sex tests have the potential to violate these provisions. However, their applicability depends on whether intersex falls within the remit of the term sex under these documents (Adair, 2011: 154). Another potential problem is the fact that such instruments do not tend to extend to non-state actors or private authorities, which may enable the IAAF and the IOC to escape challenge.

At a domestic level, Semenya could have brought a challenge against the IAAF under German law since the alleged discrimination took place in Berlin. In Germany the Constitution protects every citizen's human dignity (Article 1(1) Grundgesetz 1949). Germany is also obliged to act in accordance with the ECHR, which protects privacy under Article 8. As discussed, however, this would only apply to a public authority, which may fall short of capturing the IAAF. There may be potential redress under South African law, against the ASA, an IAAF-recognised national federation, since they admitted errors in their handling the Semenya case. As in *Sagen* however, the ASA may be considered to be the wrong defendants.

Another route could be under medical law. The practice of sex testing in sport is inconsistent with the controls placed on genetic testing in a medical setting (Wiesemann, 2011: 216). The UNESCO International Declaration on Human Genetic Data (2003) demands that consent is obtained for the collection of human genetic data (Article 8(a)). The UNESCO Universal Declaration on the Human Genome and Human Rights (1997) also states that 'no one shall be subjected to discrimination based on genetic characteristics that is intended to or has the effect of infringing human rights, fundamental freedoms and human dignity' (Article 6). It could be argued that this should extend to sport since sports bodies can offer no compelling reason for sex testing. The sport policies also subject athletes to hormone treatment for intersex conditions, as has been allegedly the case with Semenya. There may be legal matters surrounding whether they are legitimately undergoing this for health and safety reasons or instead, for unsustainable reasons pertaining to sport (Cooper, 2010: 263).

Without legitimate justifications for the existence of sex testing, perhaps they should be legally banned as is the case in Norway for instance (Macaulay *et al.*, 2010: 26; Tannsjo and Tammburini, 2000: 121). During the Lillehammer Olympic Games, the IOC was therefore denied permission to conduct sex tests. This is supported by the Canadian Academy of Sports Medicine (CASM), who propose that sex testing should be eliminated entirely since it does not serve a useful purpose. Their position statement recommends that individuals who have developed greater than average muscle mass due to training or due to any of the

DSD conditions discussed, should be 'accepted as part of the normal range of variation' (Doig *et al.*, 1997: 8). The extent to which intersex individuals are included in sport hinges upon the acceptable range of variation by sports bodies.

Transgender

Transgender individuals are those who exhibit incongruence between their birth sex and their gender identity (Greenberg, 1999). The literature uses the term transsexual and transgender interchangeably. The term transgender will be adopted here. Extensive studies have identified microscopic nerve cells in the brain of transgender individuals that had not developed in agreement with their genitalia (see Pearlman, 1995: 867; Middle Sex, 2005). Transgender individuals reject their biological sex through a self-identified condition known as 'gender dysphoria'. The aetiology of the condition is thought to be both biological and psychological, but it is subject to theoretical debate largely centred on nature versus nurture arguments (Selvaggi and Bellringer, 2011: 275). Male to female transgender is four times more frequent than female to male (Selvaggi and Bellringer, 2011: 274). Here we will focus upon male to female transgender individuals although there are examples of female to male athletes elsewhere (Buzuvis *in* Sartore-Baldwin, 2013: 61).

This disparity is so profound for some that they seek gender reassignment surgery to permanently associate the psychological and anatomical aspects of their sex and gender. The reassignment process includes counselling, diagnosis, referral to hormone therapy, consultation with an endocrinologist, electrolysis, cross living and sex reassignment (Griggs, 1999). The treatment itself consists of three phases over a long period of time and involves several doctors with more than one operation (Sharpe, 2002). Even after the full surgery, the transgender individual will face a lifetime of supplemental hormone therapy and monitoring (Whittle, 2004: 20).

Just as with intersex, transgender challenges the conventional paradigms of sex and gender and as a result they have historically struggled for legal and social recognition in their new identity.

Legal recognition of transgender

In Britain, the leading legal approach taken to transgender individuals emanates from the decision in *Corbett v Corbett* [1970] 2 ALL ER 33, which decided that sex is determined at birth and transgender individuals cannot be identified under their new sex in any aspects of their lives. In the case, the extensive medical evidence concluded that 'we do not determine sex…in medicine we determine the sex in which it is best for the individual to live' (Per Professor Dewhurst in Case, para. 44). However, Ormrod J only selected parts of this evidence to reinforce the notion that sex was not a choice in the eyes of the law (Cowan, 2005: 74).

The practice of sex differentiation at birth is particularly problematic for intersex individuals because it only takes into account the external genitalia of the newborn. For transgender, whereas civil registration of birth takes place within a number of days after the birth, 'sex differences in the brain only become manifest by the age of 3–4 years postnatally' (Gooren, 1993: 135). The likelihood of a contradiction occurring between the genitalia and the brain is slim (1:10,000 males and 1:30,000 females) and external genitalia determination is therefore usually accurate but it does leave transgender individuals in an isolated position.

Corbett was challenged by the ECtHR in *Goodwin v UK (2002) 35 EHRR 18* who urged the UK courts to reform the law and consider social and psychological traits when determining gender identity. Despite this, the House of Lords followed Ormrod J's decision in *Bellinger v Bellinger* [2003] 2 ALL ER 593, which followed over 30 years after *Corbett*. There was an acceptance that social attitudes have changed and evolved but this made no impact on the outcome.

Following *Goodwin*, criticism and pressure from ECtHR prompted the UK Government to introduce legislation allowing legal recognition of a gender change. The GRA gave transgender individuals the right to marry in their new gender, apply for substitute birth certificates and be legally recognised for parenthood by artificial insemination through the process of an application for a gender recognition certificate, which was ultimately determined by a Gender Recognition Panel (s. 1(3) and Schedule 1 GRA). This legislation has now been replaced by the UK EA (s. 7) and demonstrates a clear attempt to break down social barriers and promote inclusiveness in society (Patel, 2008).

Sport examples

Transgender has received increasing media attention as former boxing promoter Frank Maloney publically announced her new transgender identity as Kellie Maloney in 2014. She seemed to receive positive support from the competitive world of sport.

On the field however, sports bodies previously adopted the sex determination at birth logic. A number of governing bodies have been forced to amend their female at birth requirement to accommodate for transgender athletes. For instance, in 2001 the Canadian Cycling Association (CCA) and the Union Cycliste Internationale (UCI), suspended male to female transgender athlete Michelle Dumaresq's licence to compete. In 2002, they re-issued it to her after accepting that her new birth certificate classified her as female. She represented Canada in the 2002 World Mountain Biking Championship in Austria (Addelman, 2004).

In 2005, the Ladies' Golf Union (LGU) for British amateur golf announced that it would allow male to female golfers to compete by changing its sex at birth requirements. 37-year-old Mianne Bagger, who was born in Denmark and raised in Australia, became the first golfer who was born a boy to be granted full playing rights on the Ladies' European Tour in October 2004 after being previously denied (Anon, 2005).

In October 2010, 57-year-old Lana Lawless was a male to female transgender golfer legally recognised under California law. She was denied membership into the Ladies Professional Golf Association (LPGA) because of their 'female at birth' player requirements. Lawless brought an action against the LPGA and the Long Driver's of America (LDA) firstly arguing that failure to include her constituted an infringement of Californian civil rights law since the LPGA are a 'business establishment' under the legislation (*Lana Lawless v the Ladies Professional Golf Association and the Long Driver's of America* United States District Court Case Number CV10 4599 DMR). She argued that the requirement constituted unfair competition under the legislation and that the defendants interfered with her ability to economically benefit from participation in the events (Dolan Law Firm, 2010).

The Federal Court Action was dismissed following an out-of-court settlement. The parties appeared to resolve the matter and, in addition, the LPGA voted to remove the 'female at birth' requirement from its by-laws (Rodenberg, 2010). In relation to sex determination at birth, both the law and sport have shifted their attitude and approach to transgender individuals.

In 2013, US mixed martial arts (MMA) transgender fighter Fallon Fox was subject to criticism and debate within the sport, with some arguing that she should not be permitted to compete because she possesses a physical advantage over women (McNeil, 2013). Her continued inclusion was dependent upon a licence approval. The Association of Boxing Commissions (ABC) adopted guidelines for the participation of transgender athletes in MMA and boxing. These were accepted by the Florida State Boxing Commission, which enabled Fox to compete, since most MMA fights took place in Florida. However, other States may not adopt these rules, which could create problems of future participation.

Positive examples of inclusion include American Samoan Jaiyah Saelua, who is the first transgender footballer to compete in a men's team. She classifies herself as a third gender, the Fa'afafine, which is an accepted gender category in Samoa. Born a male, she possesses feminine qualities (Callow, 2014). She receives full support from her team to compete. However, her inclusion possibly is less problematic because she was competing with men, which does not raise concerns of perceived advantage.

In June 2005, transgender Australian soccer player, Martine Delaney was permitted to continue to compete in a female league in Tasmania after a rival team questioned her registration. The Football Federation Australia (FFA) ruled that if she is legally recognised as a female then she is eligible to compete, since State laws and FFA rules prohibit discrimination. Wide policy changes also enabled transgender Canadian Cyclist Kristen Worley, to enter qualification trials for the Beijing Olympics. Although narrowly missing out, she is an active campaigner for transgender athletes.

Regulation of transgender in sport

One of the most significant challenges to the balance between inclusion and exclusion in sport in terms of transgender individuals is the notion of advantage. The legal and sporting regulation of transgender individuals in female sport maintains that male to female transgender individuals sustain advantages from their physiological skeletal frame and from their prior exposure to androgen (Gooren, 1999). These are the masculinising hormones, an example of which is testosterone as earlier described. Feminising hormones include oestrogen and progesterone. Normally speaking, men have higher levels of androgens than females do. Researchers are able to certainly identify that testosterone plays an important part in the development of secondary sex characteristics in males, as well as the promotion of muscle mass and healing and burning fat. This all leads to a lean physique which is associated with male athletes (Teetzel *in* Schneinder and Hong, 2006: 58; Wood and Stanton, 2011; Karkazis *et al.,* 2012: 8).

In the previous chapter we accepted that men tend to possess an inherent performance advantage over women due to their greater average height, muscle mass, power and haemoglobin levels, which are brought on by exposure to androgens (Gooren and Bunck, 2004: 425). This lends itself well to sports such as sprinting, rowing and swimming and would arguably produce an imbalance of competition and risk of safety if men and women competed together in sports where strength is a determinant factor. There are clear exceptions such as equestrian sports where male and female athletes perform together in all Olympic events (Tucker and Collins, 2009: 148).

Because of these physiological differences, transgender individuals are presumed to possess an unfair advantage in sport. However, just as with intersex individuals, an unfair advantage on the basis of gender is difficult to prove with certainty and instead such treatment could lead to an infringement of fundamental human rights. The tensions between the sporting and individual interest is demonstrated by the debate surrounding the inclusion of sport in the UK GRA. During the preliminary stages of its passage through Parliament, the UK GRA originally required both domestic and international sporting events to allow transgender individuals to compete in their reassigned genders, which was in line with the overall purpose of the legislation. This greatly prioritised the interests of the individual and their right to participate in any sport they are qualified to enter.

However, this caused huge debate as to whether or not gender can genuinely be reassigned. Following discussions between the government and sports governing bodies, the GRA was amended to include an exemption from sport under s. 19 GRA and to consider the participation of transgender individuals on a case-by-case basis. This has now been replaced by s. 195 EA. Lord Filkin, the British Constitutional Affairs Minister, opined that this regulation ensures ‘safe and fair competition’ (cited *in* Fairbairn, 2004).

The objectives of the EA exemption seem reasonable since fair competition and safety are legitimate pursuits. However, the rationale behind the exemption is reflective of the previous s. 44 SDA exemption, which assumes that all men are more suited to sport than all women. The exemption and explanation for the term ‘gender affected’ follows the assumption that men are better at sport than women and male to female transgender individuals in sport have an unfair advantage over born females as they retain many of the previous athletically advantageous male characteristics (Pilgrim *et al.*, 2003: 530).

The sporting position reflects this assumption and the IAAF policies on transgender have developed in recent times. Previously, the 2006 transgender policy (the 'Stockholm Consensus') detailed that in order to be eligible for participation post puberty, the athlete must have completed surgical internal and external anatomical changes, legal recognition of their assigned sex and hormonal therapy for a sufficient enough time (at least two years) to reduce any gender-related advantages. This was the first transgender policy in sport, which prompted other governing bodies to be more inclusive. However, it was criticised for being transphobic and exclusionary for those who cannot afford expensive reassignment surgery or who do not wish to undergo therapy for an extended period of time (Cavanagh and Sykes, 2006: 92; Teetzel *in* Schneinder and Hong, 2006: 68). In addition, many countries continued to legally exclude transgender individuals, making recognition by appropriate authorities largely difficult. It appeared to require more than was necessary to achieve the objective of protecting the essence of sport.

As a result of the problems with the policy, in May 2011 the IAAF introduced new regulations for transgender athletes who have undergone sex reassignment (IAAF, 2011c). The athlete is required to notify the IAAF of their reassignment by providing evidence of legal recognition, reassignment surgery and ongoing treatment and monitoring. Following an initial review, athletes are then required to submit an endocrine assessment. An expert medical panel will review these findings and offer recommendations to the IAAF on eligibility. A transgender athlete will be eligible to compete if her medical treatment following reassignment has been administered in a verifiable manner and for a sufficient length of time to minimise any advantage in women's competition (Rule 8.4 IAAF, 2011c). If an athlete does not meet these standards then the panel are required to recommend conditions under which the athlete could compete (Rule 8.6 IAAF 2011c). An athlete will undergo ongoing competition monitoring for specified period of time.

Overall, these rules are more inclusive than the previous position and offer more detail than the legal provisions presented in the EA. Although they are vaguely worded in places, the IAAF appears to create an environment where the participation of transgender individuals will be encouraged where practicable (Buzuvis *in* Sartore-Baldwin, 2013: 67).

However, the policy is subject to the same criticism as with the intersex rules because they are based upon the assumption that sex-related characteristics are the only determinate of advantage and success in sport. The policy arguably contributes to the stigma attached to transgender individuals by policing gender and femininity (Findlay, 2012; Buzuvis *in* Sartore-Baldwin, 2013; Karkazis *et al.*, 2012: 7).

Participation should be determined in a manner which is 'scientifically well founded and is fair to those who wish to engage in competition' (Gooren and Bunck, 2004: 427). With this in mind, some experts have urged high school and college sports in the USA not to follow the IAAF policy for the inclusion of student athletes (Carroll *in* Hargreaves and Anderson, 2014: 367). The National

Collegiate Athletic Association (NCAA) permits participation if the athlete has been undergoing cross-sex hormone treatments, which are designed to neutralise the effect of testosterone, for one year only (Buzivis *in* Cunningham, 2012: 27). Similar to intersex athletes, the most inclusive policy promotes self-declaration of gender identity, as adopted by the Washington Interscholastic Athletic Association (WIAA). Under this approach, no medical evidence is required (Buzuvis *in* Cunningham, 2012: 29).

The sport policies on transgender vary in their approaches from overly inclusive to unreasonably exclusive. The variation of regulation indicates that there is no simple solution to the balance between inclusion and exclusion for transgender athletes (Buzuvis *in* Cunningham, 2012: 25).

Proving advantage

During reassignment surgery, transgender individuals are placed on hormone regimes which aim to eliminate, in so far as possible, the hormonally induced secondary sex characteristics of their birth sex and secondly to induce those of the new sex (Gooren, 1999). This is achieved by reducing the effects of androgen and increasing oestrogen in the body to suppress testosterone. Oestrogen is produced in the muscle and fat and is an essential part of the sex reassignment process for male-to-female transgender individuals.

The literature and medical research is marked for its lack of clarification on the exact effects of these hormone regimes upon the athletic performance of a transgender athlete which would confirm whether there is truth in the legal and sporting concerns (Teetzel *in* Schneinder and Hong, 2006: 57). Little is known because of the variable number of factors such as genetics, hormones, training, diet and differences in sports which make it very difficult to generalise the results of studies that have usually investigated non-athlete transgender subjects.

Several studies investigate the effects of testosterone and oestrogen, but their exact function and operation in the body is ongoing in the field of science and medicine. Transgender athletes have publicly expressed how their bodies are weaker post reassignment, arguing that an advantage does not really exist (Cavanagh and Sykes, 2006: 95). Bagger claims that 'being taller, with longer arms, is an advantage with hitting the ball longer in golf…but length is not everything' (Mair, 2004). Fallon Fox questioned whether she was in fact at a disadvantage after hormone therapy following a MMA defeat. Conversely, Saelua felt that she would still retain an advantage over other women following treatment and would therefore be reluctant to compete in a female football team (Channel 4, 2014).

Based on scientific and medical research available, it is reported that during the reassignment, in some cases testosterone levels may increase and the combined oestrogen and anti-androgen therapy does not necessarily reduce spatial ability, muscle mass, strength and power, which are commonly associated with testosterone and desirable attributes in sport (Gooren, 1999; Teetzel *in* Schneider and Hong, 2006: 59). The previous anabolic effects of androgen exposure (muscle, bone and haemoglobin) in male to female transgender individuals will diminish after a period of time following oestrogen and anti-androgen regime (Gooren, 2008: 427). However, the pubertal effect of testosterone on skeletal elements, such as height and physical dimensions of the human form, including the size of feet and hands, are arguably irreversible and may therefore provide advantages in certain sports (Teetzel *in* Schneider and Hong, 2006: 59; Gooren and Bunck, 2004: 426). Larger hands facilitate a greater grip in sports, such as basketball and water polo. Larger feet may enable athletes to excel in sports such as swimming. Height is likely to provide advantages in many sports, such as volleyball and basketball.

Smaller studies have made distinctions between reassignment surgery before and after puberty. If the transgender individual has undergone sex reassignment surgery before puberty then strength is argued to be irrelevant as they experience none of the masculinising effects of testosterone. If the surgery was performed after puberty then it is argued that each individual should be evaluated case by case. The effects of puberty have framed the IAAF policy approach and impacted upon inclusion and exclusion in mixed sex participation.

A seminal study was conducted to investigate the effects of androgen deprivation in male to female transgender individuals, and androgen administration in female to male transgender individuals on testosterone levels, muscle mess, haemoglobin and insulin levels (Gooren and Bunck, 2004). The results reveal that female to male transgender individuals would be able to compete fairly as long as the testosterone levels do not create a surplus of muscle mass over exercise alone and levels are within the acceptable range for men. For male to female transgender athletes there remained an 'element of arbitrariness' since there was no conclusive evidence on whether previous exposure to testosterone influenced future physical traits (Gooren and Bunck, 2004: 428). Whilst androgen deprivation did reveal a loss in muscle area, as mentioned, the mean muscle area remained larger than women.

The study concludes that 'there will always be an element of arbitrariness in the drawing of competitive lines,' as the differences in development of every individual coupled with the nature of genetics determines how nature endows individuals for competition (Gooren and Bunck, 2004). There is a large spectrum of males with an uneven distribution of attributes suitable for sports, just as some born females are better qualified for sports than male to female transgender individuals. In addition, every sport requires expertise in different qualities.

The effect that each body has on the administration of androgen makes it difficult to say either way whether transgender individuals have an unfair advantage. The study suggests that the *average* reassigned male to female has a slight advantage over the *average* born female but certainly not over *all* born females. The requirement of 100 per cent certainty may be unreasonable. The argument for defending the level playing field is objectively reasonable yet it seems that this is pushing the test of reasonableness beyond the constraints of fairness. It is important to highlight that since small differences are critical to the outcome of sport, the data in the study was limited and could not 'provide insight into all pertinent aspects' (Gooren and Bunck, 2004: 428). Overall, there is no firm evidence to suggest that hormone therapy in transgender athletes provide them with a competitive advantage *beyond* the natural competition level in male and female sports, even though there may be an enhancement in the personal performance of the athlete competing as the opposite sex. Enhanced performance is considered not synonymous with competitive advantage.

Testosterone-related physical properties are not relevant in all sporting activities but for those which are, it will depend upon the level of arbitrariness that sport wants to accept that will determine the participation of male to female transgender individuals with other women. As highlighted, the effect of testosterone on the body continues to be investigated.

The legal and sporting approach focuses on the hormonal properties of a human body, which is entirely legitimate for the maintenance of fair play principles. However, this discussion has revealed that the reliance on these attributes alone can lead to misguided assumptions about the superiority of male characteristics in all sporting activities. This can result in the broad unreasonable exclusion of athletes on the basis of gender.

Generally speaking, we tend to selectively focus on advantage in sport with some advantages unchallenged, but others such as those associated with intersex and transgender, magnified (Karkazis *et al.*, 2012: 11). For instance, many athletes in the National Basketball Association (NBA) are known to have acromegaly or gigantism, which is a condition that over produces growth hormone, caused by a tumour in the pituitary gland. Height produces an obvious performance advantage when playing basketball. Sun Ming Ming, a Chinese player who is 7 foot 9 inches tall, reportedly has this condition (Himmelsbach, 2007). It is speculated that Olympic gold medal swimmer, Michael Phelps may have Marfan's Syndrome, which is a genetic disease which can pose serious health risks whilst at the same time creating characteristics and body features which are advantageous for swimmers (Levy, 2009; Cooper, 2010: 234; Karkazis *et al.*, 2012: 11). Consider also Australian swimmer Ian Thorpe who has advantageously large feet. As highlighted earlier, perhaps the differential treatment is accounted for by what is considered a 'natural inheritance'. Nevertheless, there must be consistency and legitimacy in the criteria used to include or exclude athletes on the basis of gender.

Breach of human rights

Determining an unfair advantage may be entirely irrelevant, and instead outweighed by the broader interest to protect the basic human rights of athletes. This is exemplified in the seminal legal case of *Dr Renee Richards v United States Tennis Association 93 Misc.2d 713, 400 NYS 2d 267*, which was one of the first public cases of transgender. As a male Richard H Raskind was ranked 13th nationally in the men's 35 years and over tennis competition and underwent reassignment surgery. After the reassignment, she entered nine women's tennis competitions and won two (Shy, 2007: 96; Cole, 1990).

Following this, the United States Tennis Association (USTA) demanded that Richards undertake the Barr body test to determine her chromosomal make up. They claimed that their primary concern was to ensure fairness (Case, para. 716). In the absence of an XX female cluster, she was debarred from entering the US Open even though Richard's surgeon personally testified that her internal organs after the surgery were 'anatomically similar to a biological woman who underwent a total hysterectomy and ovariectomy' (Case, para. 719).

In 1977 Richards brought a claim against the USTA, the United States Open Committee (USOC) and the Women's Tennis Association (WTA), claiming that by denying her the right to compete in the women's division, they had violated s. 290(3) Executive Law of the New York Human Rights Law, which declares that the State has the responsibility to act to assure that every individual within this State is afforded an equal opportunity to enjoy a full and productive life.

The WTA had also failed to rank her as a woman tennis professional, which is a pre-requisite for qualification and participation in the US Open. The Supreme Court was faced with addressing the appropriateness of the Barr body test and the critical point of performance advantage. They held that it was grossly unfair, discriminatory and inequitable to make the claimant pass a sex test in order to participate. In doing so, the USTA had contravened s. 290(3). The USTA were found to have knowingly instituted the test for the primary purpose of preventing Richards from participation (Case, para. 721). The court did not wish to criticise the test entirely but highlighted that it should not be the only criteria for determining sex.

The defendant's primary concern was performance advantage. The case includes a number of opinions from medical experts for each party, each with differing views about the level of advantage Richards may have possessed. No consensus on this matter appeared to have been reached, which is consistent with the discussion in this chapter. In any case, the court judgement was rather short and did not comment on any of the medical evidence. Instead, focus was placed on the breach of human rights. Richards was permitted to compete in the 1977 US Open following the ruling and lost in the first round. She competed at a professional level until retiring in 1981 and went on to coach Martina Navratilova.

Overall, the court followed an inclusive approach to this case, placing the balance in favour of the human right to participate in sport. Little attention was paid to the determination of advantage. The court could have offered more guidance on determining what criteria may be used to assess fairness and unfairness in sport. From a feminist perspective, another criticism of the case was the over emphasis on the traditional notions of femininity and masculinity (Nyong'o, 2010: 97; Shy, 2007: 105).

Summary

This chapter has revealed that the division of sport and society according to sex is challenged by minorities such as intersex and transgender who do not sit neatly into those categories and who do not conform to the gender attributes typically associated with man and woman. Although the classification is defensible, the previous policies in place to manage this such as sex testing, were arbitrary and infringed basic human rights. The new IAAF regulations are an improvement but continue to create questions and attract criticism as being exclusive. Whilst other far more inclusive models are proposed, an appropriate balance between inclusion and exclusion has not been achieved.

Based upon the evidence provided, there are no logical grounds to exclude intersex individuals from sport or even subject them to undergo treatment, unless their health is in danger. Whilst no known case has appeared before a court, sport should be accountable under human rights provisions. The justifications for regulating advantage in sport may be entirely legitimate, but solely determining advantage according to chromosomes or hormones is highly inaccurate and unfair.

The transgender cases inform us that what is considered natural or unnatural has an important role in determining participation. Striving for a natural representation of competitors is a legitimate ideal in principle, but in practice it is impossible to obtain (Boylan, 2008). The inconsistent approaches to advantage in sport suggest that the treatment of transgender athletes is also unreasonable.

References

Aaronson, I.A. and Aaronson, A.J. 2010. How should we classify intersex disorders? *Journal of Pediatric Urology*, XX: 1–4.

Adair, J.L. 2011. In a league of their own: the case for intersex athletes. *Sports Lawyers Journal*, 18: 121–155.

Addelman, R. 2004. All inclusive Athens. *The Varsity.CA* [online], 22 March. Available at: http://thevarsity.ca/2004/03/22/all-inclusive-athens/ [accessed 30/12/14].

Anon. 2011a. IAAF introduces new gender rules. *BBCi Website* [online], 12 April. Available at: http://news.bbc.co.uk/go/pr/fr/-/sport1/hi/athletics/9455486.stm [accessed 5/08/2011].

Anon. 2005. Golf: Transsexual to play in the British Open. *The Independent* [online] 10 February. Available at: www.independent.co.uk/sport/golf-transsexual-to-play-in-the-british-open-1529950.html [accessed 30/12/14].

Anon. 2009. South Africa takes Semenya case to UN. *CNN* [online], 18 September. Available at: http://edition.cnn.com/2009/SPORT/09/18/athletics.semenya.united.nations.gender/index.html [accessed 15/10/11].

Anon. 2010a. Caster Semenya: anatomy of her case. *The Telegraph* [online], 6 July. Available at: www.telegraph.co.uk/sport/othersports/athletics/7873921/Caster-Semenya-anatomy-of-her-case.html [accessed 01/08/10].

Anon. 2010b. Semenya eyes June return in Spain *BBCi Website* [online], 6 April. Available at: http://news.bbc.co.uk/sport1/hi/athletics/8595361.stm [accessed 01/08/10].

Anon. 2011b. Male, Female or X-third option now on Australian passports. *Travel News* [online], 19 September. Available at: www.travel-news.co.uk/2078/2011/09/male-female-or-x-%E2%80%93-third-option-now-on-australian-passports/ [accessed 15/10/11].

Ballantyne, K.N., Kayser, M. and Grootegoed, J.A. 2011. Sex and gender issues in competitive sports: investigation of a historical case leads to a new viewpoint. *British Journal of Sports Medicine*. 3 May: 1–4.

Boylan, F.J. 2008. The XY Games. *The New York Times* [online] 3 August. Available at: www.nytimes.com/2008/08/03/opinion/03boylan.html?pagewanted=1&_r=1 [accessed 10/08/10].

Buzuvis, E.E. 2011. Caster Semenya and the Myth of the Level Playing Field. *The Modern American*, 6: 36–42.

Callow, J. 2014. "Football is too good a game to ruin with discrimination" [online] 1 May. Available at: www.thefa.com/news/2014/may/jaiyah-saelua-next-goal-wins [accessed 05/08/14].

CAS. 2014. Latest News. Hyperandrogenism: Dutee Chand appeals to the CAS. *Court of Arbitration for Sport.* [online], 9 October. Available at: www.tas-cas.org/en/general-information/news-detail/article/hyperandrogenism-dutee-chand-appeals-to-the-cas.html [accessed 30/12/14].

Cavanagh, S.L. and Sykes, H. 2006. Transsexual Bodies at the Olympics: The International Olympic Committee's Policy on Transsexual Athletes at the 2004 Athens Summer Games. *Body and Society*, 12(3): 75–102.

Channel 4, 2014. Meet the world's first international transgender footballer [online] Available at: www.youtube.com/watch?v=2Kt7zQN9luw [accessed 18/02/15).

CNN. 2013. South Korean soccer star Park Eun-seon "humiliated" by gender claims. *CNN* [online] Available at: http://edition.cnn.com/2013/11/08/sport/football/south-korea-gender-boycott-football/ [accessed 30/07/14].

Cole, C.L. 1990. Double Fault: Renee Richards and the Construction and Naturalization of Difference. *Sociology of Sport Journal*, 7: 1–21.

Cooper, E.J. 2010. Gender testing in athletic competitions-human rights violations: why Michael Phelps is praised and Caster Semenya is chastised. *Journal of Gender, Race and Justice*, 14: 233–264.

Cowan, S. 2005. "Gender is no substitute for sex." A comparative human rights analysis of the legal regulation of sexual identity. *Feminist Legal Studies*, 13: 67–96.

Crincoli, S. 2011. Eligibility: The IAAF hyperandrogenism regulations and discrimination. *World Sports Law Report*, 9(6): 3–5.

Cunningham, G.B. 2012. *Sexual Orientation and Gender Identity in Sport: Essays from activist, coaches and scholars.* College Station, TX: Center for Sport Management Research and Education.

Doig, P., Lloyd-Smith, R., Prior, J.C. and Sinclair, D. 1997. *Position Statement: Sex Testing (gender verification) in Sport.* Canadian Academy of Sport Medicine (CASM).

Dolan Law Firm. 2010. *Complaint for Damages and Demand for Jury Trial. Lana Lawless* [online]. Available at: www.lgbt-lawyer.com/CM/Articles/Lawless-v-LPGA-Complaint-Filed-Endorsed.pdf [accessed 03/05/11].

Dreger, A. 2010. Sex Typing for Sports. *Hastings Center Report*, 40(2): 22–24.

Epstein, D. 2013. *The Sports Gene: talent, practice and the truth about success.* London: Yellow Jersey Press.

Fairbairn, C. 2004. *The Gender Recognition Bill [HL] Bill 56 of 2003–04.* House of Commons Library [online]. Available at: www.parliament.uk/business/publications/research/briefing-papers/RP04-15/gender-recognition-bill-hl-bill-56-200304 [accessed 30/12/14].

Fastiff, P.B. 1992. Gender verification testing: balancing the rights of female athletes with a scandal-free Olympic games. *Hastings Constitutional Law Quarterly*, 19: 937–961.

Findlay, S. 2012. Olympics struggle with 'policing femininity.' *The Toronto Star* [online] 8 June. Available at: www.thestar.com/sports/olympics/2012/06/08/olympics_struggle_with_policing_femininity.html [accessed 29/08/14].

Foddy, B. and Savulescu, J. 2010. Time to re-valuate gender segregation in athletics? *British Journal of Sports Medicine*, 45: 1184–1188.

Glazer, S. 2012. Sporting chance: litigating sexism out of the Olympic intersex policy. *Journal of Law and Policy*, 20:2: 545–580.

Gooren. L.J.G. 1993. *Biological Aspects of Transsexualism and their Relevance to its Legal Aspects.* Memorandum given at the "Council of Europe Proceedings, Transgender Individualism, Medicine and Law, XXIIIrd Colloquy on European Law" hosted in April, 1993.

Gooren, L.J.G. 1999. Hormonal Sex Reassignment. *The International Journal of Transgenderism*, 3(3), July–September.

Gooren, L.J.G. 2008. Olympic Sports and Transsexuals. *Asian Journal of Andrology*, 10(3): 427–432.

Gooren, L.J.G. and Bunck, M.C. 2004. Transsexuals and Competitive Sports. *European Journal of Endocrinology*, 151: 425–9.

Greenberg, J. 1999. When is a man a man and when is a woman a woman? *Florida Law Review*, 52: 745–768.

Griggs, C. 1999. *S/he- Changing Sex and Changing Clothes.* New York: Berg Oxford.

Hargreaves, J. and Anderson, E. 2014. *Routledge Handbook of Sport, Gender and Sexuality.* London: Routledge.

Guardian, The. 2013. Controversy hits South Korean women's football league over gender testing row – video. *The Guardian* [online] Available at: www.theguardian.com/football/video/2013/nov/08/south-korean-womens-football-gender-test-video [accessed 30/07/14].

Hart, S. 2010. Caster Semenya given all clear after gender test row. *The Telegraph* [online], 6 July. Available at: www.telegraph.co.uk/sport/othersports/athletics/7873240/Caster-Semenya-given-all-clear-after-gender-test-row.html [accessed 6/07/10].

Himmelsbach, A. 2007. Basketball skills come slowly to a 7-foot-9 center from China. *The New York Times* [online], 10 March. Available at: www.nytimes.com/2007/03/10/sports/basketball/10sun.html [accessed 12/05/11].

International Association of Athletics Federations (IAAF) 2010. Caster Semenya May Compete. [online] 6 July. Available at: www.iaaf.org/news/iaaf-news/caster-semenya-may-compete [accessed 30/12/14].

International Association of Athletics Federations (IAAF) 2011a. IAAF to introduce eligibility rules for females with hyperandrogenism. [online] Available at: www.iaaf.org/news/iaaf-news/iaaf-to-introduce-eligibility-rules-for-femal-1 [accessed 30/12/14].

International Association of Athletics Federations (IAAF) 2011b. Hyperandrogenism Rules. [online] Available at: www.iaaf.org/about-iaaf/documents/medical [accessed 28/12/14].

International Association of Athletics Federations (IAAF) 2011c. Transgender Rules. [online] Available at: www.iaaf.org/mm/Document/AboutIAAF/Publications/05/98/75/20110430053236_httppostedfile_SRRegulations%28Final%29-AMG-30.04.2011_24293.pdf [accessed 23/06/11].

Karkazis, K., Jordan-Young R., Davis G. and Camporesi S. 2012. Out of bounds? A critique of the new policies on hyperandrogenism in elite female athletes. *The American Journal of Bioethics*, 12(7): 3–16.

Kessel, A. 2010. Caster Semenya returns to the track in triumph after year in limbo. *The Guardian* [online], 15 July. Available at: www.guardian.co.uk/sport/2010/jul/15/caster-semenya-returns [accessed 11/08/10].

Kimmel, M. 2009. The bigotry of the binary: the case of Caster Semenya. *The Huffington Post* [online] 24 August. Available at: www.huffingtonpost.com/michael-kimmel/the-bigotry-of-the-binary_b_267572.html [accessed 12/08/10].

Larson, S. 2011. Intersexuality and gender verification tests: the need to assure human rights and privacy. *Pace International Law Review*, 23(1): 215–248.

Levy, A. 2009. Either/Or. Sports, sex and the case of Caster Semenya. *The New Yorker* [online] 25 January. Available at: www.newyorker.com/reporting/2009/11/30/091130fa_fact_levy?currentPage=1 [accessed 11/08/10].

Ljungqvist, A., Martínez-Patiño M.J., Martínez-Vidal A., Zagalaz L., Díaz P. and Mateos C. 2006. The history and current policies on gender testing in elite athletes. *International SportMed Journal*, 7(3): 225–230.

Longman, J. 2009. South African runner's sex verification result won't be public. *The New York Times* [online], 19 November. Available at: www.nytimes.com/2009/11/20/sports/20runner.html?_r=1&ref=caster_semenya [accessed 10/08/10].

Macaulay, C.M, Hamidi, M. and Treunicht-Naylor, K. 2010. Gender verification testing: necessary for the integrity of international athletics, or inexcusable breach of personal privacy? *Medicine and the Law University of Western Ontario Medical Journal*, 79(1), Spring: 25–27.

Mair, L. 2004. Sex-changer golfer puts the game's rulers in a legal bunker. *The Telegraph* [online], 14 February. Available at: www.telegraph.co.uk/news/worldnews/europe/denmark/1454346/Sex-change-golfer-puts-the-games-rulers-in-a-legal-bunker.html [accessed 15/02/04].

Marchant, J. 2011. Women with high male hormone levels face sport ban. *Nature* [online] 14 April. Available at: www.nature.com/news/2011/110414/full/news.2011.237.html [accessed 29/08/14].

McNeil, F. 2013. Fallon Fox Fighting for Equality. *ESPN* [online] 24 May. Available at: http://espn.go.com/mma/story/_/id/9306162/mma-transsexual-fallon-fox-fighting-cage [accessed: 31/08/14].

Menon, Y. 2010. Denied the finish line: Sex verification testing for intersex athletes under the International Association of Athletics Federations. *The Dukeminier Awards Best Sexual Orientation and Gender Law Review*, 9(1): 389–423.

Middle Sex 2005. [Television] A. Thomas, Channel 4, 26 May.

Nau, J.Y. 1992. France: gender tests for athletes. *The Lancet*, 339(8789), 8 February: 354.

Nyong'o, T. 2010. The unforgivable transgression of being Caster Semenya. *Women and Performance: a journal of feminist theory*, 20(1): 95–100.

O'Reilly, I. 2010. Gender Testing in Sport: a case for treatment? *BBCi Website* [online] 15 February. Available at: http://news.bbc.co.uk/1/hi/in_depth/8511176.stm [accessed 30/07/14].

Olsen-Acre, H.K. 2007. The use of drug testing to police sex and gender in the Olympic Games. *Michigan Journal of Gender and Law*, 13: 207–236.

Patel, S. 2008. Transsexuals in sport: inclusiveness and the level playing field. *Anglia Ruskin University Papers in Law Series* [online]. Available at: www.anglia.ac.uk/ruskin/en/home/faculties/alss/deps/law/research/papers_in_law_series.html [accessed: 30/07/14].

Patel, S. 2009a. *Transgender and Sport: A UK perspective.* Oral presentation given at the "Ithaca College Sport, Sexuality, and Culture Conference" hosted by Ithaca College, USA in March 2009.

Patel, S. 2009b. *The level playing field: balancing inclusion and exclusion in sport.* Oral presentation given at the "SRLA 22nd Annual Conference on Sport, Physical Activity, Recreation and Law" hosted by the Sport and Recreation Law Association in San Antonio, Texas, USA, March 2009.

Patino, M.J.M., Padorno C.M., Vidal A.M., Sánchez Mosquera A.M., García Soidán J.L., del Pino Díaz Pereira M. and Touriño-González C.F. 2010. An approach to the biological, historical and psychological repercussions of gender verification in top level competitions. *Journal of Human Sport and Exercise*, 5(3): 307–321.

Pearlman, L. 1995. Transsexualism as metaphor: the collision of sex and gender. *Buffalo Law Review*, 43: 835–872.

Pilgrim, J., Martin, D. and Binder, W. 2003. Far from the finish line: Transsexualism and the athletic competition. *Fordham Intellectual Property, Media and Entertainment Law Journal*, 13: 495–549.

Ritchie, R., Reynard, J. and Lewis, T. 2008. Intersex and the Olympic Games. *Journal of the Royal Society of Medicine*, 101: 395–399.

Rodenberg, R.M. 2010. Gender policies and impact of litigation: Lawless v LPGA. *World Sports Law Report*, 8(12): 6–7.

Samuels, A. 2004. Gender Reassignment. *Medico-Legal Journal*, 72(4): 151–152.

Sartore-Baldwin, M.L. 2013. *Sexual Minorities in Sports – prejudice at play*. Boulder, CO: Lynne Reinner.

Schneider, A.J. and Hong, F. 2006. *Doping in Sport: Global Ethical Issues*. London: Routledge.

Selvaggi, G. and Bellringer, J. 2011. Gender reassignment surgery: an overview. *Nature Review Urology*, 8 May: 274–281.

Sharpe, A.N. 2002. *Transgender Jurisprudence: Dysphoric Bodies of Law*, 3rd Edition. London: Cavendish Publishing.

Shy, Y.L.A. 2007. "Like any other girl": male to female transsexuals and professional sports. *Sports Lawyers Journal*, 14: 95–110.

Simpson, J.L., Ljungqvist, A., Ferguson-Smith, M.A., Chapelle, A., Elsas L.J., Ehrhardt, A.A., Genel, M., Ferris, E.A. and Carlson, A. 2000. Gender Verification in the Olympics. *Journal of the American Medical Association*, 284(12): 1568–1569.

Smith, D. 2009. Caster Semenya row: 'who are white people to question the makeup of an African girl? It is racism' *The Guardian* [online], 23 August. Available at: www.guardian.co.uk/sport/2009/aug/23/caster-semenya-athletics-gender [accessed 01/09/09].

Tannsjo, T. and Tamburrini, C. 2000. *Values in Sport*. London: E & FN Spon.

Tucker, R. and Collins, M. 2009. The science and management of sex verification in sport. *South African Journal of Sport Medicine (SAJSM)*, 21(4): 147–150.

Wamsley, K.B. 2008. *Sport and Transitioning/ Transitioned Athletes*. [online] Available at: www.athletescan.com/Images/Publications/Transitioning%20Athlete%20Project/Social%20Science%20Literature%20on%20Sport%20and%20Transitioning-Transitioned%20Athletes.pdf [accessed: 01/09/10]

Whittle, S. 2004. *The Transgender Debate: the crisis surrounding gender equality*. London and New York: Cassell

Wiesemann, C. 2011. Is there a right not to know one's sex? The ethics of gender verification in women's sports competition. *Journal of Medical Ethics*, 37: 216–219.

Wood, R.I. and Stanton, S.J. 2011. Testosterone and Sport: current perspectives. *Hormones and Behaviour*, 61(1): 147–155.

Zaccone, L.A. 2010. Policing the policing of intersex bodies. *Brooklyn Law Review*, 76(1): 385–438.

6 Disability

Disability sport historically emerged as a method of therapeutic rehabilitation for patients. For instance, the Paralympic Games originated in 1948 in Stoke Mandeville, England and were organised by neurosurgeon Sir Ludwig Guttmann. They were primarily a means of rehabilitation for war veterans with spinal cord injuries (Guttmann, 1976).

Disability sport has since evolved into a successful and innovative industry which produces elite-level athletes focused on performance instead of participation alone. The Paralympic Games, which is an abbreviation for the parallel Olympics, is an elite event designed for those with physical impairments. The Special Olympics is designed for athletes with intellectual disabilities and the Deaf Olympics includes athletes with hearing impairments, both focused on social inclusion and participation.

Paralympic sports rely heavily on new technological developments such as prosthetic limbs and racing wheelchairs (Burkett, 2010: 216; Koenen *in* Gilbert and Schantz, 2008: 139). Technology therefore comes hand in hand with disability sport for quasi-therapeutic means.

However, the performance, governance and management of disability sport remains separate from what may be considered 'mainstream' or non-disabled categories of sport. Essentially two versions of sport exist. This division is viewed as necessary to match ability and ensure the safety of athletes where the physical or intellectual capacity of athletes may be imbalanced. In addition, the use of mechanical aids for assisted living may produce practical problems of integration as well as concerns over performance advantage. The Paralympic Games and the Olympic Games have historically remained segregated, with separate governing bodies who each promote and protect their own values. The Olympic motto implies exclusivity (faster, higher, stronger) whilst the Paralympic motto is more reflective of its origins (spirit in motion). Although media coverage and investment in disability sport has increased and influenced change, the division continues to exist. The rationale for this separation is that mainstream governing bodies lack expertise to deal with disability sport.

At the same time, this division may be covertly maintained to reflect standards of normality in sport. Disabled athletes have historically been considered abnormal and not suited to competitive sport because of their deviation from the norm.

As discussed in Part I, within our ableist culture social, political and media-driven attitudes have contributed towards the association of disabled individuals with stigma (Cherney and Lindemann *in* Hundley and Billings, 2009: 196). This may account for the generally low levels of participation in sport, particularly elite sport amongst individuals with disabilities (De Jong *et al.*, 2010: 18). Whilst these attitudes have shifted somewhat, there is still a clear tendency to focus on the misfortune of disabled individuals, which is reflective of the previous medical model of disability. Such institutionalisation has resulted in disabled groups accepting the image of themselves (Nixon *in* Thomas and Smith, 2009: 8).

Based upon these justifications for segregating non-disability and disability sport, the aim of this chapter is to assess the legitimacy and fairness of this division, investigating whether this categorisation is a necessary objective of the essence of sport or whether this can lead to the unreasonable exclusion of disabled athletes. The divisions are challenged by physically and intellectually disabled athletes who attempt to move from the peripheral of sport and into elite mainstream sport, which was not necessarily designed for disabled athletes. Such challenges are increasing as technology and science advances, causing these categories to become blurred. This chapter will explore the regulatory approach to dealing with such cases and whether there are appropriate mechanisms in place to balance inclusion and exclusion.

Oscar Pistorius

The case of Oscar Pistorius is 'possibly without precedent' (CAS 2008/A/1480 *Pistorius v IAAF*: 2). His story has challenged our traditional notions of human ability and began to blur the lines between non-disabled and disabled individuals (Longman, 2007). Pistorius is a bilateral trans-tibial amputee sprinter who was born without fibulae, the outer leg bones between the knee and ankle. His lower legs were amputated when he was 11 months old, and he began walking with his first prosthetic carbon fibre limbs six months later. At the age of 16 he was fitted with a 'Cheetah Flex-Foot' prosthesis, designed for sprinting by the Icelandic company Ossur. Each leg is a flat piece of carbon fibre which is shaped into a 'J' shape. The historical advancement of prosthetic limbs has mostly been associated with the military (Bidlack, 2009: 618). The flex foot prosthetic used by Pistorius, was first seen in elite sport in 1998 (Nolan, 2008: 125).

In 2004 at the Athens Paralympic Games, Pistorius won bronze medal in the 100 metre race, and a gold medal with a world record in the 200 metre race. He holds the sport class T44 world records in the 100, 200 and 400 metres and has also competed in a number of IAAF-sanctioned events against non-disabled runners.

In early 2007 he finished second in the 400 metre race at the South African non-disabled national championships. In March 2007, the IAAF Council decided to introduce an amendment to IAAF competition Rule 144.2 with the intention of regulating and banning the use of technical devices:

> (e) Use of any technical device that incorporates springs, wheels or any other element that provides the user with an advantage over another athlete not using such a device.
>
> (IAAF, 2008a)

Pistorius was invited to participate in the Norwich Union Glasgow Grand Prix, which was due to take place in June 2007. However, the IAAF intervened and withdrew this invitation due to the ambiguity of the use of his prostheses. It was disputed whether they were technical devices which were prohibited under Rule 144.2(e). An initial analysis of videotape footage of Pistorius' stride length when running proved inconclusive on the subject of whether the prostheses provide an advantage. Instead, an IAAF-commissioned study was prepared by Professor Brüggemann and colleagues at the German Sport University in Cologne.

The IAAF study

The study tested Oscar's biomechanical movements when he runs and aimed to determine whether the Cheetah legs gave him an advantage over non-disabled competitors (IAAF, 2008b; CAS, 2008; Zettler, 2009: 372). The tests evaluated his 'spring movement' and also his 'oxygen intake and blood lactate metabolism over a 400 metre race simulation' (Case, para. 4). Published in an IAAF press release, some of the main test results concluded that:

- Pistorius was able to run at the same speed as intact athletes using 25 per cent less energy.
- Highly significant differences were found between the below-knee spring mechanics (vertical ground reaction forces and vertical impulses) of an amputee using prosthetics and an athlete with natural legs.
- It was recorded that the mechanical advantage of the prosthetic limb compared with the healthy ankle joint of a non-disabled athlete is higher than 30 per cent (IAAF, 2008b).

Following this, in January 2008 (Decision 2008/01 of the IAAF Council) the IAAF banned him from further participation on the grounds that his prosthetics constitute a 'technical device' which offers him a clear mechanical advantage over other competitors, in discordance with Rule 144.2(e). Pistorius contested this decision and took his appeal to CAS who explored the following factors. The scientific detail presented is significant to the case analysis.

The process leading up to the IAAF decision

In relation to the study conducted by the IAAF, CAS found that instructions were made to Professor Brüggemann to test only Pistorius running in a straight line after the acceleration phase, which is his fastest stage. This created a distorted view of advantage and disadvantage. It was found that the IAAF deliberately limited the involvement of Dr Robert Gailey who was a scientist nominated by Pistorius for the study. The study summary, which was published on the IAAF website, was found to contain a number of errors. Finally, the IAAF did not seem to follow appropriate procedural rules for voting on an athlete's eligibility. The details of Pistorius' eligibility were already released before all votes had been received (Case, para. 8).

This study was heavily criticised by experts who argued that Pistorius' performance may not have been analysed against appropriate measures, controls and variables (Zettler, 2009: 375; Youngsteadt, 2008). Opponents of the study highlight the failure to explore this matter in a more 'holistic' manner rather than focusing on advantage only. CAS concluded that the study did not address the central question of whether or not the prostheses provided Pistorius with an overall *net* advantage or disadvantage, which was needed to decide this case.

Was the IAAF decision wrong in finding a contravention of Rule 144.2(e)?

Given that the study findings were inconclusive on whether the prostheses provide an advantage, the IAAF had no grounds to find Pistorius in contravention of the rule. CAS concluded that the introduction of the new competition rule was made deliberately to exclude Pistorius, and not, as argued by the IAAF, because they were concerned about spring technology in running shoes (Case, para. 6). Furthermore, the wording of the section was 'a masterpiece of ambiguity' (Case, para. 10; Camporesi, 2008: 639; Charlish and Riley, 2008).

Unlawful discrimination

Pistorius claimed that the IAAF had breached its obligations of non-discrimination by failing to seek alternative arrangements which might permit him to participate in IAAF-sanctioned events on an equal basis with all non-disabled athletes. He claimed that his fundamental human rights were breached, including equal access to Olympic principles and values (Case, para. 9). The court needed to consider whether or not Pistorius was competing on an equal basis with other athletes not using the Cheetah prostheses, as disability laws only require that an athlete be permitted to compete on the same footing as others (Case, para. 9).

CAS referred to the CRPD to highlight that being a signatory to this places an obligation on a State to refrain from acts which would defeat the object and purpose of the Convention. However, since the IAAF is governed by the laws of Monaco, this is not applicable since Monaco has not enacted the principles of the CRPD.

CAS found the CRPD to be of little application since if it is found that Pistorius has no advantage with his prostheses then he will be permitted to compete on an equal basis. If there is evidence of an advantage then the CRPD does not assist. On this basis, CAS found no unlawful discrimination.

Since he was prohibited from competing in an event in the UK, which is a signatory to the CRPD, perhaps the UK could have placed pressure on the IAAF to ensure that they act consistently with the Convention if it was applicable.

Furthermore, under the EA 2010 there is a duty to make reasonable adjustments when the disabled person is at a disadvantage to a non-disabled person (s. 20). However CAS highlighted that the applicability of equality legislation is limited here since the case falls on whether Pistorius has an unfair advantage over non-disabled athletes.

Pistorius study

In order to decide the case, CAS considered results of the study commissioned by Pistorius, which contradicted the IAAF study results. The team found fundamental flaws in the IAAF study. Not only did the study test broader elements, but also it found that:

- Pistorius fatigued normally and in the same manner as non-disabled sprinters;
- He used the same oxygen amounts as able-bodied runners at a sub-maximal speed and thus did not have a metabolic advantage; and
- Finally that 'anaerobic energy supply cannot be quantified which invalidates the IAAF finding that Pistorius has a 20 per cent energy advantage at 400 metre race speeds' (Rice University, 2008).

There is an overall lack of certainty surrounding the subject of advantage through the use of prosthetic limbs in sport. The alleged advantage which Pistorius has firstly relates to the energy expenditure and loss whilst running and, secondly, concerns the advantages gained through the use of the properties of the blades compared with intact limbs (Jones and Wilson, 2009: 126). Little is still truly known about the effect of the prosthetics on amputee running, primarily because there is limited scientific research conducted on the biomechanics of amputee runners, particularly with both missing legs (Longman, 2007). It is difficult to test the Cheetahs because an athlete cannot run with and then without them. Brian Frasure, US Paralympic sprinter is one of the only potential examples. He was training to make his college track team when an accident left him a single leg trans-tibial amputee. As an amputee he was not able to run as fast as he could before the accident. It is claimed that he had to work 50 per cent harder than other athletes (Thomsen, 1999). He used a shin and foot prosthetic, called the Sprint Flex III. However, he was not bilateral amputee using the Cheetah model like Pistorius, which makes the comparison difficult.

Yet, independent studies of the Cheetahs and similar prostheses generally reveal a contradiction in the IAAF findings that the Cheetahs confer energy-related advantages to users (Zettler, 2009: 377; Weyand *et al.*, 2009; Nolan, 2008; Grabowski *et al.*, 2010). There are many disadvantages to sprinting on carbon fibre legs. For instance, Pistorius requires '30 metres to gain his rhythm. His knees do not flex as readily, limiting his power output. His grip can be unsure in the rain. And when he runs into a headwind or grows fatigued, he must fight rotational forces that turn his prosthetic devices sideways' (Per Ampie Louw,

Pistorius' coach *in* Longman, 2007). During the start and the acceleration phase of a race, an amputee athlete is limited to remaining upright as they set out of the blocks. This restricts the production of the necessary horizontal force in comparison with non-disabled athletes (Jones and Wilson, 2009: 127).

Overall, advantage or disadvantage cannot be proved with certainty (Zettler, 2009: 378). There is no conclusive evidence which proves an overall net advantage to amputee athletes using the prosthetics.

CAS decision

Taking the Pistorius study into account, CAS upheld the appeal on the grounds that no advantage could be established. CAS held that the IAAF cannot prohibit something without scientific evidence which proves a metabolic or physical advantage. The Cheetah device has been used for a decade yet no sprinter using them had run faster than non-disabled runners, until Pistorius. CAS stated that the tests conducted in Germany were distorted and inaccurate and the IAAF procedures were controversial.

Following eligibility, despite falling short of qualification for the Beijing Olympics in 2008, Pistorius became the first double amputee athlete to compete at the London Olympics in 2012. At the IAAF World Championships in Daegu 2011, he just missed out on the 400 metre final. He was also a member of the South African 4x400 relay team. The IAAF permitted him to compete in the team only if he ran the first leg. This was reportedly imposed to ensure the safety of other athletes (Anon, 2008). However, the final was raced without Pistorius even though he was the second fastest South African runner at the 400 metres in 2011. Little commentary has been provided on this incident.

The international regulatory approach taken by CAS was to include Pistorius since no advantage could be proved. As discussed in previous chapters it is extremely difficult to draw lines when science cannot provide an accurate determination of the status of performance advantage. The decision appears to be limited in three ways:

1 It specifically related only to Pistorius, and therefore future cases must appear on a case-by-case basis;
2 The decision applied only to the particular model of Cheetah Flex Foot prostheses. This was to restrict the use of future versions, which may more clearly show advantage; and
3 CAS acknowledged that the decision may only be temporary because developments in scientific knowledge or testing technology may allow the IAAF to prove that Cheetah's confer a net advantage to users in the future.

Although the case has been criticised because of these limitations it is an example of good governance. The IAAF justifications for exclusion are reasonable in principle but unreasonably executed and applied. It may be argued that they were covertly seeking to maintain the standards of normality in sport as earlier described. Even if this were the case the approach taken by CAS focused on the practical factors concerning inclusion and exclusion rather than these socio-cultural influences. In an interesting twist, the limitation is significant in light of a recent claim by Pistorius himself that another competitor, Brazilian Alan Oliveira, was gaining an unfair advantage. Oliveira won the gold medal in the T44 200 metre event at the 2012 Paralympic Games. Pistorius won the silver medal but contested that his rival was using blades which were too long and in contravention of the International Paralympic Committee (IPC) rules. The lengths of the blades are carefully calculated according to the notional height of the athlete. This is determined by the arm length of the athlete (Anon, 2012). Pistorius later apologised for his actions and the IPC confirmed that Oliveira had not breached the rules (Hart, 2012). This is perhaps a good example of the continual challenges to sporting boundaries that sport will face as a result of human progression and advancement in technology.

Proving advantage

In order to strike a balance between inclusion and exclusion, CAS focused on proving an advantage. Similarly, in 2001 in the USA, 14-year-old Hunter Scott had a left leg above the knee amputation. He was a swimmer and required a specially designed prosthetic 'swim fin' to compete in swimming league competitions. In 2001, the DeKalb-Atlanta Swim and Diving League (DASL) ruled that this device infringed guidelines prohibiting the use of such devices in competitions. The Scott family argued that the device simply provided Scott with better balance and threatened to bring legal action under the US Anti-Doping Agency (USADA). The former president of the League refused to inspect the flipper despite being offered the opportunity and instead acted in accordance with the USA Swimming codes (Lohn, 2002). A similar rule of FINA reads that: 'no swimmer shall be permitted to use or wear any device or swimsuit which may aid his/her speed, buoyancy or endurance during a competition (such as webbed gloves, flippers, fins, etc.). Goggles may be worn. Any kind of tape on the body is not permitted unless approved by FINA Sport Medicine Committee' (Rule 10.8).

However, the Georgia High School Association, which governs high school athletics, approved the device since there was no evidence that the swim fin provided extra propulsion or an advantage over other competitors. In fact, the device acted as a hindrance in many ways because it created drag, which slowed Scott down as he pushed off from the wall in competitions. The device provided him with a 'necessary balance' to compete (Lohn, 2002). The DASL and the Scott family reached a legal agreement to allow him to compete, which is consistent with the CAS decision on Pistorius.

The advantage approach has also been used in cricket. The bowling action in cricket requires an unnatural rigid arm movement rather than the natural instinct to flex the arm. In fact, if the arm is flexed then this is considered to be throwing the ball or 'chucking', which is illegal under the International Cricket Council (ICC) rules because it arguably provides an unfair advantage. The legality of bowling actions has been closely debated as a result of athletes such as Sri Lankan cricketer Muttiah Muralitharan. He suffers from a congenital deformity in his elbow which prevents him from fully extending his right arm. His unique arm rotation and wrist action became the subject of global debate. It was reported that he was bending his arm by up to ten degrees when bowling, which contravened the 2004 ICC rules stating that a bowler can only flex their elbow up to five degrees.

Following concerns by players and umpires, in 1995 he was forced to undergo a series of biomechanical tests to investigate his action further and determine whether he was throwing the ball. Experts concluded that his action was within the range of legitimacy and instead created an illusion of throwing. The tests revealed that most bowlers flex their elbows at some stage during delivery of a ball. Pakistan fast bowler Shoaib Akhtar possesses hyper mobility in both his shoulder and elbow joints which leads to the hyper extension of his arm, which prevents him from bowling with a straight arm.

Following considerable biomechanical research in the area of elbow flexion, in 2005 the ICC changed their rules to accommodate for elbow flexion of up to 15 degrees (Anon, 2004). This created a better level of consistency when determining the appropriateness of a bowling action, but may also be construed to provide disabled athletes with a competitive advantage.

More recently in 2014, Pakistan cricketer Saeed Ajmal was suspended following an illegal bowling action. It was claimed that he injured his elbow in a car crash and therefore possesses a natural kink which enables him to rotate his elbow sideways (Kingsley, 2014). This has brought into question the legitimacy of the testing procedures and of the rule itself. Instead, the development of wearable technology is being considered, which could create more accuracy in the determination of advantage (Bull, 2014).

Nevertheless, the public scrutiny that the cricketers face for alleged 'chucking' could be considered unfair and discriminatory if they have a condition or disability. Proving advantage in this way prioritises the essence of sport over principles of equality.

Casey Martin

A slightly alternative approach to inclusion and exclusion was adopted in the seminal case of *Martin v PGA Tour, Inc.*, 994 F. Supp. 1242 (D. Or. 1998). Many authors have compared and contrasted the *Casey Martin* and *Pistorius* case (Condry, 2008) because they both raise the question of whether disabled athletes using technology are disabled, able or, *too* able, therefore possessing an unfair advantage and threatening the integrity of sport.

Casey Martin was born with a rare disabling blood circulatory condition called Klippel-Trénauney-Weber (KTW) syndrome, which caused severe pain in his legs and restricted his ability to walk. During his time at university, his condition deteriorated and it was dangerous for him to walk. Not only was the pain associated with walking but there was also a risk of haemorrhaging or fracturing the tibia, which could result in the amputation of his leg. His condition was recognised as a disability under the ADA.

He played for the golf team at Stanford University with Tiger Woods. The National Collegiate Athletics Association (NCAA) and the Pacific 10 Conference granted him an exception to use a golf cart to compete in collegiate events (Liguori, 2003: 186).

After university the talented golf player attempted to turn professional by entering the Professional Golf Association (PGA) qualifying tournaments. The PGA is a non-profit organisation which sponsors professional golf tournaments. However, they refused to derogate from the hard card rules of the game (it is a PGA requirement that players walk the course during its qualifying rounds. Players are required to complete qualifying rounds to earn playing privileges on the PGA Tour [Q-School]) so as to allow him to use a golf cart. The PGA Tour Commissioner, Tom Finchem refused to alter the rules claiming that this would be an unacceptable intrusion on the integrity of golf. They were not contesting the physical disability, but that a change to the rule would give him a competitive advantage.

Martin brought a case against the PGA under the ADA in the Federal District Court. He claimed that the golf cart restriction violated Title III of the ADA by denying him a reasonable modification to accommodate his disability. Under Title III an entity is guilty of discrimination if it fails to make reasonable modifications to its policies, practices or procedures to accommodate individuals with disabilities, unless the entity can demonstrate that making such modifications would fundamentally alter the nature of such goods, services, facilities, privileges, advantages or accommodations (s. 12182 (b) (2) (a) (ii)). This was upheld by the District Court and an appeal was made to the Supreme Court. The court had to consider whether the requested modification was reasonable, whether it was necessary for the disabled individual and whether it would fundamentally alter the nature of the competition (Case, para. 660).

Application of US equality legislation

The PGA argued that the Act did not apply here since the competing players were not members of class protected by Title II of the Act, which protects individuals who are 'clients and customers' of public accommodations. The court rejected this and held that it was appropriate to classify golfers as clients or customers since they pay the PGA a substantial fee to compete in its qualifying tournaments.

The Supreme Court found that the PGA matches took place in places of public accommodation within the meaning of Title III, since the statutory definition of a public accommodation expressly included a golf course under s. 12181 (7) (L) ADA (Case, para. 670). The PGA accepted this but there has been variation in the interpretation of what falls within places of public accommodation under the ADA. Its application to membership organisations such as sports clubs raises the more general question of whether sports bodies are public or private in nature and therefore subject to equality legislation.

In *Schultz v Hemet Youth Pony League* 943 F. Supp. 1222 (C.D. Cal. 1996) the youth league baseball programme was divided into seven age brackets on the basis of a player's 'legal age.' Schultz was 11-years-old and suffered from cerebral palsy, which affects the body's muscles. He was able to walk and run with the assistance of crutches. He attempted to 'play down' in a division reserved for children aged between 9 and 10 but was refused. The court held that the Hemet Youth Pony League is a place of public accommodation since it is 'not limited to actual physical structures with defined boundaries' (Case, para. 1225). It was held that the exclusion was unsubstantiated and based upon assumed concerns of possible risk or harm. The case offered little commentary on the inclusion of an athlete with crutches.

Another approach of the courts has been to refrain from intervening in private sporting matters. In *Shepherd v United States Olympic Committee* 464 F. Supp. 2d 1072 (D. Colo. 2006) the District Court consolidated two cases involving Paralympic athletes, Mark Shepherd, a wheelchair basketball player, and Scott Hollonbeck, Jose Antonio Inguez and Jacob Heilveil who were elite wheelchair racers. USOC offers Athlete Support Programmes, which includes various types of grants, tuition assistance and health insurance benefits. USOC uses criteria to distribute these benefits under its resource allocation policy. The policy states that an applicant must be eligible to represent the USA and must be one who intends to compete, if selected, in the next Olympic or Pan American Games. The athletes in the case argued that this policy was inequitable since it did not offer benefits to Paralympians and was only open to Olympians. They claimed that this violated Title III ADA and s. 504 of the Rehabilitation Act 1973 (Case, para. 1076).

The court denied that USOC constituted a place of public accommodation since their training facilities were only accessible to those already selected by the national governing bodies of Olympic, Pan American or Paralympic teams (Case, para. 1083). Furthermore, they felt that the *Casey Martin* case failed to address the question of whether places of public accommodation to which non-disabled athletes do not have 'full and equal enjoyment' to, also fall within Title III. The training facilities offered by USOC were considered world class and their access was limited. Therefore the court essentially claimed that it lacked jurisdiction over USOC because their training facilities were not available to the public to be caught under this legislation (Friedman and Norman, 2009: 354). The court distinguished the case with *Casey Martin* on the basis that golf courses were available to the general public whereas USOC facilities were only available to selected teams.

The court concluded that the plaintiffs were misplaced in their attempts to use judicial branches of government to remedy inequalities since this is a matter for the legislative and executive branches (Case, para. 1086). The court also accepted that these matters fall within the exclusive jurisdiction of USOC. This was supported in *Hollonbeck v United States Olympic Committee* 513 F. 3D 1191 (10th Cir. 2008) where the Paralympic athletes in *Shepherd* appealed several of the issues to the Court of Appeals for the Tenth Circuit. The court sympathised but was reluctant to act on a matter which they felt needed to be dealt with by the legislative and executive wings of government.

It can be difficult to hold sports bodies or organisations accountable under equality legislation since the courts often interpret the public/private divide in favour of a sports entity. However, in *Casey Martin* the court accepted that Title III applies to athletic competitions and elite athletes for the purposes of the PGA.

Alteration to golf

Having established the applicability of the ADA, the court was required to establish whether the PGA had violated the rule. This necessitates a precise interpretation of discrimination under the Act, which permits derogation if the entity can establish that making such modifications would fundamentally alter the nature of the game. The Court identified when a reasonable accommodation may well change an activity (Case, para. 682):

1. Changing an aspect of the game for all competitors which changes the nature of the game.
2. Making a modification for one competitor which gives that competitor an advantage.

The PGA relied on this to argue that using a golf cart would alter the nature of the game. In order to determine what the fundamental nature of golf was, the court looked closely at the history and multi-levelled rules of golf. They concluded that the essence of the sport was to play the ball from the tee into a hole using a stroke or a succession of strokes. The Rules of Golf, jointly written by the United States Golf Association (USGA) and the Royal and Ancient Golf Club, apply to all levels of amateur and professional golf but say nothing about the prohibition of use of a golf cart. Instead, Appendix 1 to the Rules of Golf list a number of optional conditions, which includes that if it is desired that players walk in a competition, then the imposition of a walking rule is advised.

The Conditions of Competition and Local Rules, known as the hard card rules, apply to the PGA and do force players to walk except in the Senior Tour and in the 'open' qualifying events. Carts are also used during two of the three stages of the qualifying rounds. Incidentally, most senior players prefer to walk. The purpose of such a rule is to inject an element of fatigue into the skill of shot making (Case, para. 660; 686).

The Notice of Competitors rules cover conditions for particular tournaments and at times may authorise the use of carts to speed up play when the distance is far (Liguori, 2003: 210). In any case, the use of carts has more than likely increased the participation of the game, since they were introduced in the 1950s (Case, para. 684).

The court concluded that the walking rule found in the hard card rules, based upon an optional condition which was buried in the appendix to the Rules of Golf, cannot be considered to be an essential attribute of the game itself (Case, para. 685). The inconsistent imposition of the walking rule in tournaments further supports this. The court stated that allowing Casey Martin to use a cart is not 'inconsistent with the fundamental character of golf' since the essence of the game is shot making (Case, para. 663). The walking requirement of golf is on the periphery of golf and is not even an official rule. It was also stated that it is impossible to guarantee in golf that all players can play under exactly the same conditions or even that an individual's ability will be the sole determinant of the outcome (Case, para. 663). Testimony from a professor in physiology was heard identifying that since golf is a low intensity sport, 'fatigue from the game is primarily a psychological phenomenon in which stress and motivation are the key ingredients' (Case, para. 687).

Further, participation would not fundamentally alter the game because Casey Martin would not benefit from any advantage, since it was accepted by the court that due to the chronic physical pain Casey Martin endured when he walked, he suffered greater fatigue and exhaustion syndrome than a non-disabled golfer.

Court decision

Overall, in a 7–2 decision, the court held that the PGA had violated the provisions of the ADA, and granted a permanent injunction requiring them to allow Martin to use a cart. Justice Stevens wrote the majority opinion whilst Justice Scalia and Justice Thomas filed a dissenting opinion raising some important commentary relevant to the balance between inclusion and exclusion in sport.

In Justice Scalia's dissent, he argued that the Supreme Court will find it difficult to determine which rules of a competitive sport are fundamental when the governing body of the sport contends that they are. He argued that the PGA should have the autonomy to decide what rules they wish to impose in a competition. He claimed that the courts were trespassing in an area where they do not belong as reflected in the *Shepherd* and *Hollenbeck* cases. He closed by warning that the case would lead to a 'totally equal world', which was something which George Orwell warned against in his novel *Animal Farm* (Case, para. 705). He referred to the court's decision as 'Kafkaeseque' and 'Alice in Wonderland'. Although this dissent may appear eccentric, this is reflective of the wider sports regulation debate. It is important that a balance is struck between inclusion and exclusion in sport so that legal intervention does not negatively influence the essence of sporting activity.

Fundamental alteration approach

The 'fundamental alteration' approach adopted in *Casey Martin* has produced some valuable footprints for the determination of inclusion and exclusion. The US courts have upheld that the ADA does not require entities to change their basic nature, character or purpose insofar as that purpose is rational, rather than a pretext for discrimination (Olinger Case, para. 1005). For instance, interestingly, the day after the Ninth Circuit ruled in favour of *Casey Martin*, the Seventh Circuit came to a conflicting decision in *Olinger v United States Golf Association* (USGA) 205 F.3d 1001 (2000). Ford Olinger suffered from bilateral avascular necrosis, a condition which hinders his ability to walk. He brought a claim under the ADA to allow him to ride a golf cart whilst competing in the US Open. The USGA do not allow the use of golf carts during the US Open and require player to walk during a round. The CA affirmed the District Court decision and held in favour of the USGA, on the grounds that allowing him to use a cart would alter the nature of the game. Walking in this case was deemed to be an important tradition of the game, according to testimonies of past and present professional golfers in the case. The District Court ruled that the nature of the competition would be fundamentally altered if the walking rule was eliminated because it would remove stamina from the set of qualities designed to be tested in golf. In addition, conditions that affect a golfer's performance such as fatigue, heat and humidity, were considered to be important to competition (Case, para. 1006). The literature contends that in light of *Casey Martin, Olinger* was incorrectly decided.

A fundamental alteration approach has been reasonably applied in cases such as *Kuketz v Petronelli* 821 NE 2d 473 (Mass. 2005) where a wheelchair racquetball player requested to participate in an non-disabled league and also requested permission to have two bounces of the ball as opposed to the single bounce allowed to non-disabled players. The official rules of racquetball state that the objective of the case is to win each rally and that the player loses a rally when he is unable to hit the ball before it touches the floor twice (Case, para. 356). The defendant general manager of the athletic club refused Kuketz the opportunity to compete in the non-disabled league primarily because of safety concerns that non-disabled athletes would not be accustomed to the movements and extra equipment of a wheelchair athlete if they were permitted to compete (Case, para. 357). Furthermore, the two bounces would fundamental alter the rules of the game. The court supported these arguments and held that the modifications sought by Kuketz would create a new game with new strategies and new rules which would fundamentally alter an essential aspect of the sport (Case, para. 365). This case was distinguished from *Casey Martin* since the essence of golf was shot making, which was not affected by the use of a golf cart.

Another example of reasonable exclusion is in *Knapp v Northwestern University* 101 F.3d 473 (7th Cir. 1996) where the university refused to allow Knapp to play on the school's Division 1 basketball team based on the team physicians determination that Knapp was medically ineligible because of his increased risk of cardiac death, even though he was implanted with a cardio defibrillator in his abdomen to regulate his condition. This exclusion took place even though his parents were willing to sign liability releases and had his own team of experts to testify that the level of risk was acceptable. Knapp sued Northwestern arguing that he was discriminated against because of this actual or perceived disability. The Seventh Circuit reversed the District Court decision, and concluded that Knapp should be excluded on the basis that 'legitimate physical qualifications may in fact be essential to participation in particular programs' (Case, para. 483). The case raises an important point that the determination of inclusion or exclusion from sport on the basis of sex, gender, disability or race must be based upon justifiable reasoning instead of subjective evaluations or good faith belief (Weston, 2005: 151). In this case, the court held that the decision must be reasoned and rational 'with full regard to possible and reasonable circumstances' (Case, para. 484).

Fundamental alterations to essential aspects of sport have also been considered in a number of cases concerning age rules and athletes with intellectual disabilities. Age categories in sport are imposed to balance physical and intellectual ability between athletes for the protection of safety and competitive advantage and to maintain uniformity of standards. They are usually considered essential to sporting regulations. In light of this, it has been held in some of the US decisions that the participation of a student, who has been held back a certain number of years because of an intellectual learning disability, is likely to infringe essential age rules in sport, which would constitute a fundamental alteration, modification or waiver.

For example, in *Pottgen v Missouri State High Sch. Activities Association*, 40 F.3d 926 (8th Cir.1994) a student with learning disabilities had repeated two school grades and entered the fourth grade as a 19-year-old. The student was considered ineligible to compete in interscholastic sports (basketball, cross-country and baseball) in accordance with the MSHSAA by-law 232.0, which concerns age standards. The aim of this restriction is to disallow competitive advantage to teams using older athletes, protect younger athletes from harm and to discourage student athletes from delaying their education to gain athletic maturity and experience (Case, para. 658). The MSHSAA refused to permit a waiver of this rule because it would cause administrative burdens and expenses. The District Court held in favour of the athlete since competitive advantage was *de minimis* and neither was there a safety risk (Case, para. 661). However the CA reversed this decision and concluded that the by-law was an essential requirement in high school interscholastic programmes (Case, para. 929).

This decision was followed in *Sandison v Michigan High School Athletic Association* 64 F. 3d 1026 (6th Circuit. 1995) where two high school students with learning disabilities were held back one year in school as a result of their learning disabilities. The MHSAA regulations forbid students over 19 years playing sports. The aim of the rule was to safeguard athletes against injuries arising from competing against average and oversized athletes, and to prevent average athletes from gaining a competitive advantage. This rule restricted the students from competing in track and cross country. The District Court decision to include the athletes was reversed on appeal where the court held that a waiver of the rule would be unreasonable and fundamentally alter the MHSAA regulations. In addition they held that the exclusion was solely by reason of age and not disability (Case, para. 1035).

Similarly in *McPherson v MHSAA Inc.* 119 F. 3d. 453 (6th Circuit 1997), the MHSAA handbook stated that a high school athlete cannot compete in any branch of athletics if he or she has been enrolled in grades 9-12 for more than eight semesters. The claimant was a basketball player with a learning disability who did not comply with this requirement and was therefore ineligible. The purpose of the rule was to 'create a fair sense of competition by limiting the level of athletic experience and skill of the players in order to create a more even playing field' (Case, para. 12). In addition, the rule sought to prevent age fraud, which was referred to as 'red shirting'. The MHSAA contended that there were narrow circumstances available for a waiver to this rule. The District Court decision in favour of the athlete was reversed on appeal. Relying on the previous case the court held that the rule was neutral and necessary (Case, para. 54 and 47).

Interesting commentary concerning administrative and financial burden was raised by the courts in these cases. The athletes asserted that their average athletic skill would not fundamentally alter the sports programme. However, the courts held that placing a responsibility on bodies such as the MHSAA to make individual determinations about competitive advantage would constitute an undue burden because of the range of factors that this would encompass (Case, para. 57). The courts highlighted the difficulties of making case-by-case assessments of student abilities and favoured average age standards.

On the other hand, the dissent judge in *Pottgen* argued that an individual approach should be taken to essential eligibility requirements because this would find that the student was not a threat to safety and not at an advantage (Case, para. 931). Broadly speaking about statutory interpretation, the dissenting Judge Arnold accepted that if a requirement is 'essential' to a programme or activity, then a waiver or modification cannot be reasonable. However, he advocated that we must determine what is meant by 'essential' (Case, para. 932).

This dissent was persuasively followed and a more individualised approach was supported in cases such as *Cruz v Pennsylvania Interscholastic Athletic Association* 157 F. Supp. 2d 485 (E.D. Pa. 2001) where a 19-year-old student with learning difficulties sought a modification to the age rules to be included into interscholastic wrestling, football and track. Section 1(1) of the Pennsylvania Interscholastic Athletic Association (PIAA) by-laws stipulated that students over the age of 19 were restricted from competing in interscholastic sports to protect younger athletes from the dangers and imbalance of older athletes who are perhaps larger, stronger, more mature and experienced, and to maintain uniformity of standards. The reasoning in *Casey Martin* was followed and it was held that the student would not fundamentally alter the nature of football and track. Whilst the rule was considered to be essential, a waiver or modification was viewed as reasonable and necessary. The position of wrestling was not so clear but it was agreed that the determination of a fundamental alteration should be made on an individual basis (Case, para. 499).

A similar age rule in *Dennin v Connecticut Interscholastic Athletic Conference Inc.* 913 F. Supp 663, 670 (D. Ct. 1996) restricted a 19-year-old student with Down's Syndrome from participating in intercollegiate swimming. The Connecticut Interscholastic Athletic Conference (CIAC) denied him a waiver but allowed him to compete as a non-scoring exhibition swimmer. On this basis, his relay team would be unable to earn points if he participated. The court found the dissent in *Pottgen* persuasive (Case, para. 668) and it was held that no advantage was present since the student was the slowest swimmer in the pool. Neither was there a safety concern because it was a non-contact sport (Case, para. 669). The imposition of a waiver would not constitute an undue burden on the CIAC. The court did highlight that in some cases this determination may be more complex 'depending on the sport in question, the size, agility, strength and endurance of the individual, and whether the quality of his/her athletic capacity is enhanced by his/her age beyond 18' (Case, para. 669).

The courts have revealed two approaches to the constitution of a fundamental alteration to an essential aspect of sport. On the one hand, the individual, case-by-case approach favours the athlete but involves a complex consideration of a range of factors relating to an athlete's physical and non-physical make up. On the other hand, the average approach produces a uniformity of standards across sports bodies and organisations, but is likely to lead to inaccuracies about advantage as we have seen. It is clear from the contrasting decisions in the different courts that what is essential to a sport is not a universal concept and can be very subjective.

The use of assisted devices in sport

Sporting equipment continually presses the boundaries of sport performance (Mullins *et al.*, 2000: 123). The sport and regulatory approach taken in cases such as *Pistorius*, *Hunter Scott*, *Casey Martin*, *Olinger* and *Kuketz* needs to be aligned consistently with the approach taken to the general use of assisted devices which are aimed at providing athletes with a competitive advantage in sport.

For instance, altitude stimulators, such as hypoxic chambers, hypoxic tents and dedicated training resorts, create controlled environments to help athletes adapt their oxygen efficiency in different altitude locations (Armstrong *in* Mottram, 2011: 355; Hard, 2010: 547). The legality of these methods have been criticised on the grounds that such facilities provide athletes with a competitive advantage and pose safety risks to the health of athletes (Greely, 2004: 114). However, in January 2007, following detailed consultation on the hypoxic chambers, WADA approved the recommendation of their scientific committee not to add them to the 2007 List of Prohibited Substances and Methods (WADA, 2006). The treatment of minority athletes, who use technology for therapeutic means, is challenged in an arena where advantage is constantly being sought and accepted by increasing advancements in technology.

Consider also athletes who have a pacemaker fitted, a hip prosthesis (Van Hilvoorde and Landeweerd, 2008: 108) or the procedure of laser eye surgery (Buzuvis, 2011: 39). Tiger Woods underwent two laser-assisted *in situ* keratomileusis (LASIK) procedures to improve his vision beyond 20/20. Before surgery, he was considered to be legally blind without glasses or contact lenses. He did not enjoy lenses since they blurred his eyes and negatively affected his performance (Zaccone, 2010: 426). This procedure was deemed to be an acceptable human enhancement.

Another example of welcomed advancements is the development of textiles by brands, such as Nike, who have made significant advances in their clothing and footwear to provide athletes with an advantage (Burkett, 2010: 215; Lu, 2008: 626). In 2004, Speedo® introduced the first 'Fastskin' full body swimsuit, which was modelled on shark's skin, and consisted of Lycra® or elastane covering either a part or whole of the body. It is suggested that this technology reduces friction and pressure drags, which is beneficial for swimmers (Chatard and Wilson, 2008: 1149; Craik, 2011: 73). A number of concerns were raised about the legitimacy of these suits and whether they contravened FINA Swimming Rule 10.8. Controversy surrounded whether they were assistive devices which enhance performance or whether they were simply swimming costumes. Many studies concluded that the use of the suits provided statistically significant benefits to swimmers (Zettler, 2009: 379).

Following pressure on FINA to clarify their regulations, FINA's congress voted to ban full-length swimsuits and polyurethane suits in January 2010 (FINA, 2009a; FINA 2009b). The subsequent decision to tighten regulation is positive but the swimsuits have arguably changed swimming and led to some believing that a technological doping age is taking place (Wood, 2008: 1; Randall, 2009: 2048).

Upon these examples, the challenge for the balance between inclusion and exclusion is and will be identifying the match between the technology and the athletes' essential requirements. One important distinction to make here is that disabled athletes using assisted devices are doing so for therapeutic reasons (Wolbring, 2008: 154). There is no current consistent approach to balancing inclusion and exclusion in relation to the use of technology and instead this determination may be driven by standards of normality and acceptance in sport. Some of the justifications for maintaining the categories of disabled and non-disabled sports are based upon protecting these sporting values. However, it is fair to say that neither athletes nor sporting activity can be considered 'normal.' Elite athletes possess attributes which give them a super ability, which also places them as abnormal, 'varying from extreme sized sumo wrestlers to extremely undersized gymnasts' (Van Hilvoorde and Landeweerd, 2008: 104). The difference is that elite athletes with abnormal super abilities are celebrated in our society, compared with disabled athletes who are treated with caution because their participation may pose safety concerns or create an unfair advantage. These are legitimate concerns but need to be supported by factual evidence.

Summary

This chapter reveals that the division between disabled and non-disabled sport is predominantly based upon concerns of safety and competitive advantage. The approaches of the courts to disability cases has been mixed. There has been a continued reluctance to intervene in some sport matters. Where intervention has taken place, the courts have tended to adopt either the advantage or fundamental alteration model to determine inclusion or exclusion. The balance appears to lie upon the absence or presence of scientific evidence to support a claim.

However, making any of these determinations requires a high degree of subjectivity, which leads to a number of inconsistent outcomes and decision. Many of the US court decisions concerning age rules were reversed and included dissenting opinions because of the complexity involved in ascertaining whether a disabled athlete is likely to alter the essence of a sport and provide an unfair advantage, and whether an age rule is a fundamental aspect of a sports programme.

The cases have produced interesting discussions concerning the appropriate balance between inclusion and exclusion for disabled individuals. There remains a desire to protect the standards of normality, which is being driven by what is acceptable in sport.

References

Anon. 2012. Pistorius Paralympics gripe: How long can blades be? *BBCi Website* [online], 3 September. Available at: www.bbc.co.uk/news/magazine-19465118 [accessed 30/07/14].

Anon. 2004. Chucking rules set to be changed. *BBCi Website.* [online], 10 November. Available at: http://news.bbc.co.uk/sport1/hi/cricket/3998397.stm [accessed 01/05/07].

Anon. 2008. Relay safety fears over Pistorius. *BBCi Website* [online], 15 July. Available at: http://news.bbc.co.uk/sport1/hi/olympics/athletics/7508399.stm [accessed 16/07/08].

Bidlack, C. 2009. The Prohibition of Prosthetic Limbs in American Sports: the issues and the role of the American with Disabilities Act. *Marquette Sports Law Review.* 19(2): 613–637.

Bull, A. 2014. Saeed Ajmal: latest clampdown in cricket's "chucking" debate may be last. *The Guardian* [online] 12 August. Available at: www.theguardian.com/sport/2014/aug/12/the-spin-saeed-ajmal-cricket-chucking-debate [accessed 10/09/14].

Burkett, B. 2010. Technology in Paralympic Sport: performance enhancement or essential for performance? *British Journal of Sports Medicine*, 44: 215–220

Buzuvis, E.E. 2011. Caster Semenya and the Myth of the Level Playing Field. *The Modern American*, 6: 36–42.

Camporesi, S. 2008. Oscar Pistorius, Enhancement and Post-Humans. *Journal of Medical Ethics*, 34(9): 639.

Charlish, P. and Riley, S. 2008. Should Oscar Run? *Fordham Intellectual Property, Media and Entertainment Law Journal*, 18: 929–957.

Chatard, J.C. and Wilson, B. 2008. Effect of Fastskin Suits on Performance, Drag and Energy Cost of Swimming. *Medicine and Science in Sports and Exercise*, 40: 1149–1154.

Condry, S.N. 2008. *Disability, Sport and the Limits of Law.* M. Phil, University of Stirling, School of Law.

Craik, J. 2011. The Fastskin Revolution: from human fish to swimming androids. *Culture Unbound: Journal of Current Cultural Research*, 3: 71–83.

De Jong, R., Vanreusel, B. and Van Driel, R. 2010. Relationships between mainstream participation rates and elite sport success in disability sports. *European Journal of Adapted Physical Activity*, 3(1): 18–29.

FINA 2009a. PR58. *FINA Bureau Meeting.* [online] 28 July. Available at: www.fina.org/H2O/index.php?option=com_content&view=article&id=976:pr58-fina-bureau-meeting&catid=197:2009&Itemid=248 [09/09/11].

FINA 2009b. PR59 *FINA Bureau Meeting.* [online] 31 July. Available at: www.fina.org/H2O/index.php?option=com_content&view=article&id=975:pr59-fina-bureau-meeting&catid=197:2009&Itemid=248 [accessed 09/09/11].

Friedman, J.L. and Norman, G.C. 2009. The Paralympics: yet another missed opportunity for social integration. *Boston University International Law Journal*, 27: 345–366.

Gilbert, K. and Schantz, O.J. 2008. *The Paralympic Games: empowerment or side show?* Maidenhead: Meyer and Meyer Sport.

Grabowski, A.M., McGowan, C.P., McDermott, W.J., Beale, M.T., Kram, R. and Herr, H.M. 2010. Running-specific prostheses limit ground force during sprinting. *Biology Letters*, 6: 201–204.

Greely, H.T. 2004. Disabilities, Enhancements, and the Meaning of Sports. *Stanford Law and Policy Review*, 15: 99–132.

Guttmann, L. 1976. *Textbook of Sport for the Disabled.* Aylesbury: HM&M Publishers.

Hard, M. 2010. Caught in the net: athletes' rights and the World Anti-doping Agency. *Southern California Interdisciplinary Law Journal*, 19: 533–563.

Hart, S. 2012. Oscar Pistorius 'sorry' for criticising Alan Oliveira's blades after Paralympics 200m defeat. *The Telegraph* [online], 3 September. Available at: www.telegraph.co.uk/sport/olympics/paralympic-sport/9516818/Oscar-Pistorius-sorry-for-criticising-Alan-Oliveiras-blades-after-Paralympics-200m-defeat.html [accessed 30/07/14].

Hundley, H.L. and Billings, A.C. 2009. *Examining Identity in Sports Media.* London: Sage Publications.

International Association of Athletics Federations (IAAF) 2008a. *IAAF Competition Rules 2008. [online], Available at:* www.iaaf.org/mm/Document/imported/42192.pdf [accessed 07/07/10].

International Association of Athletics Federations (IAAF) 2008b. *Oscar Pistorius – Independent Scientific study concludes that cheetah prosthetics offer clear mechanical advantages.* [online], 14 January. Available at: www.iaaf.org/news/Kind=512/newsId=42896.html [accessed 01/07/08].

Jones, C. and Wilson, C. 2009. Defining advantage and athletic performance: The case of Oscar Pistorius. *European Journal of Sport Science.* 9(2): 125–131.

Kingsley, P. 2014. Saeed Ajmal: the bowler caught out by cricket's rules over chucking. *The Guardian* [online] 9 September. Available at: www.theguardian.com/sport/shortcuts/2014/sep/09/saeed-ajmal-bowler-cricket-chucking-throwing-pakistan-spin [accessed 10/09/14].

Liguori, D.J. 2003. Fore! The Supreme Court tees off a standard to apply the Americans with Disabilities Act to professional sports in PGA Tour, INC, v Martin. *Widener Law Journal.* 12: 185–219.

Lohn, J. 2002. Standing Tall. *Swimming World and Junior Swimmer*, 11(43), November: 32–34.

Longman, J. 2007. An Amputee Sprinter: Is he disabled or too abled? *The New York Times* [online], 15 May. Available at: www.nytimes.com/2007/05/15/sports/othersports/15runner.html [accessed 18/01/08].

Lu, A. 2008. Do new materials make the athlete? *In Science*, 321, 1 August: 626–626.

Mottram, D.R. 2011. *Drugs in Sport*, 5th Edition. London: Routledge.

Mullins, B.J., Hardy, S. and Sutton, W.A. 2000. *Sport Marketing.* Illinois: Human Kinetics.

Nolan, L. 2008. Carbon fibre prostheses and running in amputees: A review. *Foot and Ankle Surgery*, 14: 125–129.

Randall, D.L. 2009. Ethics in Practice. *The Journal of Bone and Joint Surgery*, 91(8), August: 2048–2054.

Rice University 2008. *Study Revives Olympic Prospects for Amputee Runner.* [online] Available at: www.rice.edu/nationalmedia/news051608oscar.shtml [accessed 11/08/09].

Thomas, N. and Smith, A. 2009. *Disability, Sport and Society: an introduction.* London: Routledge.

Thomsen, I. 1999. Hitting His Stride Again. *Sports Illustrated* [online], 18 October. Available at: http://sportsillustrated.cnn.com/vault/article/magazine/MAG1017342/index.htm [accessed 20/07/10].

Van Hilvoorde, I. and Landeweerd, L. 2008. Disability or Extraordinary Talent – Francesco Lentini (three legs) versus Oscar Pistorius (no legs). *Sport, Ethics and Philosophy*, 2(2): 97–111.

Weston, M.A. 2005. The Intersection of Sports and Disability: analysing reasonable accommodations for athletes with disabilities. *Saint Louis University Law Journal*, 50: 137–163.

Weyand, P.G., Bundle, M.V., McGowan, C.P., Grabowski, A., Brown, M.B., Kram, R. and Herr, H. 2009. The fastest runner on artificial legs: different limbs, similar function? *Journal of Applied Physiology*, 107: 903–911.

Wolbring, G. 2008. Oscar Pistorius and the future nature of Olympic, Paralympic and other Sports. *Script-ed*, 5(1), April: 139–160.

Wood, J. 2008. Record Breaking or Rule Breaking? *Materials Today* [online]. 11(6), June: 1–1.

World Anti-Doping Agency (WADA) 2006. *WADA Executive Committee Approves the 2007 Prohibited List.* [online], 16 September. Available at: www.wada-ama.org/en/News-Center/Articles/WADA-Executive-Committee-Approves-the-2007-Prohibited-List/ [accessed 11/09/10].

Youngsteadt, E. 2008. "Blade Runner" Back on Track. *Science Now* [online] 20 May. Available at: http://news.sciencemag.org/sciencenow/2008/05/20-02.html [accessed 20/07/10].

Zaccone, L.A. 2010. Policing the policing of intersex bodies. *Brooklyn Law Review*, 76(1): 385–438.

Zettler, P. J. 2009. Is it cheating to use Cheetahs? The implications of technologically innovative prostheses for sports values and rules. *Boston University International Law Journal*, 27: 367–409.

7 Race

In Part I we introduced the complex concept of race, highlighting that our human differences between us are largely brought about by evolutionary adaptation and further exaggerated through culture. When race is used as a term to describe this process then it is a valid construct. Problems begin to emerge when human differences are explained using misguided or even false assumptions about entire populations (Winant *in* Back and Solomos, 2000: 678). This can lead to acts of racism or exclusionary behaviour. There are many historical overt examples of individuals and groups treated differently because of their race, which includes physical characteristics, geographical origin, religion, culture and behaviour. These practices extended to sporting activity and in the 1936 Berlin Olympics Adolf Hitler attempted to exert white Nazi superiority over non-white athletes. In addition, until the 1990s in the USA, golf clubs enforced exclusionary policies which denied African Americans from membership (Gable and Johnson *in* Quirk, 1996: 251).

In modern society, the protection of race within the international human rights regime (UDHR, ICERD), the regional provisions (ECHR) and domestic legislation (UK EA, US Civil Rights Act) has imposed criminal and civil legal sanctions on acts of racism or racial abuse. Sport is not exempt from this and has also overtly moved away from discriminating on the grounds of race.

Given this legal framework, this chapter sits separately from the areas of sex, gender and disability. Thus far we have focused on contentious cases of inclusion and exclusion in competitive sport. Race is less contentious since any form of exclusion based on race would infringe human rights legislation and outweigh sporting interest. That is not to say that discriminatory behaviour does not still take place. There are some examples of overt exclusion in sport such as racial abuse, which continues to imbalance inclusion and exclusion. There are many instances of more covert expressions of race in sport such as racial stacking and restrictions upon religious and cultural expressions. As a result of misguided stereotypical assumptions about suitability to sporting activity, pockets of under-representation and over-representation of minority groups in sport have also emerged.

In the context of race, it is often the culture of sport which clashes and tends to lead to an imbalance between inclusion and exclusion. This chapter will demonstrate the limits to regulatory mechanisms in changing cultures and attitudes.

Overt practices: racial abuse

Racial abuse 'works to isolate a particular section of the community and carries with it violent and damaging undertones' (Long, 2000: 126). It has the effect of creating an exclusionary culture within sports, and leads to athletes lacking a sense of belonging. Holland (1995) reveals that many athletes of minority backgrounds learn to live with any abuse which they may receive, as a means of having a successful career in sport. In modern times racial abuse on social media has become an increasing problem for athletes. Even more concerning is the growth of racism within 'banter'. Such behaviour is excused on the basis that no harm is intended and it is inoffensive. This is evidenced in cricket where 'sledging' is used as an excuse for racial abuse amongst competitors (Long, 2000: 127).

In October 2010, the EU Agency for Fundamental Rights (FRA) published a report documenting findings of research on racism, discrimination and exclusion in amateur and professional sport in Europe (FRA, 2010). It found incidents of racism, anti-semitism and anti-gypsyism in football and basketball across the EU. In most cases, the report highlighted that the prohibition of discrimination was not adequately enforced in sport. The current frequency of race-related incidents in English football reinforces the findings of this report. For instance, whilst not central to this discussion, overt racism continues to manifest itself amongst spectators in football. In February 2015, a group of Chelsea FC fans forcefully prevented a black man from boarding a train in Paris, as they chanted, 'we're racist, we're racist, and that's the way we like it' (Anon, 2015). Within this cultural setting, three recent affairs on the pitch amongst the athletes have prompted the FA to review its sanctions for racism offences.

The first of these high-profile incidents took place in October 2011 when Chelsea captain John Terry was accused of aiming a racial slur at Queens Park Rangers player Anton Ferdinand during a football match. Whilst this behaviour does not directly exclude athletes from sport on the grounds of race, it creates an exclusionary environment. The case was referred to the criminal court and also investigated by the FA. The court cleared Terry of any charges of racial abuse given the absence of proof beyond reasonable doubt that he intended to racially abuse Ferdinand (*R v John Terry*, Westminster Magistrate's Court, 13 July 2012, unreported).

Conversely, in October 2012 the FA Independent Commission found Terry guilty, applying the civil burden on the balance of probabilities (The Football Association v John George Terry, Ruling of the Full Regulatory Commission, 4 October 2012). He was issued with a four-match ban and fined £220,000 (Anon, 2012). The Commission held that Terry was not 'racist' but found that his words infringed FA Rule E.3, which states that a participant should always 'act in the best interests of the game and shall not act in any manner which is improper or brings the game into disrepute or use any one, or a combination of, violent conduct, serious foul play, threatening, abusive, indecent or insulting words or behaviour' (FA Rule E3 (1)). If there is a breach of this rule including any reference to a person's 'ethnic origin, colour, race, nationality, faith, gender, sexual orientation or disability' then an increased sanction will be considered (E3 (2)).

In December 2011 Liverpool FC striker Luis Suarez received an eight-match ban and a £40,000 fine from the FA for racially abusing Manchester United FC defender Patrice Evra, contrary to Rule E3. The difference of punishment between Terry and Suarez was justified on the basis that Suarez repeatedly used an abusive word (Conway, 2014a). Chief Executive of the Professional Footballers' Association (PFA), Gordon Taylor expressed that just because it is a football pitch it is not a vacuum and the law of the land applies (Anon, 2011). Following these incidents, the FA revised their penalties. Players found guilty of racial abuse or any other form of discrimination, will receive minimum ban of five matches. A further offence will lead to an automatic minimum ban of 10 matches, including a financial penalty (Conway, 2014a).

The third incident took place in December 2013 when West Bromwich Albion player Nicholas Anelka performed an anti-semitic quenelle hand gesture (an inverted Nazi salute) during a football match. The player denied the use of the gesture as racist, arguing that it was 'anti-system' and in support of a friend, a French comedian. However, the comedian already faced racially aggravated charges for this gesture. The Commission banned him for five matches and an £80,000 fine for an aggravated breach of misconduct. Anelka's employers lost their football shirt sponsorship with Zoopla as a result of his actions and he was subsequently sacked for gross misconduct. The FA will again review its policies in light of this incident (Conway, 2014b).

The actions of the sports bodies in these cases have been under close scrutiny and they appear to have been keen to display a strict approach to racism in sport, more so than the courts it would seem. However, the trio of incidents expose a deeper cultural problem inherent within sport which is more difficult to eradicate. The athletes seem to act above the law, abusing their positions to express themselves using racially offensive behaviour (Hyde, 2014). It may be the case that firmer intervention by the courts is required to deal with this inherency. For instance, in 2007, lower league football player Tom Gosling was charged by the Cambridgeshire FA for racially abusing an opponent during a match. He was issued with a 42-day ban and £50 fine. The incident was reported for Suffolk police where, by contrast, the Magistrates Court found him guilty of using racially aggravated threatening behaviour and imposed a football banning order for three years.

In contrast to the criminal law approach to racial abuse, the civil law approach draws upon equality legislation. Three employment-related cases demonstrate this. In the first case of *Sterling v Leeds Rugby League Club* [2001] ISLR 201 a rugby league player was successful in his claim for direct race discrimination by his club after claiming that he was excluded from selection because of his race and that he was victimised by the club. In support of the claimant, the court highlighted that the victimisation resulted from a failure to appreciate that race discrimination could be unconscious and ill intentioned. Similarly, in *Hussaney v Chester City FC* 15 January 2001 No. EAT/203/98, a youth squad member brought a successful claim against his club for racist and offensive remarks made about him by the first team manager.

The case of *Singh v The Football League, The Football Association and others* (unreported, December 2001, ET Case No. 5203953/99*)* concerned an Asian football referee who successfully brought a claim against the FA and others. The removal of Mr Singh from the National List of Referees amounted to racial discrimination. They also found evidence of unfair dismissal by the FL (Case, para. 30.2).

These three well-documented cases further highlight the legal mechanisms in place to address racial abuse in sport. Whilst the courts successfully identified elements of behaviour which were racially motivated, it is concerning to consider that there may be closed door instances where this takes place without challenge.

Sport approach

In order to overcome long-term discrimination in sport, there appears to be 'small pockets of good practice' amongst sports governing bodies and networks (Asians in Football Foundation [AFF], 2005: 6). The FRA Report (2010) highlighted the sport-specific initiatives in place to eradicate racism and named Union of European Football Associations (UEFA) as a model of good practice for combating racism through its partnerships with organisations such as the Football Against Racism in Europe (FARE) network and through its regulations (p. 26). Chapter 3 evaluated the general impact of sport equality policies on the balance between inclusion and exclusion in sport.

The 'Let's Kick Racism Out of Football' campaign in 1994 attempted to encourage fans to counter racism in the stands and to challenge its normalisation in the sporting culture of football. The campaign stood as protection for spectators or participants in football from racial abuse or harassment (Carrington and McDonald *in* Houlihan, 2008: 237). The campaign expanded to cover racism in all areas of the sport and shifted a focus from ethnic minorities in sport, to the perpetuators of racism. In 1997, further developments led to introduction of a new organisation named 'Kick it Out', which received financial support from the PFA, the FA, the Football Association Premier League (FAPL) and the Football Trust. The campaign extended beyond professional football (Kick it Out, 2000) and was complemented by the formation of anti-racism groups such as the Show Racism the Red Card charity, which seeks to combat racism through educational resources and workshops targeted at young people (Dixon *et al.*, 2014). However, the campaign has been criticised as limited and failing to target internal structures and institutional power imbalances within sport (Magowan, 2012; Dixon *et al.*, 2014: 2).

Following the emergence of a number of racist incidents in football across Western Europe in 2004, the King Baudouin Foundation and Nike introduced the 'Stand Up Speak Up' (SUSU) campaign in 2005. It was highlighted that racist incidents tend to surface and receive a lot of attention, but then disappear until another high-profile incident arises. This makes it difficult to maintain awareness of racism in sport and society (King Baudouin Foundation and Nike, 2009: 5). The SUSU was therefore launched to empower football fans to voice opposition to racism in football on an international stage. Black and white interlocking wristbands, which were worn by fans and players across Europe, formed the symbol of the campaign (King Baudouin Foundation and Nike, 2009).

The Kick it Out campaign influenced other sports to follow such as the 'Tackle It – Tackle Racism in Rugby League' campaign in rugby league, which was established in 1996 in response to research suggesting that racism was a 'small but significant' concern in the sport (Carrington and McDonald *in* Houlihan, 2008: 239). Similarly, in cricket, the England and Wales Cricket Board (ECB) appointed the Racism Study Group in 1998 who reported on the realities of racism in cricket. The quantitative data were useful and expressed the views of respondents on particular topics but it failed to address significant matters concerning the existence of racism in the sport. Few measures were implemented from the report and it has been disregarded as 'an empty cynical document' (Marqusee, 1994). The 'Hit Racism for Six' campaign in 1996 and the 'Clean Bowl Racism' publication in 1999 appeared to do the same and whilst accepting that race was important, it did little to explicitly accept the presence of any racism in cricket.

Overall, despite the increase in the number of policies and initiatives in this area, it seems that 'all the evidence confirms that change in behaviour at the highest levels of the game still lags lamentably behind any real change in attitude or in stated policy' (AFF, 2005: 6). The recent incidents highlighted above, clearly reflect this lack of connection between policy commitments and active shifts in racial abuse in sport. Kick it Out defended their position, stating that 'we are not a decision-making organisation with power and resource as some people think', which may highlight the main problem with equality campaigns (Magowan, 2012).

The FRA Report (2010: 59) suggests that there exists a general lack of awareness and deniability of these pertinent factors within sport (Long, 2000; Lusted, 2009). This has resulted in 'colour blind complacency' (Dixon *et al.*, 2014: 2). For instance, the presence and dominance of black athletes in sports such as basketball and American football leads to the idea that no racial tensions exist in these sports. In reality these demographics raise important points about over-representation in sport. In addition, the existence of 'novel' high-profile athletes from minority groups leads many sports to believe that no racism exists in their fields (Long, 2000: 124). For instance, in rugby league there have been minority black and Asian athletes who participate in the sport (such as Ellery Hanley, Martin Offiah and Ikram Butt), but, generally speaking, rugby suffers from disproportionate representation as well as overall low representation of Asian and black athletes (Long *et al.*, 1997: 252; Arnot, 2009).

The FRA Report (2010) concludes that racist incidents, which are mostly in the form of racist abuse, are a continuing problem, but are being addressed through legislation and policy. However, the balance between inclusion and exclusion is also affected by under-representation, which is less pronounced (FRA, 2010: 45). This is a more covert and unconscious topic within race and sport (FRA, 2010: 51).

Covert practices: over-represented or under-represented?

Representation in elite-level sport is an area of inclusion and exclusion that is less clear. Whilst research conducted on the statistics of sports participation and ethnic minority participation suggests that many groups are under-represented (a cursory observation of sports competitions would also tell us this), possible explanations for this can only be speculative as race is a factor which sport tends not to deal with directly or openly. The historical background of sports such as cricket, which was heavily influenced by the British Empire, offers some insight into certain practices today, but it is difficult to pinpoint the exact causes of over- or under-representation in certain sports.

One compelling argument is that minority groups receive disproportionate sporting opportunities, which means that there is a lack of representative role models to encourage youngsters to pursue certain sports (Long *et al.*, 1997: 255). Whilst these hold a lot of strength, the further question is why they receive fewer opportunities. In football, for instance, few Asian footballers play in the English Premier League, but there is certainly not a lack of passion for football amongst young British Asians at a recreational level (Burdsey, 2007).

Another persuasive explanation is the impact of racial stereotypes in society which have filtered into sport and now become an indistinguishable element of sporting culture. Consistent with the previous chapters, these stereotypes have influenced the landscape of sports participation and affected the balance between inclusion and exclusion in sport on the basis of sex, gender, disability and race. Within modern sport contemporary expressions of exclusion in the form of covert behaviour have evolved. Such behaviour is reflective of the ways in which physical and non-physical differences can be applied and often misinterpreted in particular contexts to treat individuals differently. This is often referred to as racial stereotyping which involves the general judgement of a particular race or group that becomes a part of their identification and influences the way in which they are treated.

Since sport is built around human differences and human performance, stereotypes become an inevitable indicator of athletic performance and suitability to sport. Hoberman (1997: 116) explores the range of stereotypes attached to athletes from the cool and calculating Scandinavian traits, to the German athlete as strong and efficient. These examples become dangerous when they are used to select athletes for inclusion and/or justify exclusion.

For instance, in the 1990s, it was widely thought that 'Afro Caribbeans are good sprinters; Asian girls were unable to adopt certain postures; Afro Caribbeans are sinkers in water; Asian men have double jointed wrists enabling them to play stick sports' (Hoberman, 1997: 124). The iconic film entitled White Men Can't Jump is understood in a society in which the vast majority of NBA players are black men (Goldberg and Solomos, 2002: 261).

The consequence of these racial stereotypes is the covert or unconscious disproportionate distribution of minority athletes in particular sports. Whereas black athletes have often been celebrated for their athletic abilities and have a prominence in many sports, South Asian individuals are not considered to be athletic and are less visible at an elite level. This is consistent with Alexander (*in* Back and Solomos, 2000: 220) who contends that African Caribbeans and Asians have been placed in opposition to each other as objects of 'irreconcilable versions of cultural difference.' On the one hand, black athletes are pigeon-holed into positions in sport, whereas Asian athletes are excluded because of their perceived athletic inability.

Black Athletes and racial stacking

The success of black athletes has led to suggestions that they are far superior in certain athletic activities because of their African descent (Entine, 1999). This racial proposition is reflected in sport records, with East Africans dominating marathon running, and Jamaican athletes of West African descent dominating sprinting records (Epstein, 2010).

This hypothesis presumes that dominance in sport is attributed to genetic and physiological characteristics attached to racial populations, with advantageous traits found within the African population (Price, 1997). Scientists and writers have long investigated whether there is a connection between ethnicity and athletic success, with theories which tend to be framed around the nature versus nurture debate (Epstein, 2013). There is no conclusive evidence on the existence of specific athletic genes. It is increasingly accepted that 'the inherited components of complex traits, like athleticism, is most often the result of dozens or even hundreds or thousands of interacting genes, not to mention environmental factors' (Epstein, 2013: 157).

Pitsiladis, a biologist who has researched extensively in this field, locates many of the successful sprinters in the world, from a particular region of northwest Jamaica, Trelawny. Rather than a conclusive genetic explanation for this, since the genetic heritage of Jamaicans are extremely diverse, one theory is that these habitants form part of a superior stock of the fittest and strongest slaves who were historically brought from Africa to this region (see Deason *et al.*, 2012). Previously, Kane (1971) also proposed that 'slavery weeded out the weak.' In other words, he contended that black athletes were more suitable to sport physically and psychologically because they had to endure hardship during slavery. Despite the strength and belief of this argument, it has not been proved.

Another theory links West African efficiency in sport with the adaptation of genes to protect against disease such as malaria in those geographical regions (Epstein, 2013: 175). Whilst compelling, no human studies have been carried out to prove this.

Pitsiladis's research suggests that the success of Jamaican sprinters has less to do with genes and is influenced by the proactive strides taken to focus the best athletes on sprinting rather than on other sports, through dedicated talent spotting systems in Jamaica (Epstein, 2013: 174).

Ecogeographic and socioeconomic theories centre on the link between body proportions and ancestral latitude and climate, with particular builds being more favourable in certain activities (Epstein, 2013: 175; Kane, 1971; St Louis, 2004: 32). For instance, a study of the demographics of elite East African distance runners concluded that the athletes originate from a distinctive environmental and ethnic background, and they travelled further to school, mostly by running, compared with the general Kenyan population (Onywera *et al.*, 2006). The Kenyan runners are most often from the Kalenjin tribe who have a linear build suited to endurance running (Epstein, 2013: 198). Similar patterns have emerged in Ethiopia, although there is no genetic connection between them (Epstein, 2013: 208). The climate and context of the Rift Valley in Ethiopia and Kenya is considered an ideal altitude for endurance athletes, which is a favourable factor for training (Epstein, 2013: 215). However, this is not the case for all successful Kenyan or Ethiopian athletes and it would therefore be unreasonable to stereotype on this basis (Epstein, 2013: 209).

Some assertions are subject to considerable criticism, particularly those which rely on 'racist folklore rather than scientific inquiry' (Cashmore, 1982: 55). This brief discussion suggests that even science has few answers about our differences (Epstein, 2013: 207). Whilst populations do tend to cluster around geographic regions that correspond with racial classifications, such classifications are considered inadequate descriptors of the distribution of genetic variation in our species because races are so diverse (Tishkoff and Kidd, 2004).

Instead, the suggestion that black athletes are athletically superior is embedded within conventional wisdom. Commonsense has the dangerous power of interconnecting 'fact, opinion, belief, myth, impression, analysis and intuition together' in order to explain race (St. Louis, 2004: 43). Genetic or cultural differences between us are often generalised and used as a basis for discriminatory practice (Tishkoff and Kidd, 2004).

This is part of a wider scientific debate surrounding the appropriateness of the concept of race. The focus on biology reinforces a culture which constructs the black male athlete as a distinct racial category (King, 2004: 19). Some refer to the use of science in this way as 'scientific racism', which describes the tension between 'evidence based knowledge and the desire to explain, predict and improve performance that allow the race controversy to continue' (Spracklen, 2008). St Louis (2004: 35) reveals that the scientific basis for the race argument represents a 'naïve understanding of scientific procedure; and secondly, a reformulated common sense that integrate biological and cultural forms of racial description.'

The practice of identifying differences in physical ability between humans has also been termed a 'corruption of science' (Marks, 2003: 93) because these differences cannot be truly known and to make sweeping assertions about relatively insignificant genetic differences is a corruption. Upon this, the ICERD affirms that 'any doctrine of superiority based on racial differentiation is scientifically false, morally condemnable, socially unjust and dangerous, and that there is no justification for racial discrimination, in theory or in practice, anywhere.' This is supported by the European Race Directive (2000/43), which rejects theories of superiority in its preamble.

The consequences of this type of stereotyping is the deliberate placement of athletes in positions in sports on the basis of 'parroted conventional wisdom such as the belief that black footballers were no good in defence because they lacked any "bottle" ' (Long and Hylton, 2002: 93). In the past this has been referred to as racial stacking (Long *et al.*, 1997: 253). In North American sport, racial stereotyping and 'stacking' has resulted in the traditional placement of black (African American) players in non-central positions of sport, leaving white athletes in more central positions (Chappell *in* Laker, 2002: 96). Research conducted on the racial composition of all players in the Football League also uncovered elements of stacking in Britain (Maguire *in* Jarvie, 1991). The disproportionate positioning of black players in certain positions in soccer was due to the perception of managers and coaches that black players possessed certain attributes, such as speed, which were more conducive to wider positions (Chappell *in* Laker, 2002: 101). In comparison, white players have more cognitive attributes such as decision-making which made them more suited to central positions.

Within the literature there was concern over how racial stacking should be understood. It must be noted that there may be many other reasons for the disparate representation of black athletes in particular sports. For instance, representation in sport is attributed to socio-economic factors and social identity (Cashmore, 1982). Consequently, stacking should only be used as a 'preliminary tool' to identify the covert social processes at work (Maguire *in* Jarvie, 1991: 120). There continue to be many approaches to understanding this matter. For instance, King (*in* Burdsey, 2011: 39) has considered whether talent identification in football is the new form of racial stacking.

South Asian athletes

At the other end of the spectrum of racial stereotypes in sport are South Asian athletes who are under-represented in some popular sports because they are considered to be unsuited to sport. Historically they have been labelled as weak and fragile (Patel, 2010a; 2010b). These physical assumptions can be traced back to the British Empire in nineteenth-century Europe. Another stereotype of 'academic but not sporting' is usually attached to South Asian men and women. It has been documented that coaches perceive Asian parents to be less supportive of their children in sports and more focused on education. Religious practices and beliefs are also said to play a part in under-representation. It is further assumed that South Asians prefer to play, and have a natural passion, for cricket.

South Asian women in sport have typically been regarded as 'traditional' and 'passive' (Puwar and Raghuram, 2003: 69) experiencing difficulties in physical education because they are 'usually small and quite frail' (Lewis, 1979: 132). These attitudes, coupled with 'the more overt racism that these groups encounter in a sporting setting and wider social life, have combined to limit their potential sporting aspirations' (Ismond, 2003: 54).

The participation of British Asians in football provides an interesting case study to illustrate the imbalances between inclusion and exclusion in sport on the basis of race (Burdsey, 2007). In contrast to individuals of Afro-Caribbean origin, British Asians are less represented in elite football, with only a handful of players recorded (Cadden, 2010). For instance, in 2013 only eight British Asian players appeared in the top four football divisions (Sanghera, 2013). This appears in contrast to the population of British Asians in the UK today. In the 2011 Census, of the total population in England and Wales, 86 per cent were white. All Asian or British Asians count for 7.5 per cent of the total population, with all black or black British at 3.3 per cent.

The reasons for this disparity may be attributed to the factors considered above: physicality, culture and religion. These stereotypes may influence the perceptions of key decision-makers in the sport as well as the general culture of football. Whilst there is little truth in the perception of Asian groups as weak or physically unsuited to sport, there are certainly cultural differences amongst the Asian communities which may have historically influenced representation in sport.

However, new generations of British Asian individuals have begun to change this trend significantly (Patel, 2010a; 2010b). British Asian individuals are considered to be in conflict with their parent's ideals and their own religious practices and beliefs, which are said to impact upon their inclusion in sport (Valiotis, 2009: 1792). At the amateur level Asian football is very successful despite the existence of racism (Burdsey, 2007: 487). All-Asian local-level breakaway leagues have formed and this model is evident amongst black populations also.

There are positive and negative consequences of this inward movement away from 'mainstream' channels of football (Coakley and Pike, 2009: 331). Such leagues offer British Asians a chance to compete in the sport whilst there are no alternative routes elsewhere. They also contribute to a sense of belonging and inclusion on a recreational level. However, since Asian footballers tend to pursue five-a-side rather than eleven-a-side, there is an obvious a lack of professional representation and role models for younger athletes (Fleming *in* Jarvie, 1991). Few role models exist for British Asian athletes, one of only a few being Amir Khan who is a second-generation British Pakistani Muslim. He won the lightweight boxing silver medal at the 2004 Olympics and presents a challenge to the notion that Asians are not as strong as white or black athletes and the idea that they are unsuitable to contact sports (Burdsey, 2007: 617).

Another less-high-profile role model is Ambreen Sadiq, a 15-year-old female British Muslim boxer. Ambreen is Britain's first Muslim female boxer, holding the title of the ABA Female National Champion (Ambreen: The Girl Boxer, 2009). In a Channel 4 documentary, Ambreen discussed how she has had to defy her community to pursue her dream of competing. She had to contend with criticism of showing her skin, and bringing shame to her culture. The boxer aims to compete at the 2016 Olympics and prove her community wrong. In this interesting mix of sport, religion and culture, Ambreen comments on how she does not want to be the only Muslim girl and would wish more girls generally to compete in boxing. She is referred to as a role model by her Muslim friends and a pioneer by the Amateur Boxing Association (ABA) (Gledhill, 2010).

The possible reasoning behind the creation of leagues by particular racial groups could be because of a lack of confidence in local FA decision-makers to implement effective measures to eliminate racial abuse which is evident in the sport (AFF, 2005: 6). In addition, it is suggested that such leagues 'remains a way in which the community seeks to fill the gap' (AFF, 2005: 6). These initiatives reflect the passion for football amongst British Asians, and serve to break down stereotypes. However, the existence of separate leagues for separate racial categories is certainly not the solution to under-representation (AFF, 2005: 7).

In 2005, AFF published an inspirational report named 'Asians Can Play Football'. This report highlighted that despite development in football, there remains to be the lack of Asian fan base in England; the 'closed shop' approach to the appointment of senior positions in the management areas of football; and, finally, the under-representation of Asian professional footballers at English clubs. The report celebrates the progress which has been made in particular pocket communities in the UK (e.g. Albion Sports Juniors in Bradford; Luton United) but confirms that there remains to be a considerable lack of connection between enjoying football and pursuing a career in it.

Some argue that with low representation at top level, the game will suffer at an inclusion and business level (AFF, 2005: 7). At an international level it is interesting to see that many players represent Pakistan or India instead of England, possibly because that may be the only way they will have the opportunity to complete at an international level. In 1998 it was predicted that it will take up to 30 years before we see an Asian heritage youngster player represent England at football (McGuire and Collins, 1998: 76). In 2013, the FA planned to publish a report outlining a strategy to increase the participation of British Asians in all aspects of football, which was delayed (Sanghera, 2014). Instead, the inclusion of Asian athletes playing football has been incorporated into the FA Inclusion and Anti-Discrimination Plan.

Just as is the case with black athletes, South Asian athletes have not been overtly excluded from sport on the basis of their race. However, the lack of representation of this population in sports such as football suggests that the balance between inclusion and exclusion in sport is managed by cultural forces which are influenced by general stereotypes about racial groups.

Whilst not the focus of this book, black and minority ethnic (BME) individuals also suffer from low representation in non-competitive sport positions. Increasingly apparent is the disparity between the presence of black athletes on the field of play in English football and American football, and the absence of diversity in the management positions of those sports. The possible reasons for this could be attributed to institutional racism, covert exclusion and stereotyping. Or, perhaps it is simply a proportionate representation of the BME population (see Cashmore and Cleland, 2011). The introduction and success of the Rooney Rule in the NFL in the USA has brought further attention to this issue and it has been suggested that a version of the rule should be introduced in the UK in order to actively encourage equality in English football (see Corapi, 2012). The Rooney Rule has forced NFL teams to interview at least one minority candidate for a senior coaching position. Whilst this is not without its drawbacks, it has prompted cultural change by threatening legal action and financial penalties.

Clashes between sport and religion

The concept of race encompasses non-physical differences between us such as cultural and religious beliefs and values. These values are protected under human rights legislation. Article 18 UDHR reads:

> Everyone has the right to freedom of thought, conscience and religion; this right includes freedom to change his (*sic*) religion or belief, and freedom, either alone or in community with others and in public or private, to manifest his religion or belief in teaching, practice, worship and observance.

These manifestations can include wearing religious dress or accessories, particular dietary requirements and rituals or customs. Whether these are recommendations or obligations under the faiths are subject to interpretation. At times these manifestations have come into conflict with aspects of the dominant culture and the rules of sport. Article 18(3) ICCPR and Article 9(2) ECHR highlight that a human's right to manifest his or her religion or belief is not absolute and may be limited as are prescribed by law and are necessary in the interests of safety, order, health or moral or the fundamental rights and freedoms of others. In other words, there may be justifiable restrictions under these necessity provisions to limit the right to the manifestation of one's religious beliefs or values.

One example of the tension between inclusion and exclusion in this context concerns the rules of boxing and the participation of a Muslim male with a full beard. The visual marker of a full beard holds symbolic significance in many religions including Hinduism, Sikhism, Islam and Judaism. It is considered by some a mandatory requirement to fulfil their obligations of their faith (Cottrell, 2010). However, it arguably contravenes the rules of boxing. The International Boxing Association (IBA) stipulates in its medical handbook that:

> Beards are a potential danger and are therefore prohibited. During clinches the beard can get into the opponent's eye and can cause corneal abrasions. Facial stubble is likewise dangerous and boxers must be clean shaven with no moustaches.
>
> (AIBA, 2009)

Upon this safety concern, all boxers must be clean shaven. However, Sikh individuals have been exempt from this rule when competing in England due to an amendment enforced by the Amateur Boxing Association of England (ABAE, 2009 Section 6 Control of Bout: 54).

In January 2009, 25-year-old Muslim boxer Mohammed Patel was prevented from competing by the ABAE because he had a beard. He challenged this on the grounds that it was discriminatory and inconsistent with the treatment of Sikh athletes who are permitted to tie back hair with a net (Mitchell, 2009). The ABAE ruled that the exemption for Sikh boxers is no longer applicable and the rules were now in line with the AIBA rule (AIBA, 2009). The ABAE national child protection and equity manager, Barry Jones, contended that 'it has nothing to do with race, only health and safety' (Nye, 2010). Furthermore, it was argued that referees required sight of the face for cuts during the fight. Little commentary exists on this case.

This row is not new and has appeared in professional boxing when British Danny Williams fought Vitali Klischko for the World Boxing Council Championship. He refused to trim his beard and was not willing to compromise his religious beliefs (Lawton, 2004). Joe Frazier was ordered to trim his beard before his fight with Joe Bugner, but his refusal was on vanity grounds rather than religious (Lawton, 2004). In 1998 the AIBA refused entry of three Afghan boxers into the world championships because they refused to shave their beards.

In professional boxing, specific rules relating to facial hair are negotiated in the contracts for the fights between the parties (Cottrell, 2010). In fact, they have been allowed to compete with facial hair for over 20 years (Nye, 2010). Cottrell (2010) highlights the inconsistencies of the amateur rules with the professional rules. In professional boxing it seems an accepted part of the culture that boxers will intend to inflict abrasions on their opponents as an underhand technique, similar to diving in football. It would seem that they are then at greater risk from harm than amateur boxers. To support this is the fact that amateur boxers have to wear head guards. Cottrell (2010) argues that the essence of boxing is to land a punch in the permitted target areas. The risk of corneal abrasions is an intrinsic risk of the sport, not a risk brought about from a beard.

Such a restriction in sport maybe a potential infringement of Article 18 ICCPR and Article 9 ECHR. It would firstly need to be established whether the beard is actually a manifestation of a belief and whether that right has been interfered with through a restriction. This restriction may be justified if it can be proved that it is necessary to protect health and safety of competitors. For instance, there have been a number of UK employment cases forbidding beards in factories producing food on the grounds of health, safety and hygiene (*Singh v Rowntree MacKintosh Ltd* [1979] ICR 554; *Panesar v Nestle Co Ltd* [1980] ICR 144; Hill, 2005). The balance between inclusion and exclusion here will depend upon the necessity of the rules restricting the use of beards in boxing.

Another example involves religious clothing and accessories. The protection of the right to wear the religious hijab under Article 18 and Article 9 has produced litigation in many areas including employment and education. The headscarf is worn as an expression of one's Muslim identity although its obligation under the faith is subject to interpretation. In a sporting context, the hijab has conflicted with sporting rules regarding equipment and clothing (See Smith and Wrynn *in* Hargreaves and Anderson, 2014: 61). In 2007 in Canada, 11-year-old Asmahan Mansour refused to remove her hijab during a football tournament. She was requested to do so by the referee who had acted in response to the Quebec Soccer

Association ruling which prohibits the wearing of a veil or other religious items. This is in accordance with FIFA Law 4 (the player's equipments), which stipulates that 'a player must not use equipment or wear anything which is dangerous to himself or another player (including any kind of jewellery)'. It was reported that the decision was made on the grounds of the safety of athletes including the possibility of strangulation by wearing the hijab. Mansour left the tournament in protest of this restriction.

FIFA's rule marking strand, the International Football Association Board (IFAB), decided not to take any action on the rule prohibiting veils in competition and favoured the interpretation of Law 4 even though it does not explicitly refer to religious dress. One FIFA official was reported saying that 'there is nothing prohibiting hijabs in the laws of the game…head gear is permitted as long as it is not considered dangerous by the referee' (Ravensberg *et al.*, 2007).

The matter was raised again in April 2010 when FIFA refused the Iran Women's National Football Team entry into the 2010 August Youth Olympic Games in Singapore because they wore headscarves (Anon, 2010). The decision was made by the IFAB and based upon FIFA Law 4.

This appeared to be inconsistent with other athletes such as Ruqaya Al Ghasara of Bahrain who in 2008 wore a 'hijood' for track events, a breathable form-fitting hood designed for athletes. Following pressure on FIFA from members of the Iran Football Federation, in May 2010 the decision was overruled. In a compromise, the girls wear a cap which covers their heads to the hair line but does not extend below the ears to cover the neck (Fatteh, 2010). However, problems continued in 2011 when the team were banned from competing in their qualifying match for the London Olympics 2012. A FIFA official claimed that the headgear was inappropriate.

In December 2011 FIFA's ruling Executive Committee agreed to put forward a proposal to lift the ban on the hijab. One of the FIFA vice presidents, Prince Ali bin Al Hussein campaigned for the sanction of a safe, Velcro-opening instead of pin secured headscarf for players and officials. He argued that there had been no cases of injuries incurred by the use of a headscarf, and drew parallels with accepted practices of long hair and Chelsea FC goalkeeper Petr Čech who adorns a protective cap due to a head injury (Warshaw, 2012). Although this proposal received criticism from several French groups, in March 2012 IFAB unanimously agreed to overturn the ban on the headscarf and compromised on an alternative pin-less design. The IOC also resolved a similar matter by permitting the use of modified head cover (Donnelly and Donnelly, 2013: 15).

At the regional level the ECtHR addressed a related matter in the French case of *Dogru v France* [2008] ECHR 1579. A secondary school student in France refused to remove her headscarf during sport classes. The school decided to expel her for failing to actively participate in physical education and sport classes. The school internal rules stipulated that pupils must wear clothing which complies with health and safety rules and they must attend sport classes in the appropriate clothes. The parents of the student failed in their claims against the school in the French courts and appealed the decision to the ECtHR (Steiner *et al.*, 2007: 616).

The government argued that its interference with the manifestation of the religious belief pursued a legitimate aim of protecting the rights and freedoms of others and protecting public order. This was upheld by the EctHR and there was no violation of Article 9 ECHR. The Court highlighted that 'the State may limit the freedom to manifest a religion, for example by wearing an Islamic headscarf, if the exercise of that freedom clashes with the aim of protecting the rights and freedoms of others, public order and public safety' (Case, para. 17).

Upon this discussion, there may be instances when religious freedoms may be restricted by existing rules in sport. However, in order to avoid contravening equality legislation, these rules must be necessary and must pursue a legitimate aim. Sports bodies must ensure that their rules exist to protect the essence of sport and are not in place to perpetuate stereotypes about religious faiths or ideals.

English-only speaking rules in sport

Another expression of our non-physical differences is language and communication. In recent years, women's professional golf has seen an increase in the number of international players competing in the sport, particularly originating from South Korea. In 1998 Si Ri Pak became the first Korean player to join the LPGA and win a major championship. This influenced the growth and gradual domination of South Korean athletes. This increase of international players presented new challenges to the traditional LPGA Tour.

In August 2008, the LPGA proposed a new rule which required all players on the tour to speak English when they are speaking publicly with the media and interacting with playing partners during pro-am events. International players would be tested and if they failed to pass an oral English test then they would face indefinite suspension (Claussen, 2010: 136). It is suggested that the rule was targeted at Far East Asian players since it was announced at a mandatory meeting of the Korean players.

The rule was never intended to be public but was leaked by Golfweek magazine. The LPGA then felt that they needed to respond to the criticism they faced. Their intentions were to require players with at least two years' experience on the tour to have sufficient skills in English to manage media interviews, to deliver victory speeches and speak with amateur partners in pro-am competitions (Lloyd, 2009: 183). The reasoning behind this rule was reportedly to satisfy corporate sponsors, to further increase the marketability of the tour itself and to help international players succeed financially.

The LPGA were met with hostility following the foreseeable discriminatory effects of the rule (Claussen, 2010). Since the LPGA are based in the USA, under US law an English-only rule may be justified if it is needed as part of a 'business necessity' (Lloyd, 2009). However, the courts have allowed the rule in the workplace in only limited instances thus reflecting the narrow scope of this defence. The LPGA rule does not appear to meet this standard in any case. The rule reflects a type of employee control which was 'stifling' and 'limiting' (Lloyd, 2009: 189). When determining business necessity the courts tend to look at the central aspect of the employee's job. In relation to golf, it seems that the central part of the job is to play the sport, and test athletic ability, rather than speak English.

The sports community described the rule as an unnecessary restriction and overbearing. The LPGA may argue that the rule is necessary given the perceived negative impact which international players have had on the tour. For instance, in 2003, LPGA player Jan Stephenson stated in an interview with Golf Magazine that 'Asian's are killing our tour' as a result of their 'lack of emotion, their refusal to speak English when they can speak English' (Blauvelt, 2003). These opinions are stereotypical, based upon the assumption that Far East Asian players are unmarketable, dull to watch and fail to provide excitement in the game of golf (Shin and Nam, 2004: 224). The LPGA departed from these proposals following criticism but a version of the rule remains an option (Associated Press, 2008).

This language rule presents itself as an overt and covert form of unreasonable exclusion. Whilst on the outside the LPGA were concerned about marketability, there is evidence to show that in reality it is based upon the reluctance of women's golf to embrace the globalisation of the sport. It is difficult to see how speaking English is a necessary requirement of a professional sport. The rule has the potential to contravene Article 2 UDHR, which protects the rights and freedoms of every individual without distinction of language.

Summary

This chapter has explored instances when human differences based upon evolutionary adaptation and culture can present challenges to the traditional sporting culture and at times the rules of sport. Where an individual is overtly or covertly excluded from sport as a result of these differences, international, regional and domestic equality legislation plays an important role in protecting human rights from discriminatory treatment.

There are no legitimate reasons to exclude an individual from participating in sport on the basis of their race. Incidents concerning racial abuse have been appropriately sanctioned by sports governing bodies and/or the law. These cases do however illustrate that overt racial abuse continues to exist within the structures of sport. This is contributing to an exclusive sporting culture, which impacts upon participation in sport. As the FRA report (2010) highlighted, sports governing bodies and figures within sport appear to be denying the existence of racism in sport making it a difficult matter to confront.

Where there is no legitimate reason to exclude an athlete on the grounds of race, then this results in unjustifiable exclusion as demonstrated above. However, exclusion may be reasonable on the grounds of safety. Whilst the safety of athletes is a legitimate objective to pursue, the AIBA, ABAE and FIFA rules lack clarity on the type of safety threats which are presented by religious beards and hijabs. The IFAB decision to include the Iran Women's football team is a positive move forward.

The disproportionate representation of minority black athletes and South Asian athletes reflects a general lack of awareness of the under-representation of minority athletes in sports (FRA, 2010: 28). This chapter has offered some insight into this and revealed that the scientific understanding of our physical differences have often been stretched or misused to create perceptions about a population's suitability for sporting activity. This may have resulted in the over- or under-representation of minority athletes. In order to counteract the effects of this unconscious practice, eligibility and selection rules in sport need to be transparent and based upon ability alone. The role of the law in regulating the unconscious and covert practices within the sporting culture is difficult since it may be limited in changing attitudes and traditional perceptions. However, as illustrated by the racial abuse cases and the introduction of the Rooney Rule in the USA, the law can create conditions in society which favour the growth of tolerance and education (Howard, 2010: 69).

References

ABAE 2009. *Rules of Boxing*. [online]. Available at: www.abae.co.uk/aba/assets/File/rules_of_boxing.pdf [accessed 19/11/2010].

AIBA 2009. *Medical Handbook of Olympic Style Boxing Seventh Edition*. [online]. Available at: www.aiba.org/documents/site1/docs/AIBA%20Medical%20Handbook%202009%20final%20with%20foreword.pdf [accessed 9/11/2010].

Ambreen: The Girl Boxer 2009. [Television] Century Films for Channel 4, 22 January.

Anon. 2010. FIFA makes its Islamophobia official and ban Iranian women for donning the Hijab *From a Left Wing Website* [online], 3 April. Available at: http://fromaleftwing.blogspot.com/2010/04/fifa-makes-its-islamaphobia-official.html [accessed 4/05/10].

Anon. 2011. John Terry to be charged over Anton Ferdinand race row. *BBCi Website* [online], 21 December. Available at: www.bbc.co.uk/news/uk-england-london-16284813 [accessed 21/12/11].

Anon. 2012. John Terry defence 'improbable, implausible and contrived'. *BBCi Website* [online], 5 October. Available at: www.bbc.co.uk/sport/0/football/19842795 [accessed 31/07/14].

Anon. 2015. Film shows Chelsea fans in Paris Metro incident. *BBCi Website* [online], 18 February. Available at: www.bbc.co.uk/news/uk-31514168 [accessed 19/02/15].

Arnot, C. 2009. Trying Times. *The Guardian* [online] 28 October. Available at: www.guardian.co.uk/society/2009/oct/28/ikram-butt-interview-rugby-community [accessed 10/09/10].

Asians in Football Forum (AFF) 2005. *Asians Can Play Football: another wasted decade* [online] September. Available at: www.furd.org/resources/Asians%20Can%20play%20football.pdf [accessed 03/01/12].

Associated Press 2008. LPGA won't suspend players over English-speaking requirements. *ESPN* [online] 7 September. Available at: http://sports.espn.go.com/golf/news/story?id=3570957 [accessed 12/11/11].

Back, L. and Solomos, J. 2000. *Theories of Race and Racism: a reader.* London: Routledge.

Blauvelt, H. 2003. Stephenson to play with seniors, says Asians hurt LPGA. *USA Today* [online] 9 October. Available at: www.usatoday.com/sports/golf/champions/2003-10-09-stephenson-champions_x.htm [accessed 21/02/12].

Burdsey, D. 2007. *British Asians and Football.* London: Routledge.

Burdsey, D. 2011. *Race, Ethnicity and Football: Persisting Debates and Emergent Issues.* London: Routledge.

Cadden, P. 2010. Cardiff boss Dave Jones gives Michael Chopra the green light to play for India *The Mail Online* [online] 18 November. Available at: www.dailymail.co.uk/sport/football/article-1330678/Cardiff-boss-Dave-Jones-gives-Michael-Chopra-green-light-play-India.html#ixzz15iWf5fuO [accessed 19/11/10].

Cashmore, E. 1982. *Black Sportsmen.* London: Routledge and Kegan Paul.

Cashmore, E. and Cleland, J. 2011. Why aren't there more black football managers? *Ethnic and Racial Studies*, 34(9): 1594–1607.

Claussen, C.L. 2010. The LPGA's English proficiency rule. *Journal of Legal Aspect of Sport.* 20(2): 136–150.

Coakley, J. and Pike, E. 2009. *Sports in Society, Issues and Controversies.* London: McGraw Hill.

Conway, R. 2014a. FA introduces five-match minimum bans for racial abuse. *BBCi Website* [online] 16 May. Available at: www.bbc.co.uk/sport/0/football/22547598 [accessed 31/07/14]

Conway, R. 2014b. FA to review bans for racism offences after Anelka verdict. *BBCi Website* [online] 1 March. Available at: www.bbc.co.uk/sport/0/football/26399284 [accessed 31/07/14]

Corapi, J. 2012. Red card: using the National Football League's 'Rooney Rule' to eject race discrimination from English professional soccer's managerial and executive hiring practices. *Fordham Intellectual Property, Media and Entertainment Law Journal*, 23(341): 341–395.

Cottrell, S. 2010. Boxing: Freedom of religion and rules on safety. *World Sports Law Report*, 8(2), February: 12–13.

Deason, M. *et al.* 2012. Importance of mitochondrial haplotypes and maternal lineage in sprint performance amongst individuals of West African ancestry. *Scandinavian Journal of Medicine and Science in Sports*, 22: 217–223.

Dixon, K., Lowes, J. and Gibbons, T. 2014. Show racism the red card: potential barriers to the effective implementation of the anti-racist message. *Soccer and Society*, pp. 1–15.

Donnelly, P. and Donnelly, M. 2013. *The London 2012 Olympics: A gender equality audit.* University of Toronto: Centre for Sport Policy Studies Research Reports.

Entine, J. 1999. *Taboo: Why black athletes dominate sports and why we're afraid to talk about it.* New York: Public Affairs.

Epstein, D. 2010. Sports Genes. *Sports Illustrated* [online] 17 May. Available at: http://sportsillustrated.cnn.com/vault/article/magazine/MAG1169440/index.htm [accessed 10/08/10].

Epstein, D. 2013. *The Sports Gene: talent, practice and the truth about success.* London: Yellow Jersey Press.

Fatteh, P. 2010. Iranian girls soccer teams no longer banned. *The Muslim Observer* [online] 13 May. Available at: http://muslimmedianetwork.com/mmn/?p=6183 [accessed 1/10/10].

FRA (The European Union Agency for Fundamental Rights). 2010. Racism, ethnic discrimination and exclusion of migrants and minorities in sport: a comparative overview of the situation in the European union [online]. Available at: http://fra.europa.eu/sites/default/files/fra_uploads/1207-Report-racism-sport_EN.pdf [accessed 11/05/11].

Gledhill, R. 2010. Ambreen Sadiq, Muslim boxer, aims to combat prejudice to succeed in the ring. *The Times* [online] Available at: www.timesonline.co.uk/tol/sport/more_sport/boxing/article6997531.ece [accessed 19/11/2010].

Goldberg, D.T. and Solomos, J. 2002. *A companion to racial and ethnic studies*. Malden: Blackwell.

Hargreaves, J. and Anderson, E. 2014. *Routledge Handbook of Sport, Gender and Sexuality*. London: Routledge.

Hoberman, J. 1997. *Darwin's Athletes: how sport has damaged Black America and preserved the myth of race*. New York: Houghton Mifflin Company.

Holland, B. 1995. 'Kicking racism out of football': an assessment of racial harassment in and around football grounds. *Journal of Ethnic and Migration Studies*, 21(4), October: 567–586.

Houlihan, B. 2008. *Sport & Society: a student introduction*. London: Sage Publications.

Howard, E. 2010. *The EU Race Directive*. London: Routledge.

Hyde, M. 2014. Nicolas Anelka likely to up the 'anti' after FA's quenelle charge. The Guardian [online] 22 January. Available at: www.theguardian.com/football/blog/2014/jan/22/nicolas-anelka-fa-charge-quenelle-gesture [accessed 31/07/14].

Ismond, P. 2003. *Black and Asian athletes in British sport and society: a sporting chance?* Basingstoke Palgrave Macmillan.

Jarvie, G. 1991. *Sport Racism and Ethnicity*. London: The Falmer Press.

Kane, M. 1971. An assessment of 'black is best.' *Sports Illustrated* [online] 18 January. Available at: http://sportsillustrated.cnn.com/vault/article/magazine/MAG1084501/index.htm [accessed 10/08/10].

Kick It Out. 2000. *Part of the Game? An examination of racism in grass roots football*. Kick it Out.

King Baudouin Foundation and Nike 2009. *Stand Up Speak Up the Story 2005–2009*. King Baudouin Foundation.

King, C. 2004. Race and Cultural Identity: playing the race game inside football. *Leisure Studies*, 23(1), January: 19–30.

Laker, A. 2002. *The Sociology of Sport and Physical Education*. London: Routledge Falmer.

Lawton, J. 2004. Boxing: beard row is a storm in a shaving cup for Williams. *The Independent* [online] 9 December. Available at: www.independent.co.uk/sport/general/boxing-beard-row-is-a-storm-in-a-shaving-cup-for-williams-680773.html [accessed 1/10/10].

Lewis, T. 1979. Ethnic Influences on Girls PE. *British Journal of Physical Education*, 10: 132.

Lloyd, A.T. 2009. You're next on the tee, just remember to speak English! Could the LPGA really force players to learn and speak English? *Sports and Entertainment Law Journal*, 9(1): 181–217.

Long, J. 2000. No Racism Here: A preliminary examination of sporting innocence. *Managing Leisure*, 5(3): 121–133.

Long J. and Hylton K. 2002. Shades of White: an examination of whiteness in sport. *Leisure Studies*, 21: 87–103.

Long, J., Carrington, B. and Spracklen, K. 1997. Asians cannot wear turbans in the scrum: explorations of racist discourse within professional rugby league. *Leisure Studies*, 16: 249–259.

Lusted, J. 2009. Playing games with 'race': understanding resistance to 'race' equality initiatives in English local football governance. *Soccer and Society*, 10(6), November: 722–739.

Magowan, A. 2012. Kick It Out caught in the crossfire as racism flares up again. *BBC Website* [online] 21 October. Available at: www.bbc.co.uk/sport/0/football/20001544 [accessed 02/09/14].

Marks, J. 2003. *What it means to be 98% Chimpanzee.* London: University of California Press.

Marqusee, M. 1994. *Anyone but England: cricket and the national malaise.* London: Verso.

Mcguire, B. and Collins, D. 1998. Sport, Ethnicity and Racism: The experience of Asian heritage boys. *Sport, Education and Society*, 3(1): 79–88.

Mitchell, K. 2009. Bearded Muslim boxer cries foul over board's treatment of Sikhs. *The Guardian* [online] 22 December. Available at: www.theguardian.com/sport/2009/dec/22/mohammed-patel-boxers-beards-abae [accessed: 02/09/14].

Nye, C. 2010. Bearded amateur boxers fight ban. *BBCi Website* [online] 13 January. Available at: http://news.bbc.co.uk/1/hi/8451615.stm [accessed 1/10/10].

Onywera, V.O., Scott, R.A., Boit, M.K. and Pitsiladis, Y.P. 2006. Demographic characteristics of elite Kenyan endurance runners. *Journal of Sports Sciences*, 24(4): 415–422.

Patel, S. 2010a. *Using Lived Experiences to Explore Inclusion and Exclusion in Sport: the case of the British Indian Female.* Oral presentation given at the 'Sport and society conference' hosted by the University of British Columbia, Vancouver, Canada in March 2010.

Patel, S. 2010b. *Inclusion and Exclusion in Sport through Lived Experiences.* Oral presentation given at the 'Conference on law, policy and the Olympic movement' hosted by Ithaca College in the Ithaca College London Centre, UK in May 2010.

Price, S.L. 1997. Is it in the Genes? *Sports Illustrated* [online] 8 December. Available at: http://sportsillustrated.cnn.com/vault/article/magazine/MAG1011594/index.htm [accessed 10/08/10].

Puwar, N. and Raghuram, P. 2003. *South Asian Women in the Diaspora.* Oxford: Berg.

Quirk, C. E. 1996. *Sports and the Law.* New York: Garland Publishing Inc.

Ravensberg, J., Cobb, C. and Corbett, R. 2007. Hijab soccer ban upheld. *The Gazette* [online] 4 November. Available at: www2.canada.com/montrealgazette/news/story.html?id=0875380c-b5cc-491a-afca-6d4b6229c225&p=1 [accessed 11/08/11].

Sanghera, M. 2013. British Asians in football: FA steps up recruitment drive. *BBCi Website* [online] 29 October. Available at: www.bbc.co.uk/sport/0/football/24593671 [accessed 31/07/14].

Sanghera, M. 2014. FA's Asians in football plan delayed until 2015. BBCi Website. [online] 22 May. Available at: www.bbc.co.uk/sport/0/football/27208873 [accessed 31/07/14].

Shin, E.H. and Nam, E.A. 2004. Culture, gender roles, and sport: the case of Korean players on the LPGA Tour. *Journal of Sport and Social Issues*, 28(3), August: 223–244.

Spracklen, K. 2008. The holy blood and the holy grail: myths of scientific racism and the pursuit of excellence in sport. *Leisure Studies.* 27(2), April: 221–227.

St. Louis, B. 2004. Sport and common-sense racial science. *Leisure Studies*, 23(1): 31–46.

Steiner, H.J., Alston, P. and Goodman, R. 2007. *International Human Rights in Context.* 3rd Edition, Oxford: Oxford University Press.

The Football Association v John George Terry, Ruling of the Full Regulatory Commission, 4 October 2012. Available at: www.bbc.co.uk/sport/0/football/19845841 [accessed 14/08/14].

Tishkoff, S.A. and Kidd, K.K. 2004. Implications of biogeography of human populations for 'race' and medicine [online] *Nature Genetics*, 36(11). Available at: www.nature.com/ng/journal/v36/n11s/full/ng1438.html [accessed 01/08/14].

Valiotis, C. 2009. Runs in the outfield: The Pakistani diaspora and cricket in England. *The International Journal of the History of Sport*, 26(12), September: 1791–1822.

Warshaw, A. 2012. Velcro's dramatic save leads football to life ban on hijab. *The Independent* [online] 4 March. Available at: www.independent.co.uk/sport/football/news-and-comment/velcros-dramatic-save-leads-football-to-lift-ban-on-hijab-7534753.html [accessed 21/03/12].

Part III

Striking the balance

8 Exploring key themes

The aim of this chapter is to comparatively analyse the legal and non-legal cases explored throughout Part II. The main findings will be displayed in tables and figures to extract patterns and trends which have emerged from the regulatory approaches to inclusion and exclusion across the areas of sex, gender, disability and race. Table 8.1 presents the major sports rules and criteria which have had a restrictive effect upon minority athletes. Figure 8.1 graphically plots the overall outcome of all of the cases within an inclusion/exclusion grid. Tables 8.2 and 8.3 support this with some basic statistical analysis. Using these tools, impressionistic conclusions can be drawn about the consistency between the regulatory approaches across the four areas.

The thematic evaluation of the cases will enable us to identify deficiencies and good practice in the approaches to inclusion and exclusion and to establish the factors which tend to affect the balance. It is important to note that this book has presented only a selection of cases concerning inclusion and exclusion in the areas of sex, gender, disability and race. Any inferences which are drawn from this analysis are limited to the sample of cases studied.

Analysis of the sports rules/practices concerning inclusion and exclusion

Consistent across all of the cases explored is the exclusion of an athlete as a consequence of a restrictive rule or criteria which has been imposed by a sports body, local authority, sports league or school board. Some rules have an exclusionary impact upon minority individuals even though this may not necessarily be their aim. The formulation and application of sports rules are broad and their general purpose is to protect the essence of sporting activity by placing boundaries upon participation and competition (Meier, 1985; Wild, 2009: 1357; Loland, 2002). Rules are multi-levelled and can be intrinsic to the sport, such as 'in game' rules concerning the playing of the activity, or extrinsic rules, dealing with matters outside of the game itself. Generally speaking, the rules identified throughout Part II are all underpinned by scientific, evolutionary and cultural understandings of human beings. They provide sports with their identity, value and structure. Governing bodies have a responsibility to protect and guard these rules to ensure that any changes or modifications do not threaten the essence of sporting activity.

Throughout the cases, sport bodies have consistently protested that these rules exist to satisfy a sport specific need or objective. These objectives include imposing categories to match ability, regulating advantage in sport, maintaining standards of safety and competition and protecting the sporting culture. Table 8.1 illustrates the type of rules which have emerged from the cases and indicates which rules seek to achieve these interconnected objectives. Part II has established that these objectives can be legitimate and contribute towards defining the essence of sporting activity. However, there are instances when the objectives conflict with the inclusion or exclusion of an athlete on the basis of their physical and non-physical differences. The sport approach to this has generally been to defend these objectives and view them as necessary, but by doing so they are not always appropriately balancing inclusion and exclusion.

Categories

Striking a balance between inclusion and exclusion in sport is essentially concerned with the management of the physical and non-physical differences

Table 8.1 Overview of intrinsic and extrinsic sports rules, and their objectives

	Rule objective			
Sports rules	*Categories*	*Advantage*	*Safety*	*Sporting culture*
Event selection rules (e.g. Olympics)	✓			✓
Male only club memberships	✓			✓
Boxing and wrestling licenses	✓		✓	✓
Sex segregation rules	✓	✓	✓	✓
Sex testing and female at birth rules	✓	✓	✓	✓
Hormone based gender verification policies	✓	✓		✓
Self-declaration gender rules	✓			
Technical aids and devices rules		✓		
Golf cart rules		✓		✓
Cricket bowling laws		✓		
Age division rules	✓	✓	✓	
Resource allocation policies	✓			✓
Official sports rules (e.g. Racquetball)		✓		✓
Medical eligibility checks			✓	
Player conduct rules				✓
Sport dress codes			✓	
English speaking only rule				✓

which exist between human beings. The social, legal and sporting approach to this management is the formation of categories which help us better understand and organise the world in which we live. As we have highlighted throughout, categorisation and classification is not a new process and human obsession with divisions in everyday life, has permeated into fields such as sport.

Table 8.1 illustrates that rules which seek to maintain categories are those concerning the division between men and women, and between disabled and non-disabled athletes. The division of human beings along these superficial lines may be considered discriminatory in any other employment or social context and in contravention of equality legislation. In sport these categories are discriminatory by nature but accepted because the essence of sporting activity is to differentiate winners and losers precisely based upon differences. The categories also provide a structural framework within which sport can operate.

Consequently, where an individual wishes to compete in a category which was not typically designed for them, or they are not considered a typical participant, the sporting approach has been to initially exclude them in order to protect the essence of sport. The sporting rationale behind this is to make competition fair by ensuring the safety of competitors (the precautionary principle), matching ability for equal competition (advantage and age), avoiding significant rule changes, providing the best possible entertainment and generating the best economic value (Jones and Howe, 2005: 142). A strict approach is therefore taken to the maintenance of these divisions in sport.

Whilst it is reasonable to impose categories in sport, the lines along which these categories are formed have been challenged by minority athletes such as those explored in Part II. In addition, the rules that seek to support these categories have been criticised as being unnecessarily exclusive. The categories of sport appear to be formed by making a series of assumptions about populations, which derive from evolutionary, scientific and cultural understandings of human beings. Over time they have become rigid and have become placed within a sport Doxa where they are taken for granted. Conventional wisdoms tend to become mixed up within scientific reference and therefore lead to false assumptions about suitability to sport (St. Louis, 2004; Marks, 2003). Part II has revealed that often these assumptions have unconsciously evolved to become the truth (McFee, 2011). As science and culture progresses, our understanding of human ability and difference has significantly developed. At times, therefore, a gap exists between the traditional categories of sport and the realities of the modern athlete. The appropriateness of some of the categories has been questioned as a result of the imbalances between inclusion and exclusion across the four areas.

Comparatively, there are no rules explicitly dividing athletes on the basis of their race, which implies that race is viewed differently from sex, gender and disability. However, there are pockets of over- and under-representation of different groups, which suggests that invisible categorisation is also taking place.

Advantage

Table 8.1 reveals that a large proportion of the rules which conflict with minority athletes seek to regulate performance advantage and eliminate unfair advantages. From the cases we can infer that an advantage in sport can be grouped as a natural inherent advantage, or an artificial enhancement of the body. Within these two types of advantage, there is a wide spectrum of instances where advantage is deemed fair or unfair; permitted or prohibited.

Preventing unfair advantage in sport is an essential objective which goes to the core of sport's purity. It is an entirely legitimate and necessary aim to pursue in order to protect the essence of sport. However, there are significant problems with the application and enforcement of rules which seek to achieve this objective, as evidenced throughout Part II. The commonalities across the four areas are that advantage is based upon presumed assumptions which are not always accurate or scientifically sound. For instance, women, intersex and transgender athletes are treated on the basis that men are physiologically stronger than women and possess preferable characteristics which provide them with an advantage in sport. Disabled athletes have been differentiated on the grounds that any use of equipment or any abnormality in their sport skills will provide them with an unfair advantage over 'normal' athletes. Different racial groups have been labelled as being naturally advantaged or disadvantaged for sport as a result of the presumed inherent characteristics which they may possess. The inclusion or exclusion of these minority athletes therefore rests upon generalised sporting assumptions, which may have elements of truth, but are broadly applied unfairly and discount a wide range of other factors which may provide advantage in sport.

The persistence on eliminating unfair advantage in these cases has created a suspicious environment, where anyone outside of what is considered normal or acceptable, is treated exclusively or discriminatorily at times. Sport has failed to accept that proving an unfair advantage is often impossible and almost unnecessary.

The achievement of this objective across the four areas has been inconsistent and disproportionate because of the subjectivity involved in determining what is fair or unfair, acceptable or unacceptable, natural or unnatural. This has led to the unreasonable exclusion of innocent minority athletes in sport who appear to be getting caught within the regulatory nets which are cast for catching deliberate cheats.

One of the reasons for this position is the lack of clarity within the regulations themselves. Many of the rules fail to define advantage in their sport, which contributes towards this uncertainty. In addition, as scientific knowledge and technology advances, the cases have highlighted an absence of legitimate scientific underpinning in some of the policies, which has led to conventional wisdom alone determining eligibility.

Sport tends to selectively tolerate natural and artificial advantages with some advantages unchallenged and celebrated, but others stigmatised and excluded. As raised throughout Part II, the differential and selective treatment of athletes based upon sex, gender, disability and race is accounted for by what is considered a natural inheritance. The WADA code defines a person as a 'natural person' and refers to an athlete's 'natural talents' (WADA, 2015). However, as science and technology progresses, it is becoming increasingly unclear what this means.

It would appear that one of the biggest challenges in overcoming shortfalls in the rules regulating advantage is whether sports bodies adopt a case-by-case approach to advantage or whether they formulate rules based upon 'average' standards relating to physical and non-physical differences. There are positive attempts by sports bodies to review rules and provide more clarity when regulating natural and artificial advantages deriving from innocent athletes. However, shortfalls remain and rules continue to be criticised as being driven by suspicion instead of truth.

Safety: the precautionary principle

Table 8.1 indicates that rules which significantly affect inclusion and exclusion tend to concern safety matters. Ensuring compliance with safety rules is a valuable part of the essence of sport. These rules serve to satisfy more than one objective and the categories between physical and non-physical human differences in sport are justified on the basis that they protect athletes from any foreseeable risks or harm which may ensue if ability is not matched. These include risks from the activity, the safety of bodily security/health and the safety of other athletes. In addition, the selective nature of fair and unfair advantages is to some extent explained by the level of risk involved in each case (Wild, 2009: 1365).

The core of this precautionary principle is paternalism, which can be applied in a hard or soft way and is determined by who is considered to be at risk by society. It is suggested that safety arguments exclude athletes by raising a sense of fear that vulnerable adults may get hurt (Fields, 2005: 118). At times this application has been unequal because of the subjectivity involved in determining who is at risk. The constitution of 'risk' or something which is a hazard to us in society is in itself considered to be a 'social construction' (Laurendeau and Adams, 2010: 437; Lupton, 1999). This is usually influenced by assumptions originating from scientific research and conventional wisdom. In addition, the principle has conflicted with liberalism, which is the autonomy of athletes to 'trade their liberty or risk their bodily integrity for some other value, possibly economic' (Anderson, 2010: 141).

The safety rules in the sample explored appear to be either based upon the assumption of average strength differences, or the assumption of hazardous risks caused by unfamiliar devices, aids or dress codes.

Part II accepted that where strength is a determinant factor and where strength can be accurately differentiated and measured, it is legitimate to divide along the lines of sex, gender and age since safety, strength and fair play come hand in hand. The essence of sport would be lost if the competition was one sided because factors such as strength were unequal. However, there are a number of instances when such justifications have not been related to the objective of protecting the safety of the athlete and have therefore been disproportionate.

Sex segregation rules, boxing and wrestling licences, sex testing and female at birth rules and gender-verification policies are based upon a gender-specific approach. Women have been offered more bodily security protection from physical harm or activity such as sport because they are perceived to be weaker than men. The broad and over-generalised application of this assumption leads to the unreasonable exclusion of athletes. Furthermore, the selective application of the safety rules is incompatible with principles of equality and freedom.

Age rules also follow an assumption of strength approach, which is based upon average age abilities and physiques. This has led to assumed concerns of risk or harm which are not always substantiated and instead unreasonably exclude disabled athletes. However, the alternative approach of reviewing each case individually may place impossible burdens on sports bodies and may cause difficulties in classifying athletes as we have seen.

Safety rules which seek to regulate devices, aids or dress codes are based upon the assumption of hazardous risks caused by these unfamiliar items in sport. This has impacted upon the participation of disabled athletes and those who practice particular religious faiths. Whilst such safety concerns may be legitimate and reasonable, as in *Kuketz*, they tend to lack clarity and any hard evidence of risk. The rules are often unrelated to the objective of protecting safety and instead a common theme across the four areas is that safety rules act as a smoke screen for discriminatory behaviour.

Overall, the precautionary principle is a legitimate rationale upon which to determine inclusion and exclusion as we have seen in the cases presented. The sporting approach to safety is largely fair but requires more neutrality and transparency in how it is applied and who it is applied to.

Sporting culture

Navigating between and across rules and practices in sport is challenging because of the sporting culture. Table 8.1 suggests that an implicit objective of some of the rules is to protect the historical culture of a sport, and to uphold traditional norms or attitudes. This is often a covert expression of inclusion and exclusion. Whilst this is a legitimate objective to pursue, it can have a negative effect upon inclusion and exclusion when the rules seek to protect traditions and norms which are no longer reflective of a modern society and may in fact be discriminatory.

As we have seen throughout, the rules of sport carry with them a set of assumptions about our physical and non-physical differences. These have had the effect of creating ideas about a population's suitability or unsuitability to sport. As they develop and strengthen they have created a generic benchmark of what are considered to be 'norms' within sport. Reinforcing this are the silent and unspoken customs and rules which serve to imbalance inclusion and exclusion. Sport is comfortable with its norms and traditions as we have seen and these form the historical status quo of sporting activity.

The rules which seek to uphold sex and gender norms are based upon the idea that men are physiologically better suited to sport than women, who are considered to be weaker and need more protection from harm. The underlying historical principle behind some of those rules is that women should not participate in sport on or off the field. Reinforcing this is the idea that only feminine-looking women are accepted within society. These norms have contributed towards a sexist, transphobic and homophobic sporting culture, which has affected the participation of female, intersex and transgender athletes.

Disability norms in sport derive from the historical medical model of a disabled individual as being incapable, devious and passive. Norms here are based upon the difference in ability between disabled and non-disabled athletes and the operation of sports which were created for non-disabled individuals. Society and sport have been built around standards of normality and disabled athletes challenge those standards. The protection of the sporting culture can have a detrimental effect on the participation of disabled individuals since their inclusion prompts sport to evaluate traditional norms and realign notions of ability. Without legitimate justification for rules which seek to exclude on the basis of tradition, sport is acting incompatibly with equality legislation.

Rules exist to maintain race norms, which are based upon a range of amalgamated factors such as physical appearance, skin colour, geographical location, environment, religion and culture, beliefs and practices, language, behaviour and science. Influenced by all of these elements, race norms tend to create stereotypes of those suited or unsuited to sport. These have evolved over time and become accepted as part of the sporting culture. It is difficult to provide accurate explanations for under- and over-representation of particular racial groups, but it is speculated that the sporting culture, which has developed attitudes towards race and racism, influences participation.

As these norms progress, they become mixed up with casual derogatory references to individuals on the basis of their sex, gender, disability or race and this breeds an abusive culture within sport which is accepted as part of the essence, but leads to discriminatory practices. Consistent throughout the cases is the attachment of stigma to minority groups, which has contributed towards this abuse.

Sport tends to fear the unfamiliar, which is reflective in the cases. This book has been concerned with challenging some of the traditional cultures and norms of sport to ensure that inclusion and exclusion is based upon legitimate criteria which are focused upon ability and merit. There is however a lack of awareness or denial by sports bodies that there is any conflict. In addition, there is a general lack of transparency in the construction and application of rules in sport. This is leading to a failure at an institutional level to provide appropriate actions for positive change (Bell, 2008: 12). Short of legal intervention, it is argued that the sporting culture will be hard to overcome.

Analysis of the regulatory approach to inclusion and exclusion

Figure 8.1 collectively plots the sex, gender, disability and race legal and non-legal cases to identify whether the overall outcomes resulted in inclusion or

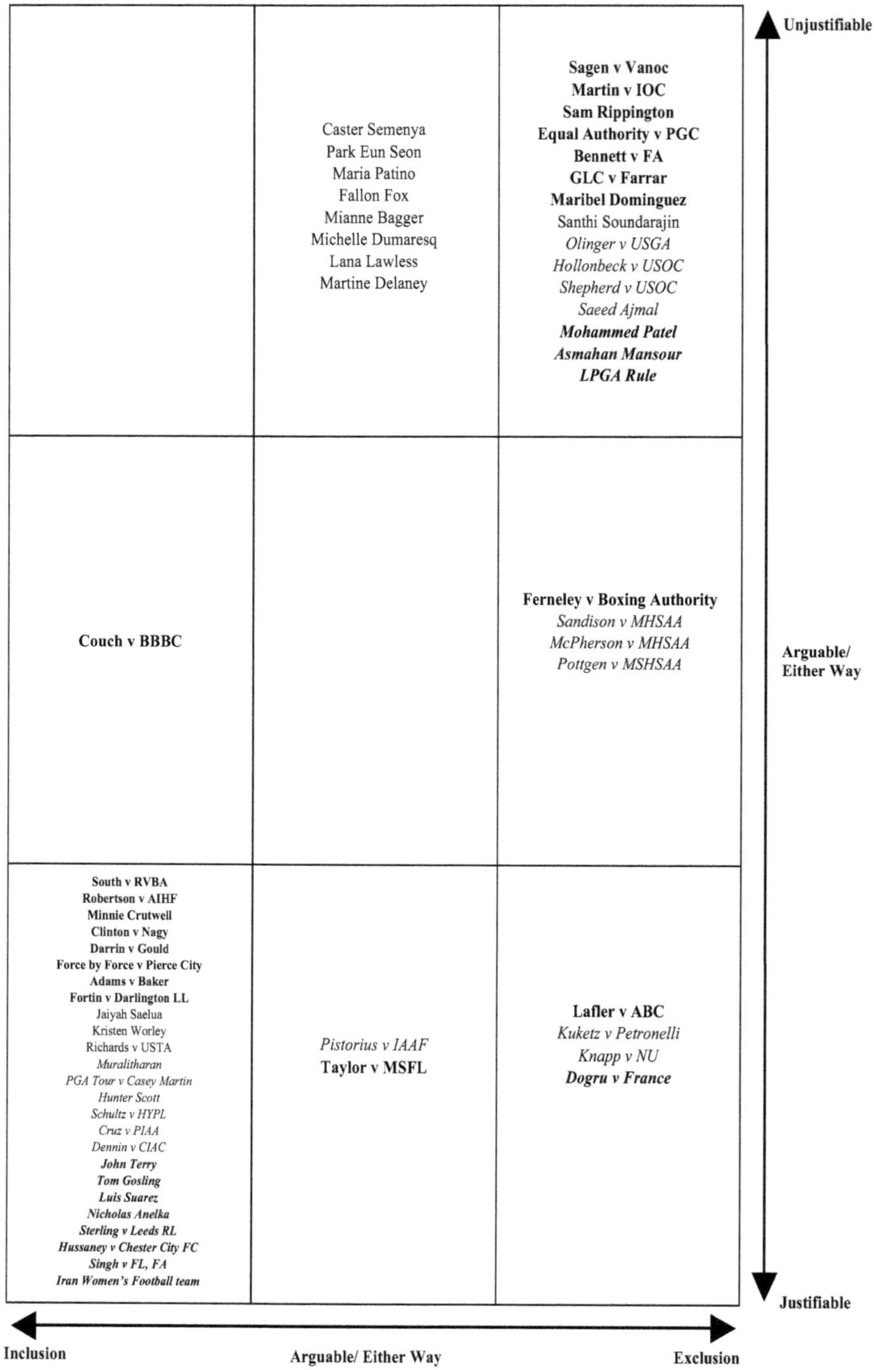

Figure 8.1 The outcome of all sex, gender, disability and race cases examined

exclusion, whether this decision was justifiable or unjustifiable, or arguable/either way. When analysing the effectiveness of the balance technique for determining rights, graphical methods have been pursued elsewhere in the literature also (Rivers *in* Pavlakos, 2007). The cases presented in Figure 8.1 are coded:

Bold text – sex
Roman text – gender
Italic text – disability
Bold italic text – race

Supporting Figure 8.1 is Table 8.2, which illustrates the percentage of sex, gender, disability and race cases which appeared within each category of inclusion and exclusion. Omitted from the analysis are those cases which were used as comparators and not explicitly concerning sex, gender, disability and race.

Table 8.2 The percentage of sex, gender, disability and race cases which fall within inclusion and exclusion

<table>
<tr><th></th><th>Sex</th><th>Gender</th><th>Disability</th><th>Race</th><th colspan="2">Total % of cases</th></tr>
<tr><td>Justifiable inclusion</td><td>42</td><td>25</td><td>38</td><td>67</td><td>42</td><td rowspan="3">53</td></tr>
<tr><td>Justifiable inclusion/exclusion</td><td>5</td><td>0</td><td>6</td><td>0</td><td>3</td></tr>
<tr><td>Justifiable exclusion</td><td>5</td><td>0</td><td>13</td><td>8</td><td>7</td></tr>
<tr><td>Arguable/either way inclusion</td><td>5</td><td>0</td><td>0</td><td>0</td><td>2</td><td rowspan="3">8</td></tr>
<tr><td>Neutral</td><td>0</td><td>0</td><td>0</td><td>0</td><td>0</td></tr>
<tr><td>Arguable/either way exclusion</td><td>5</td><td>0</td><td>19</td><td>0</td><td>7</td></tr>
<tr><td>Unjustifiable inclusion</td><td>0</td><td>0</td><td>0</td><td>0</td><td>0</td><td rowspan="3">39</td></tr>
<tr><td>Unjustifiable inclusion/exclusion</td><td>0</td><td>66</td><td>0</td><td>0</td><td>14</td></tr>
<tr><td>Unjustifiable exclusion</td><td>37</td><td>8</td><td>25</td><td>25</td><td>25</td></tr>
<tr><td>Total % of sex, gender, disability and race cases</td><td>32</td><td>20</td><td>27</td><td>20</td><td colspan="2">Total number: 59</td></tr>
</table>

Justifiable decisions

Of the 59 legal and non-legal cases explored, Figure 8.1 displays a large cluster of sex, disability and race cases which fall within justifiable inclusion. A higher overall percentage of cases are located within the justifiable categories (53 per cent), with 42 per cent of these falling within justifiable inclusion.

In the legal cases, the court decisions generally appear to have been reached by interpreting legislation and sports rules in a manner which achieves a balance between the rights of athletes and the specific nature of sport. A balanced and literal approach has been taken to the interpretation of such legislation by the judges, to ensure that the meaning of the provisions is not stretched beyond their primary objective (*South* Case, para. 34). The courts have acted in a way which seeks to overcome any ambiguities in the legislation by eradicating generalised cultural assumptions about suitability to sport, and instead focus on the individual. In *Force by Force* Judge Roberts states that 'the idea that one should be allowed to try – to succeed or to fail as one's abilities and fortunes may dictate, but in the process at least to profit by those things which are learned in the trying – is a concept deeply engrained in our way of thinking; and it should indeed require a 'substantial' justification to deny that privilege to someone' on the basis of their differences (Case, para. 1031). This reaches the heart of the balance between inclusion and exclusion in sport and is particularly reflective of the US legal approach to these cases.

In addition, the courts have limited their decisions and promoted the need for an individual or case-by-case approach to inclusion and exclusion. This is confirmed by the justifiable arguable/either way case of *Taylor* where the courts set out the boundaries to age rules concerning mixed-sex competition. Justice Morris advocated that the courts consider the relative differences in strength between the sexes, the nature of the sport and the age group, and whether the differences bear any significance (Case, para. 29). He went onto highlight that sport governing bodies should be lawfully allowed to adopt such rules but at the same time the girls themselves should have the right to free choice. Similarly in *Pistorius,* the decision was limited since CAS accepted that developments in scientific knowledge or testing technology may create advantages in the future.

In the evaluation of the balance between inclusion and exclusion, many courts have applied a proportionality test to determine whether the exclusionary sports rule or policy satisfies an important government objective and is directly related to that objective. The principles set out in equality legislation have therefore been implicit throughout some of the legal analysis of rules.

Another consistent approach taken by the courts in these justifiable decisions is the reliance on scientific or medical evidence to determine inclusion or exclusion. Where an exclusionary rule or practice is unsubstantiated, unsupported and cannot be proved, then the courts tend to favour the athlete. Equally, where there is evidence to support the rule then the courts will conclude that the exclusion is justifiable as demonstrated in only 7 per cent of the cases explored.

Figure 8.1 also reinforces the fact that race discrimination and racial abuse are unequivocally incompatible with equality legislation. Most of the race cases follow a justifiable inclusionary agenda eventually, with the courts/tribunals/ sports bodies making a positive overt stance against such behaviour.

However, whilst the sport decisions in the non-legal cases may have been inclusive, the manner in which these took place has not necessarily been satisfactory. The approach tends to be to initially exclude based upon suspicion, which has led to the derogatory treatment of minority athletes throughout their investigation. In this sense, it may be misleading to conclude that all of these decisions in this category have been wholly inclusive, given the covert nature of some practices in sport.

Unjustifiable decisions

At the other end of the scale, Table 8.2 displays a large percentage of outcomes from each area that are unjustifiable and did not adopt a balanced, evidenced-based, individual approach (39 per cent). Medical evidence was ignored in some cases and instead participation seemed to be based upon cultural and traditional assumptions about suitability to sport. In addition, sports rules seem to apply disproportionately to unjustifiably exclude minority individuals. The desperate need to protect the essence of sport by governing bodies has resulted in illegitimate practices, such as sex testing, which infringe human rights.

The placement of most of the intersex and transgender cases in the unjustifiable category is an example of the unsatisfactory nature of the treatment of these athletes. Whilst many of them were eventually included, their treatment was unreasonable and exclusive. The sport policies which seek to include them are conditional and heavily criticised.

Generally speaking, the accountability of sports bodies under the law has rested upon the level of intervention that the courts take in inclusion and exclusion cases. For instance, the application of human rights legislation has been limited by the treatment of sports bodies as private entities. A consistent theme across the legal approach to inclusion and exclusion has therefore been the autonomy of sports bodies to make determinations about inclusion and exclusion through self-regulation and autonomy. This has been appropriate in some cases where sports rules are legitimate, but has produced uncertain results as this category emphasises. In these cases, the courts consistently argued that it lacked jurisdiction or the sports body was not accountable under legislation since it was a private and exclusive body.

Justice Scalia's dissent in *Casey Martin* provides a justification for this legal position of non-intervention. He argued that the PGA should have the autonomy to decide what rules they wish to impose in a competition (Case, para. 705). Conversely, Pregerson J in his dissent in *Martin* argued that the Olympic Games are not a private club since they adopt policies aimed at encouraging all athletes to participate and they operate under a congressional charter (Case, para. 682). They therefore offer a 'quasi-public service'. He did not accept that the California legislature would have intended a major public event such as the Olympic Games to be free to discriminate against a class of participants on the basis of protected characteristics. In addition, he was not satisfied that the IOC had presented compelling social justifications for female exclusion. As a result, he concluded that the opportunity to tip the scales of justice in favour of equality may have slipped away. Pregerson's dissent reinforces the idea that sport is not exempt from the reach of the law of the land.

The difficulty of determining the appropriate level of intervention may be responsible for the host of contradictory messages throughout these unjustifiable decisions, which represented a legal struggle to intervene in sporting matters, even though there was an identification of discriminatory practice (Patel, 2010). The lack of legal pressure on cases involving the activities of the IOC may be for political and economic reasons (Patel, 2010). The courts may have been compelled to maintain strong links for future Olympic opportunities in their respective nations. The Olympic Games as a product provides the IOC with significant power and authority to exercise a regulatory function as a private entity, and essentially apply whichever rules they wish, even if this means that they are operating in a manner which is not accountable to fundamental norms such as human rights and equality. The approach of the courts has been to generally delegate power to the governing bodies to deal with sporting matters. However, this responsibility is dependent upon power being exercised in good faith.

Figure 8.1 and Table 8.2 demonstrate that whilst most decisions are acceptable and justifiable, many continue to lack any justifiable reasoning. This indicates that inclusion and exclusion in sport remains imbalanced and needs to be addressed.

Arguable/either way decisions

Although no neutral cases exist, the balance between inclusion and exclusion is not entirely simple since 8 per cent of the decisions are arguable/either way, which are neither justifiable nor unjustifiable. This suggests that a complete balance will always be difficult to achieve.

For instance, where the courts have adopted an inclusionary, interventionist approach, at times they have prioritised the fundamental rights of the athletes and disregarded valuable scientific and medical evidence which may justify an athlete's exclusion as in *Couch* and *Ferneley*. Few cases successfully strike a balance between equality and the essence of sport. This is particularly evidenced where participation concerns advantage as discussed earlier. The courts have adopted a case-by-case or average approach to dealing with the balance. A case-by-case approach is one where the courts identified the essence of the sport in question and determined whether inclusion would alter this essence and constitute a fundamental alteration. However, this has created inconsistencies because a case-by-case approach demands a high degree of subjectivity, as illustrated by the opposing decisions of *Casey Martin* and *Olinger.* It is equally argued that an individual approach places undue burden on sports bodies.

Instead, an average approach is therefore one where inclusion is determined based upon the average performance advantage of an individual based upon their differences. As demonstrated by the disability cases concerning age rules, however, this potentially excludes minority individuals who do not fit neatly into average categories.

Level of regulation

Having identified the problems which tend to be occurring in this area, Table 8.3 identifies the level at which decisions are being made. It locates the percentage of justifiable, arguable/either way and unjustifiable decisions which took place at a domestic, regional and international level of sport or law regulation.

Table 8.3 The percentage of decisions made by sports governing bodies and the law

		Justifiable decisions (%)	*Arguable/ either way decisions (%)*	*Unjustifiable decisions (%)*	*Total (%)*
Domestic level	Sport	10	0	10	20
	Law	34	8	15	58
Regional level	Sport	0	0	0	0
	Law	2	0	0	2
International level	Sport	5	0	14	19
	Law	2	0	0	2

The table shows that the majority of cases from the sample were decided in domestic UK, US, Australian and Canadian courts (58 per cent), with 34 per cent of the court decisions represented as justifiable. Most sport decisions were made at a domestic level (20 per cent). Little activity has occurred at a regional or international level (2 per cent). Few sport decisions took place at an international level, most of which were unjustified (14 per cent).

Summary

This chapter has analysed the regulatory approaches to inclusion and exclusion by cross-analysing the sample of sex, gender, disability and race cases. Using Tables 8.1, 8.2 and 8.3 and Figure 8.1, the following main themes have been found:

Sports rules and practices

The construction and application of intrinsic and extrinsic sports rules and practices concerning inclusion and exclusion often seek to protect the essence of sport. These have evolved over time and become part of the traditional structures of sport. Such rules can be restrictive and differentially treat individuals on the basis of their physical and non-physical differences. When challenged, the justification for these restrictions is to achieve the objectives of maintaining categories, eliminating unfair advantage, preserving safety and protecting the sporting culture. In other words, fundamental freedoms are restricted in order to protect the essence of sport.

The objectives for restricting athletes on the basis of sex, gender, disability and race do carry some legitimacy when the rules are applied fairly and transparently. However, legal and non-legal cases have arisen partly because of the inconsistency of application of the rules, the ambiguity of the wording of the rules, the lack of certainty of the intention of sports governing bodies and the misuse of scientific knowledge concerning human differences. In addition, not all rules are directly related to the sport objectives. Sport has responded positively in some circumstances, displaying a willingness to adapt or modify their rules to reflect modern sport. Where there has been a threat of legal action by some athletes, sports bodies have also been more willing to make exceptions to their rules to include an athlete. However, the culture of exclusion continues to create instances of discrimination amongst minority athletes.

Regulation and decisions

Where cases have resulted in legal challenges, the role of the law across the four areas has been to interpret equality legislation to determine whether sport is compatible with it and to assess the validity of intrinsic and extrinsic sports rules. The compatibility appears to rest upon the interpretation of the provisions of the legislation and the jurisdictional capacity of the court. Consistent with the rather poor construction of sport rules, the construction of sport exemption clauses in equality legislation has similarly been vague. The courts have been responsible for interpreting the wording of the provisions to give effect to the intention of Parliament and to determine when it is appropriate for sports bodies to rely on the exemptions. In most cases, this has been executed in a thoughtful and balanced manner which draws upon intrinsic and extrinsic material and evaluates the overall purpose of the legislation.

Table 8.3 demonstrates that the domestic law courts appear to be dealing with the majority of cases concerning inclusion and exclusion. The domestic courts have gone some way to rectify some of the ambiguous provisions. These cases have produced useful commentary on the appropriate balance between inclusion and exclusion in sport. There is also evidence of international sport federations (ISFs) managing cases at the international level but most of these decisions appear to be unjustifiable. Little activity appears to be taking place at the regional level. There is no evidence of an effective toolkit for managing inclusion and exclusion in sport or law regulation.

When analysing intrinsic and extrinsic sports rules, the courts have generally considered whether the restrictive sports rule or policy satisfies an important sport or government objective, is proportionate and is directly related to that objective in order to determine its validity and compatibility with equality legislation. There has been a general trend towards adopting a case-by-case, evidenced-based approach to assessing the rules of sport. Collectively this has led to a complex evaluation of the sports rule, policy or action which reflects a commitment to balancing inclusion and exclusion.

A consistent theme across all of the legal cases is the number of reversed decisions by higher courts, dissenting opinions in the judgments and split decisions. Within some of the cases this has led to contradictory judgments. Across the cases this has resulted in a lack of clarity on when it is appropriate for the law to intervene in sporting matters concerning inclusion and exclusion. With a small percentage of arguable/either way decisions, it appears that striking a balance between the sporting interest and the fundamental right of an athlete can be difficult to completely achieve.

One significant limitation of the law lies in its ability to control the influence of social and sporting attitudes and culture upon the formation and application of sports rules, participation and attitudes in sport. Some of the cases dealt with internally by sport may have resulted in an overt inclusive outcome but there remain shortfalls in the covert treatment of the athletes and the policies used to include them.

References

Anderson, J. 2010. *Modern Sports Law: A Textbook.* Portland: Hart Publishing.

Bell, M. 2008. *Racism and Equality in the European Union.* New York: Oxford University Press.

Fields, S.K. 2005. *Female Gladiators; Gender, Law and Contact Sport in America.* Urbana and Chicago: University of Illinois Press.

Jones, C. and Howe, P.D. 2005. The Conceptual Boundaries of Sport and Disabled: Classification and Athletic Performance. *Journal of the Philosophy of Sport*, 32: 133–146.

Laurendeau, J. and Adams, C. 2010. 'Jumping like a girl': discursive silences, exclusionary practices and the controversy over women's ski jumping. *Sport in Society*, 13(3): 431–447.

Loland, S. 2002. *Fair Play in Sport: A moral norm system.* London: Routledge.

Lupton, D. 1999. *Risk.* London: Routledge.

Marks, J. 2003. *What it means to be 98% Chimpanzee.* London: University of California Press.

McFee, G. 2011. *Ethics, Knowledge and Truth in Sports Research.* London: Routledge.

Meier, K.V. 1985. Presidential Address, Philosophic Society for the Study of Sport: Restless Sport. *Journal of the Philosophy of Sport*, XIII: 64–77.

Patel, S. 2010. Women's Ski Jumping and Olympic Programme Inclusion. *World Sports Law Report*, 8(7) July: 11–14.

Pavlakos, G. 2007. *Law, Rights and Discourse: the legal philosophy of Robert Alexy.* Oregon: Hart Publishing.

St Louis, B. 2004. Sport and Common-Sense Racial Science. *Leisure Studies*, 23(1): 31–46.

Wild, S.J. 2009. On Equal Footing: Does Accommodating Athletes with Disability Destroy the Competitive Playing Field or Level it? *Pepperdine Law Review*, 37: 1347–1392.

World Anti-Doping Agency (WADA). 2015. *The World Anti-Doping Code* [online]. Available at: www.wada-ama.org/en/resources/the-code/world-anti-doping-code [accessed 18/02/15].

9 Conclusion and recommendations for regulatory reform

This chapter formulates regulatory recommendations for overcoming deficiencies and striking a balance between inclusion and exclusion. A practical template for reformative action will be proposed for sports bodies to engage in and adapt within their sports. Underpinning this will be recommendations for effectively regulating the balance through appropriate levels of governance and with relevant legal instruments. The findings in the previous chapter highlight the absence of an appropriate toolkit for managing inclusion and exclusion. In order to rectify this, a menu of options for engagement and intervention will be offered in the pursuit of better regulation in this area. The recommendations will have respect for the social significance of inclusion and exclusion in sport and society.

As far as possible, a universal approach is proposed to ensure that human similarities and differences are treated with due respect. A universal approach does not advocate for a totally equal world as Justice Scalia feared in *Casey Martin*. It is accepted that there will continue to be over- and under-representation in sport because of the difficulty in achieving a true balance between the rights of an athlete and the essence of sporting activity. Instead, the aim of this chapter is to propose recommendations which will support a case for parity in participation.

The ladder of sport regulation

Having due regard for conceptual discussions of law and regulation, and for the sociological dialogue on inclusion and exclusion, a ladder of regulatory proposals are offered, ranging from a less-intrusive autonomous approach to sport, to an interventionist legal regulation of inclusion and exclusion. Table 9.1 presents an overview of this recommendation. This model is referred to as 'responsive regulation' where a hierarchy of regulatory strategies are offered, from a least intrusive intervention towards enforcement actions with increasing severity (Harlow and Rawlings, 2009: 242). The aim of the model is to improve regulation in this area by protecting sporting interests and exploring ways to avoid legal challenge, whilst at the same time having respect for the values of human rights and equality in sport.

Table 9.1 The ladder of regulation

Level of regulation/ intervention	*Detail and benefits*	*Drawbacks*
1 Laissez-faire	Least intrusive, best practice approach through codes of practice, education and awareness within ISFs. Little cost or time required.	Sport bodies unlikely to engage with this. Little appreciation of these issues.
2 Internal audit approach	Guidance policy approach through the IOC/FIFA. Host conferences, workshops to encourage sports bodies to conduct a sports audit, share knowledge and provide support.	No enforcement mechanism if sports bodies refuse to engage. Only succeeds if all bodies agree.
3 Regulatory approach	Establish the IADSU – focus on rule formulation, monitoring and inspection, enforcement and sanctions in the fight against discrimination in sport. Supported by the IOC, UNESCO and the Council of Europe.	Only succeeds if all bodies agree, could be costly and timely. Requires a balance between equality and specificity of sport.
4 Legal intervention	Public accountability under domestic, regional and international law. Positive engagement of equality bodies and policies through increased resources and powers.	Lack of sport expertise. Public versus private debate.

Laissez-faire approach

Good regulation thinks small scale first in order to minimise costs of compliance (Harlow and Rawlings, 2009: 248). As a minimum standard therefore, it is proposed that the balance between inclusion and exclusion is left to the ISFs themselves to manage, since they possess the necessary knowledge and expertise in their sport(s). The findings have demonstrated some good responses to notions of inclusion and exclusion by sports bodies, without the need for any legal intervention. To support this, they could additionally offer guidance within their sports for best practice in this area by formulating local codes of practice or rules of respect and raising awareness of human differences through education and training programmes for staff and athletes. This would be least intrusive, place little burden on sports bodies and would have minimal cost implications.

However, without any monitoring it is unlikely that they would engage with this process since, as we have established throughout, sport has little understanding of the factors surrounding inclusion and exclusion in sport. Similar internal policies already exist and have had little impact. They may not have the expertise to deal with this 'in-house' and are more likely to refuse to accept that their sports need to balance inclusion and exclusion more effectively. If there was engagement with this level of regulation then it may create positive conditions for participation. However, the previous chapter reinforced that the problem lies with some of the rules of sport.

Internal audit approach

Instead, an internal audit approach could be adopted. The IOC, in its capacity as a world governing body for sport, could organise and host a series of conferences and workshops to encourage sports bodies to conduct a 'sports audit'. A sports audit is a process by which sports governing bodies and decision-makers in sport review all rules and practices in their sports that concern inclusion and exclusion. The purpose of this process is to identify restrictive rules, ensure they are justified and necessary and amend where appropriate. Sport bodies should ensure that rules do not unnecessarily exclude women, intersex, transgender, disabled individuals and particular racial populations. The IOC could adopt this role as a commitment to the principles of the Olympic Charter.

Specifically, the audit seeks to provide a clearer sense of how rules concerning categories, advantage, safety and culture should be constructed, applied and regulated. The aim of the audit is to enhance the essence of sport by ensuring that eligibility and selection rules which seek to match ability, preserve competition, ensure safety, provide the best possible entertainment, generate revenue, maintain traditions and sporting cultures do not unnecessarily exclude minority individuals. The audit is an opportunity for sports to review the foundations of their sports and realign them with modern sport and society. This may necessitate a number of amendments to rules and regulations to ensure a better balance between inclusion and exclusion. At the series of conferences and workshops, the IOC could assist sport bodies in focusing on specific aspects of their rules and practices.

Categories

The sports audit will encourage a review of sport categories in light of the cases presented, to better reflect an informed, modern understanding of human differences.

For instance, in relation to sex and gender divisions, it is proposed that, where possible, a non-gendered approach should be taken to categorisation so that human differences between individual athletes can be evaluated more accurately (Reaves, 2001: 11). Given the findings, the matter which needs addressing is whether sex and gender is a relevant classification in sport and if it is, how this is best determined. This is supported by Ballantyne *et al.*, (2011) who argue that there is a need to provide an objective and relevant criteria to evaluate what separates men and women in sport. Donnelly and Donnelly (2013) conducted a gender equality audit on the 2012 Olympic Games. They recommended that the structure and rules of events are reviewed to determine whether weight, height and distance differences between men and women are still relevant and to establish consistency across sports.

Other alternatives include the promotion of mixed-sex sports participation, which eliminates the focus on gender categories (Buzuvis *in* Sartore-Baldwin, 2013: 71), or ranking according to height, weight and strength (Capel and Piotrowski, 2000: 28; Burke, 2004: 178). Some call for the introduction of 'non-sex-binary-based trans-inclusive policies' (Love *in* Hargreaves and Anderson, 2014: 376). Mixed-sex participation is offered in a number of modern alternative sports which are growing in popularity (Cohen *et al.*, 2014).

Since hormone levels are relied upon so heavily in the determination of participation, it may be the case that categories should be formed according to the hormonal balance of athletes instead of sex and gender. The introduction of the WADA Athlete Biological Passport is consistent with the focus on biological variables as a condition for participation (WADA, 2010). It is anticipated that the passport will provide a more accurate measurement of the variables of athletes, in contrast to the traditional approach of being measured against norms in the population at large (WADA, 2010).

The categories of disabled and non-disabled could also be reviewed. The imposition of age categories in sport may not be an accurate indicator of matching ability and ensuring safety, particularly when there is not always correlation between age and physical ability. It is therefore proposed that an individual approach should be adopted in cases concerning athletes with intellectual disabilities. However, this needs to be underpinned by scientific evidence and should not place unreasonable burdens upon the sports body to make determinations about physical or intellectual ability.

The rules dividing disabled and non-disabled sports concern legitimate practical matters of integration when a disabled athlete attempts to compete in non-disabled categories, which were not necessarily designed for them. However, these considerations should be evidence based, rather than being driven by broad generalities and applying stereotypical assumptions about the capabilities of disabled athletes. It is likely that the main challenges to these categories will be the acceptance of the use of technology in sports. Athletes such as *Pistorius* and *Hunter Scott,* prompt a new way of thinking about human beings which should be encouraged in the sports audit.

New categories are proposed where there is no restriction on the use of technologies in sport (Burkett, 2010: 219). It may be the case that the sports audit will encourage the introduction of new forms of sport (Francis, 2005: 128; Lenk, 2007).

The invisible categories which divide racial groups in sport are difficult to audit since they occur unconsciously and are embedded within the sport Doxa as we shall discuss further shortly. However, if sports rules are constructed accurately, transparently and achieve legitimate objectives, it is anticipated that this will lead to a more precise use of human differences when drawing lines in sport. Overcoming inclusion and exclusion on the basis of race is concerned with creating an open environment where populations are judged on their athletic ability rather than their presumed suitability.

Realistically, it is unlikely that current categories will be entirely abandoned in our lifetime. Resolving category issues will have serious implications on the economic value of sport (Francis, 2005). However, re-thinking categories of sport will at least begin to challenge the concept of the human body and the sporting body and acknowledge the existence of changing times (Nixon, 2007: 421). The sports audit encourages sports bodies to begin to at least review the categories of sport under modern regimes. Kane (1995) advocates for the deconstruction of categories by viewing sport as a continuum instead. Where categories remain, perhaps self-declaration should be encouraged, particularly in relation to sex and gender, to determine classification.

Rules regulating advantage

We have seen that the objective of regulating advantage in sport is integral to the essence of sport. In response to the findings, the audit encourages sport to construct rules which precisely define the scale of advantage in their sports including the conduct that is to be regulated, as well clear definitions of important terms (adapted from Solomon *et al.*, 2009: 256). Definitions of fair, unfair, natural, artificial advantage are not currently available within the construction of the rules. The sports audit aims to ensure that when these words are used, they are defined in the context of the sports in which they exist. It is proposed that a workable scale is produced which would indicate a fair or unfair advantage. This is constantly changeable but it is necessary to formulate a policy which is capable of producing consistency. A clearer definition will ensure that all potential advantages are reviewed.

The audit will encourage sports bodies to review the scale of natural and artificial advantages in their sports to better reflect significant developments in science and technology. Sports bodies should employ rules which are based upon current scientific knowledge when regulating advantage rather than selectively tolerating particular forms of advantage. Regulatory bodies in sport and the law need to rely on 'good science' to determine advantage in sport rather than stereotypes and irrational concerns (Cooper, 2010: 262). Relying on accurate scientific knowledge will at least ensure that rules are consistently applied to natural and artificial advantages and minimise the subjectivity involved in determining what is considered natural or unnatural in sport. Perhaps standards of normality need to change and a revision of the nature of the athlete is required to reflect the realities of modern sports participation (Van Hilvoorde and Landeweerde, 2008: 98; Reaves, 2001).

Policies regulating advantage tend to be in place to prevent cheaters and intentional acts which threaten the integrity and essence of sport. We have seen that such policies tend to have a diverse effect on innocent athletes who unintentionally possess an advantage such as some female, intersex, transgender and disabled athletes. Departure from the strict approaches to advantage in sport is necessary in some cases to appreciate the reality of 'widespread biological and environmental inequality' (Kayser *et al.*, 2007: 2). Sports bodies should review their rules concerning natural and artificial advantages particularly in the context of innocent athletes. A threshold of acceptance should be outlined in order to prevent drawing arbitrary lines.

It has been suggested in the literature that unintentional advantages may be more accepted if a certain level of intentional advantage was also permitted in sport. Savulescu and Foddy (2010) express that 'we have two choices: to vainly try to turn the clock back, or to rethink who we are and what sport is...performance enhancement is not against the spirit of sport, it is the spirit of sport. To choose to be better is to be human.' A number of writers have called for a revision of the WADA Code to accept a certain level of doping (Anderson, 2013). This may in turn have a positive effect on athletes explored here.

There is already evidence of good practice by some bodies to review rules and provide more clarity in the regulation of inclusion and exclusion for minority individuals. Revised policies have shifted from exclusion to participatory parity, and wider consultation has been made with external experts in the fields of medicine and science when constructing the rules. Sport is moving towards a case by case, instead of an average approach to advantage factors.

Safety

The precautionary principle is a significant sport and society objective. In circumstances where safety is threatened, priority must be given to the protection of sport and exclusion will be deemed justifiable. This exclusion is necessary and legitimate to maintain the essence of sport. The sports audit adopts the legal approach to safety objectives and proposes that any safety rules pursue legitimate aims, are proportionate and are directly related to the aims when constructed and applied. There should be more neutrality in how the rules are applied and whom they are applied to. As highlighted, matching ability and ensuring safety should be the focus of the precautionary principle. Sports bodies should be prepared to justify exclusionary rules, which will encourage a better connection between the requirements and the purpose of rules (Weston, 2005: 163). When the rule is correctly applied, it will lead to justified inclusive or exclusive outcomes. The audit should encourage sport not to use safety as a smokescreen for discriminatory behaviour in the future.

Managing the sporting culture

The sports audit encourages implicit norms upon which rules are based, to shift to better reflect modern sport and society. Although traditional cultures and norms form an integral part of the essence of sport, many of these standards unconsciously operate to exclude athletes who are perceived as unnatural or abnormal and unsuited to sporting activity. With this in mind, the sports audit will ensure that inclusion and exclusion is determined by legitimately justified rules instead of being driven by the sporting culture.

Culture provides a context for sport but should not determine participation by itself. Sport deserves historical continuity as traditional customs certainly form part of its essence. However, there must be a process of accountability when those traditions are inaccurate and are also being used to treat individuals derogatorily. In order to avoid unnecessary under-representation and discrimination, extrinsic matters to sport concerning our sex, gender, disability and race should not be used to decide whether or not athletes are eligible to compete. Internal sporting matters concerning human differences should be evidenced based and truthful.

Regulating and managing culture is difficult because of the unconscious and invisible nature of some of the issues emerging from the sport culture, as we have seen in cases concerning race. In order to overcome this, the sports audit seeks to encourage sports bodies to take more responsibility for the cultures which surround their sports in order to produce a better balance between inclusion and exclusion in sport. This will ensure that sports bodies are operating with transparency and awareness in their sports.

The ability of sports bodies to change social attitudes and challenge stereotypes about human differences, which may no longer be accurate, will take time and require patience as social tides shift. Nevertheless, the sports audit prompts a proactive rather than reactive approach to inclusion and exclusion in sport. In terms of overt racial abuse, the social dimension of the EU White Paper proposes that sports bodies 'have procedures for dealing with racist abuse during matches, based on existing initiatives. It also recommends strengthening provisions regarding discrimination in licensing systems for clubs' (European Commission, 2007: 8). In sports such as football, a licence is required for a club or team to participate in the competition. The primary aim of licensing systems is to raise the standards of good governance in professional sports, increase financial transparency and ensure competitive balance (Hill, 2009: 259). In order to obtain a licence certain criteria need to be met, relating to safety for instance. It is recommended in the White Paper that amongst others, provisions regarding discrimination are also included in these criteria (European Commission, 2007: 53). This is reflective of the idea that the eradication of choice from the process of exclusion may be a way to deal with this and seems to be a fair recommendation to employ.

To briefly summarise, the sports audit advocates that the balance between inclusion and exclusion in sport should be based upon the liberalistic ideology of rationalism, which is associated with behaviour and actions which are based upon reason and principle, rather than a reliance on custom or tradition, or non-rational impulses (Heywood, 2003: 33). Performing a sports audit of the nature and purpose of sport itself will enable sports bodies to evaluate how appropriate sports rules are in a modern society (Stone, 2005: 389). Truth and transparency is required to purify the sporting culture and the essence of sport. The overarching aim of the sports audit is a philosophical one: the re-construction of sports rules which are based upon truth about human differences, and the application of those rules from a truth perspective (Patel, 2011). In order to achieve this truth, sports bodies need to rely on 'good science' to determine eligibility and perhaps broaden its definitions of athletes to accommodate for the diversity amongst human beings (Cooper, 2010: 262; Marshall, 2009).

However, without any enforcement or monitoring mechanisms at this stage, it seems unlikely that sports bodies will actively participate in this process and agree to undertake an audit of their rules. Furthermore, based on the findings here, it is possible that ISFs alone may not be equipped to manage this process since they often misunderstand the factors involved. The achievement of a balance between preserving sporting values whilst respecting law and equality principles may be difficult within these first two levels of the ladder because of their internalised nature.

Regulatory approach

The preferred approach to striking a balance to inclusion and exclusion is the establishment of an International Anti-Discrimination in Sport Unit (IADSU) who would act as an enforcement body for the fight against discrimination in sport. Carr has also proposed a compliance unit (2009: 175), and the European Commission have made references to engaging in a fight against discrimination in sport (European Commission, 2011). Responsive regulation should involve rule formulation, monitoring and inspection, and at its heart, enforcement and sanctions (Harlow and Rawlings, 2011: 238).

The idea of a body specifically designed to focus on inclusion and exclusion is adopted from the successful WADA model. The universal agreement to combat doping in sport has led to the creation of a uniform standard of agreed articles and provisions across sport (David, 2009: 3). WADA functions by agreement, which tends to be adopted to bring about a common approach in a particular area of activity. This approach has been described as a body of 'soft' international law even though this is not a legal body (David, 2009: 40). It is proposed that the IADSU functions in this way because it would involve a voluntary agreement under the rules of a private organisation, which could reduce intervention from the law. At the same time, there is potential for the law to play an important role in the fight against discrimination in sport (see below).

It is proposed that the IADSU follows a similar path to WADA and is initially set up by the IOC since they could earmark necessary funding for the body and also have the power to enforce this type of body upon sport globally. The body would be managed by the IOC but comprise representatives from different sports, and engage with experts in the fields of equality, law and regulation, social sciences, science and medicine and sport. Despite the shortfalls in the IOC, they have the capacity and power to drive this movement and bring panels together. In their gender equality audit, Donnelly and Donnelly (2013) advocate for the IOC to be responsible for achieving gender equality in participation.

It is accepted that this will not be a cheap process and WADA has taken a long time to develop and refine its anti-doping programme. However, given the irregularities in the case decisions analysed, there should be a commitment to this movement.

The main objective of the IADSU would be to harmonise sports rules concerning inclusion and exclusion in order to combat discrimination in sport. This could be achieved by the body taking on the responsibility of conducting the sports audit across sports. The IADSU could audit sports rules to ensure compliance with equality standards such as non-discrimination. These legal principles should underpin the function and purpose of the IADSU. This inspection of rules would follow five criteria:

1 Identify and clarify legitimate objectives of the essence of the sporting activity.
2 Review the construction of rules so that the wording is clear and unambiguous, the rule directly relates to the objectives, and understandings of human differences are accurately interpreted within the rules.
3 Ensure that the application of the rules are, where appropriate, consistent and fair across the areas of sex, gender, disability and/or race, as well as across other comparable areas.
4 Adopt an evidenced-based approach to any inclusion or exclusion of athletes.
5 Justify the rules against legal standards.

The principles of the sports audit are similar to the general rule of law. Sports governing bodies should not operate beyond the rule of law when constructing and exercising their eligibility rules and selection criteria for participation. The audit criteria form the basic principles of an IADSU anti-discrimination code of conduct, which would also achieve the major objective of harmonisation (Harlow and Rawlings, 2009: 193). Sports organisations could sign up to the code of conduct by agreement. The IOC has the power to enforce agreement to a code of conduct by making it a condition of participation into Olympic events and competitions. Failure to comply could impact upon inclusion to these sporting events.

A second main objective would be enforcement and sanctions, which distinguishes this level of regulation on the ladder. The IADSU would, by agreement, have powers to enforce changes to rules which are unjustifiable, impose penalties on sports bodies for non-compliance with the code of conduct and instruct certain standards of behaviour. In addition, the body could investigate cases of unreasonable exclusion, which can then lead to a route into CAS who could play a central role in dealing with discrimination cases (David, 2009).

What makes the WADA model persuasive is its support from governments and the law (David, 2009: 3). The UNESCO Doping Convention contains general provisions by which the States commit themselves to take steps to support the principles and regime of the WADA Code. Furthermore, it reconfirms the commitment of governments to fund half of the WADA budget (WADA, 2009). Since UNESCO is also committed to the fight against discrimination it would be reasonable to propose that they support the IADSU through the enactment of a convention on anti-discrimination in sport. This could be underpinned by the relevant principles of the UDHR. Sport is moving towards this in relation to corruption and match-fixing as we shall see below.

Despite the public significance of the WADA Code, its legal enforceability derives from the universal agreement to commit to the Code. It functions as a contractual arrangement by which sporting organisations and associations regulate themselves (David, 2009: 83). Ensuring this universal commitment to the fight against discrimination will present a challenge to this proposal. It is unlikely that an anti-discrimination movement would take place currently because governing bodies, the law and society generally is unwilling to confront the concerns presented in the sports audit with any real transparency. As highlighted, there is a general lack of awareness of any imbalance between inclusion and exclusion in sport amongst governing bodies.

A final objective of the IADSU, therefore, is to offer education and training to sports bodies and athletes, about inclusion and exclusion in competitive sport and about physical and non-physical human differences. Training could be offered to educate these groups about the importance of equality and how key legislation might apply to their sports.

David (2009: 7) highlights a number of challenges that WADA face. These surround the problem of producing harmonised standards, consistent application and interpretation of the Code provisions and consistent decision-making by tribunals around the world. Furthermore, despite significant devotion to education about doping for athletes, coaches and advisors, there continues to be ignorance in this area. It is accepted that the IADSU proposal may be perceived as ambitious as it is likely to require a significant amount of investment and time from sports bodies. However, equality and non-discrimination are fundamental principles which must be protected regardless of the industry in question.

The Council of Europe – an alternative

Lessons can be learnt from the current approaches taken by the Council of Europe, to tackle corruption and match-fixing in sport (Smith, 2011). With the adoption of two conventions against corruption in 1999, the Council of Europe have demonstrated a commitment to this problem by recommending the establishment of a WADA-like body for corruption (Council of Europe, 2008: 20). An alternative proposal for the IADSU could therefore be that the Council of Europe undertakes this role and/or supports the IADSU through networks with the IOC and other ISFs, the UN and various governments. The Council of Europe have also shown similar commitments to gender equality and elite sport and following a study in 2011, they offered a number of main recommendations to States within the Council of Europe, to promote female representation in sport (Council of Europe, 2011).

The EU Communications Document promises to support the Council of Europe with this fight against corruption in order to uphold the integrity of sport (European Commission, 2011: 12). These commitments to the fight against corruption have filtered down to the domestic level, with the establishment of a Sports Betting Intelligence Unit (SBIU) by the UK Gambling Commission and 'memorandums of understandings' between sports bodies and betting organisations (Smith, 2011, para. 57). There are also considerations for sanctions to be imposed upon those who do not complete it (Smallwood, 2012). In light of this, there is a strong argument that the Council of Europe could play a significant role in the establishment of the IADSU.

Legal intervention

Where sport cannot be protected from legal challenge and is unwilling to engage in a fight against discrimination in sport, the intervention of the law to uphold equality principles will be necessary. It is important to locate a process by which sports governing bodies can be held publically accountable for their actions which potentially impinge upon an athlete's fundamental rights, and where sport rules and regulations fall within the legal boundaries of intervention and can be appropriately critiqued for compliance and compatibility with legal provisions.

International level

Firstly, it is proposed that sports bodies comply and are compatible with fundamental human rights legislation. Since the sports rules which impact upon inclusion and exclusion seek to discriminate against human differences, it is inevitable that there will be times when these rules conflict with human rights. We have seen in Part I that there is exists an extensive body of international, regional and domestic equality legislation and provisions which seek to protect individuals from discriminatory practices on the basis of their sex, gender, disability and race. These instruments place obligations on the States who are signatories to them, to comply with the provisions and refrain from interfering in the enjoyment of human rights. These obligations should extend to the actions of international sports governing bodies, such as the IOC and FIFA. Where there are clear breaches of human rights, ISF's should be held accountable for discriminatory practices.

Human rights systems seek to bind States through obligations to which only States can become parties. Non-discrimination norms are traditionally associated with vertical obligations between the State and the individual. This places third party private entities or non-State actors such as sports bodies outside of the legal regime (Forgues, 2000). This has prompted a clear divide between public and private bodies and has created a wider debate about the relationship between human rights, the State and private entities (Rehman, 2010: 12).

There is a growing discussion in the literature about how non-State private bodies such as sport can be held accountable for human rights violations (Cooper, 2010: 259; Hunt, 1998). It is proposed that since ISF's such as the IOC and FIFA behave and function like a State, they should be held accountable under human rights legislation (Cooper, 2010: 260). One way of holding them accountable would be to supplement the existing vertical framework by imposing a system of 'horizontal obligation' or 'diagonal obligation' instead (Hessbruegge, 2005: 26).

Challenging the vertical application of human rights, which seeks to protect the private sphere from legal intervention, horizontal application demands that the State is 'constitutive of all legal relations, because law is itself a construct of the State' (Hunt, 1998: 424). The horizontal application of human rights norms would subject all law, which governs all types of legal relations, to review for compatibility with human rights. Vertical and horizontal application are two extremes: there are degrees of approach which can be achieved within this. It seems appropriate to ensure that private bodies are susceptible to human rights legislation in an age where public duties are increasingly being carried out by private or quasi-private bodies.

In addition, there is an indirect responsibility on the State to ensure that private bodies do not interfere with human rights. At the international level, international law places responsibilities upon the States rather than individuals. Although the ISFs are not signatories to international law, the States can use legislation to apply pressure on them to act fairly and legitimately. If sports bodies fail to do so, a State can retract their willingness to host or participate in sporting events. In order to do this, international law needs to be more actively enforced.

The effectiveness of equality legislation is contested across the literature because of the *sui generis* characteristics of international law (Rehman, 2010; Forgues, 2000: 256; Roy, 2007; Fasting *in* Hartmann-Tews and Pfister, 2003: 276; Neumayer, 2005). There appears to be a general trend that although the conceptual commitment to equality is evident, stronger enforceability and compliance is still required (Kluka 2008: 39). This supports Moser's (2005) concept of 'evaporation', which occurs when good policy intentions fail to be transferred through sustainable processes into practice. That said, there are examples of the positive impact of provisions such as CEDAW, the Brighton Declaration and the CRPD upon domestic legislation (McPhedran *et al.,* 2000; Brown and Connolly, 2010).

Regional level

The shortfalls in the international system may be fulfilled at the regional level, which seeks to provide a middle ground between the State and domestic institutions, and the international system which is unable to deal with individual victims of human rights breaches. The Inter-American Convention places a duty upon States to respect and ensure the rights by adopting protective measures. The ECtHR have interpreted the text and spirit of the ECHR to develop the doctrine of placing 'positive obligations' on States to ensure that they secure the rights and freedoms to everyone under their jurisdiction (Spielman *in* Oliver and Fedtke, 2007: 427).

Although these instruments do not place direct obligations upon private bodies, the Inter-American Convention has established that this positive duty extends to breaches by non-State actors (Nolan, 2009: 231). In a number of cases, the ECtHR has objected to States failing to address human rights breaches by private bodies highlighting that this can result in engaging the States responsibility under the Convention (Spielmann *in* Oliver and Fedtke, 2007: 464; Nolan, 2009: 245). In other words, a State may be indirectly liable where they fail to hold sports bodies accountable for human rights breaches. If a State has failed to secure the rights to sports bodies within their jurisdiction, it would be difficult to escape their obligations and duty to protect at the regional level.

There is great potential at a regional level for striking a balance between inclusion and exclusion in sport. Following the entry into force of the Treaty of Lisbon 2009, the EU has a new competence in sport and a commitment to combating discrimination in sport as reinforced by Article 165 TFEU and in the EU White Paper (European Commission, 2007, para. 2.6).

Commentary on the relationship between sport and Community law implies that a balance between individual and sporting interests is possible by encouraging good governance. Current focus on the application of competition law and free movement principles to sport demonstrates this. There is scope for the EU, given its recognition of fundamental rights under the Treaty on European Union (TEU) and the Charter of Fundamental Rights, to offer guidance on the application of equality law to the rules of sport.

At this level, there is also an appreciation of the specificity of sport through a more sensitive application of EC law to sport. The soft competence provided for by the TEU and the TFEU is reinforced by the White Paper. However, the White Paper offers a definition of the specificity of sport, part of which does not sit comfortably with the findings of this book (European Commission, 2007: 13);

> The specificity of sporting activities and of sporting rules, such as separate competitions for men and women, limitations on the number of participants in competitions, or the need to ensure uncertainty concerning outcomes and to preserve a competitive balance between clubs taking part in the same competitions.

The segregation of men and women's competition is explicitly referred to as specific to sport, whilst this book has provided a detailed evaluation of the limitations to binary categories dividing sex and gender. The White Paper definition fails to approach the complexities and inaccuracies of broadly dividing along sex and gender lines with any real vigour. It is in fact likely that all of the rules we are concerned with are considered specific to sport under this current regime. This should be challenged and when it comes to eligibility rules and selection criteria, this definition presents itself as a 'cop out' and another example of the law essentially escaping their responsibility to directly address particular norms of sport (Patel, 2011).

The EU approach and the White Paper contribute towards shaping good governance in sport up until the point of defining specificity. Although the concept of purely sporting rules has now been rejected, it could be argued the 'specificity of sport' is just a replacement for that concept. Whilst the EU approach accepts and respects the value of the essence of sport, it fails to accurately identify what rules are part of that essence. To exempt specific rules such as the segregation of men and women's competition is to ignore the real issues of sport that most require governance and guidance on good sports policy. Recognising that certain aspects of sport are specific and unique in nature is entirely necessary as we have established throughout. However, the approach to treat this in a special way sends out a message that discriminatory practices are accepted so long as they are specific to sport. This is not the case since all practices should pursue legitimate aims which are evidenced based and fit for purpose.

Domestic level

The findings dictate a good level of engagement of the domestic courts with decisions of inclusion and exclusion cases. In light of this it is proposed that limitations in the form of sport exemption clauses contained within domestic equality legislation should be revised and given greater thought in their construction. The UK EA exemption for instance demands greater justification for differential treatment in sport. The previous chapter reveals that the interpretation and application of these vague provisions by the courts has been mostly balanced and thoughtful. There is a role for sport-specific exemptions because they respect the essence of sporting activity and accept that sporting activity operates in a different manner. However, the provisions need to be evidenced based and accurate, consistent with the proposals under the sports audit.

The US, Australian and UK courts have reasonably interpreted legislation to determine compatibility with sports rules and they have gone some way to rectify some of the ambiguous provisions. In the absence of references to sport within international and regional provisions as we have identified, the courts should adopt a position which is in line with the overall purpose of the legislation rather than in a way which is inconsistent with human rights.

The US Title IX model is not without its problems but it has provided great opportunity for minorities in sport and demonstrates a strong commitment to the balance between inclusion and exclusion (Williams, 2013). Similarly, the US ADA has been applied to sport in a manner which balances the interests of the athletes with the special nature of sport.

The Rooney Rule in the USA is a response to Title VIII of the Civil Rights Act and demonstrates positive action against discrimination in sport. It may not be a perfect solution, but engaging private employers to adopt positive measures to prevent discrimination in the workplace or face legal and financial penalties, is a persuasive model for balancing inclusion and exclusion. Where invisible barriers are hindering progress, the law has a pivotal role to play in forcing change.

At a domestic level, a level of horizontality should also be applied to interpret the UK HRA in a way which broadens its application to all law rather than just public law (Hunt, 1998). Similar matters of compatibility and compliance are continuously arising out of the defamation and libel actions concerning the right to free speech and privacy. As we have seen, the HRA is not drafted in a way which seeks to apply to all law. However, it is suggested that by explicitly making courts and tribunals bound by the HRA, it imposes a duty on them to act compatibly with the Convention when they develop common law, including private disputes between private parties (Hunt, 1998). There is some degree of horizontal application as a result of this. Furthermore, if there is a failure at a domestic level, an individual can seek reference to the regional courts.

Generally speaking, the enforcement of equality legislation will be necessary when there are breaches of fundamental rights. At an international, regional or domestic level the focus of enforcing human rights legislation is for the protection of the individual. Since sports bodies play an increasingly public role in the enjoyment of the fundamental rights for athletes they should be subject to equality legislation where they fail to demonstrate that restrictive rules pursue a legitimate aim proportionately. The principles set out in the UDHR seek to protect human rights in any field and this should be given more effect. In addition, from a governance perspective, following the principles set out within equality provisions, such as proportionality, can contribute towards a better execution of the sports audit and can encourage sports bodies to operate in a more transparent manner.

Equality bodies and policies

Existing equality bodies, such as the Equality and Human Rights Commission (EHRC) in the UK, should also support the enforcement of equality principles in sport. They are a non-departmental public body, established under the EA, comprising experts in the field of sex, gender, disability and race. Their mandate is to challenge discrimination and protect and promote human rights. They have enforcement powers to conduct inquires about specific matters, conduct assessments to test compliance with the EA, intervene in legal proceedings and serve compliance notice. However, their powers apply only to public authorities, which may not currently extend to sport. That said the EOC (which was replaced by the EHRC) played a significant part in ensuring that s. 44 SDA was considered dead law. Equality bodies could therefore play a role in ensuring sports bodies are compliant with equality legislation, if their remit was extended.

As we have seen throughout, there has been good progress through the introduction of equality policies across sport. However, their effectiveness has been subject to criticism. More resources and power should be given to equality organisations in order to enable them to enforce these policies and achieve positive outcomes.

Overall, the drawbacks to this legal intervention are that the law lacks expertise to deal with sport-specific issues. However, the EU regional level is developing competence in this area despite the shortfalls in the White Paper definition of specificity. At the same time, fundamental principles are much more important than sporting interests and when they are violated, there should be accountability for those actions, which this level proposes to offer, particularly if sport as a whole is not willing to engage in a fight against discrimination. A consistent theme throughout the cases is that, short of legal intervention, the culture of exclusion in sport will be slow to change.

Conclusion

This book has engaged in a critical evaluation of inclusion and exclusion conceptually and in practice. The overarching aim has been to strike a balance between inclusion and exclusion in competitive sport by offering regulatory recommendations for reform in the management of human differences in sport. In order to ensure that sports bodies construct and apply rules and practices which preserve the essence of sport whilst at the same time recognising and respecting fundamental values, a range of recommendations along a ladder of regulation are proposed. The options vary on a scale from self-regulation of sports bodies through a best practice and internal audit approach, to the establishment of the IADSU who would act as enforcers in the fight against discrimination in sport. Where sport is not willing to engage with this process, there is an argument for the legal regulation of sports bodies through public accountability under equality legislation. This could be conducted in hard or soft way, and there are positive developments at the EU regional level of sports regulation to ensure that the specificity of sport is recognised by the law. The ladder of regulation seeks to offer a range of options for the mutual engagement of sports bodies and/or the law in this area. The degree of intervention by the law will depend upon the level of commitment to sport in the fight against discrimination.

References

Anderson, J. 2013. Doping, sport and the law: time for repeal of prohibition? *International Journal of Law in Context*, 9(2): 135–159.

Ballantyne, K.N., Kayser, M. and Grootegoed, J.A. 2011. Sex and gender issues in competitive sports: investigation of a historical case leads to a new viewpoint. *British Journal of Sports Medicine*, 3 May: 1–4.

Brown, K.J. and Connolly, C. 2010. The role of law in promoting women in elite athletics: an examination of four nations. *International Review for the Sociology of Sport*, 45(3): 3–21.

Burke, M. 2004. Radicalising Liberal Feminism by Playing the Games that Men Play. *Australian Feminist Studies*, 19(44): 169–184.

Burkett, B. 2010. Technology in Paralympic Sport: performance enhancement or essential for performance? *British Journal of Sports Medicine*, 44: 215–220.

Capel, S. and Piotrowski, S. 2000. *Issues in Physical Education.* London: Routledge Falmer.

Carr, S. 2009. Title IX: an opportunity to level the Olympic playing field. *Seton Hall Journal of Sports and Entertainment Law*, 19: 149–180.

Cohen, A., Melton, N.E. and Peachey, J.W. 2014. Investigating a Coed Sport's Ability to Encourage Inclusion and Equality. *Journal of Sport Management*, 28(2): 220–235.

Cooper, E.J. 2010. Gender testing in athletic competitions-human rights violations: why Michael Phelps is praised and Caster Semenya is chastised. *Journal of Gender, Race and Justice*, 14: 233–264.

Council of Europe 2008. *Why Sport is Not Immune to Corruption* [online]. Available at: www.coe.int/t/dg4/epas/Source/Ressources/EPAS_INFO_Bures_en.pdf [accessed 01/08/12].

Council of Europe 2011. Gender Equality and (Elite) Sport. Available at:

www.coe.int/t/dg4/epas/resources/texts/INF25%20Gender%20equality%20and%20elite%20sport.pdf [accessed 02/01/14].

David, P. 2009. *Guide to the World Anti-Doping Code: A Fight for the Spirit of Sport.* Cambridge: Cambridge University Press.

Donnelly, P. and Donnelly, M. 2013. *The London 2012 Olympics: A gender equality audit.* Centre for Sport Policy Studies. University of Toronto. Available at: http://physical.utoronto.ca/docs/csps-pdfs/donnelly-donnelly—olympic-gender-equality-report.pdf [accessed 02/01/14].

European Commission 2007. *White Paper on Sport* [online]. Available at: http://ec.europa.eu/sport/documents/wp_on_sport_en.pdf [accessed 01/04/12].

European Commission. 2011. *Developing the European Dimension in Sport* [online]. Available at: http://ec.europa.eu/sport/news/doc/communication/communication_en.pdf [accessed 07/06/11].

Forgues, C. 2000. A Global Hurdle: the implementation of an international non-discrimination norm protecting women from gender discrimination in international sports. *Boston University International Law Journal*, 18: 247–272.

Francis, L.P. 2005. Competitive Sports, Disability, and Problems of Justice in Sports. *Journal of the Philosophy of Sport*, 32: 127–132.

Hargreaves, J. and Anderson, E. 2014. *Routledge Handbook of Sport, Gender and Sexuality.* London: Routledge.

Harlow, C. and Rawlings, R. 2009. *Law and Administration.* Cambridge: Cambridge University Press.

Hartmann-Tews, I. and Pfister, G. 2003. *Sport and Women: social issues in international perspective.* London: Routledge.

Hessbruegge, J.A. 2005. Human Rights Violations Arising from Conduct of Non-State Actors. *Buffalo Human Rights Law Review*, 11: 21–88.

Heywood, A. 2003. *Political Ideology: an introduction.* 3rd Edition. New York: Palgrave Macmillan.

Hill, J. 2009. The European Commission's White Paper on Sport: a step backwards for specificity? *International Journal of Sport Policy and Politics*, 1(3): 253–266.

Hunt, M. 1998. The horizontal effect of the human rights act. *Public Law*, pp. 423–443.

Kane, M.J. 1995. Resistance/transformation of the oppositional binary: exposing sport as a continuum. *Journal of Sport and Social Issues*, May: 191–217.

Kayser, B., Mauron, A. and Miah, A. 2007. Current anti-doping policy: a critical appraisal. *BMC Medical Ethics* [online] 8(2). Available at: www.biomedcentral.com/content/pdf/1472-6939-8-2.pdf [accessed 11/08/08].

Kluka, D.A. 2008. *The Brighton Declaration on Women and Sport: A management audit of process quality.* Ph.D thesis, University of Pretoria, South Africa.

Lenk, C. 2007. Is Enhancement in Sport Really Unfair? Arguments on the concept of competition and equality of opportunities. *Sport, Ethics and Philosophy*, 1(2): 218–228.

Marshall, C. 2009. The Humiliation of Caster Semenya. *Eureka Street* [online] 31 August. Available at: www.eurekastreet.com.au/article.aspx?aeid=16058 [accessed 1/08/10].

Moser, C. 2005. Has Gender Mainstreaming Failed? *International Feminist Journal of Politics*, 7(4): 576–590.

Neumayer, E. 2005. Do International Human Rights Treaties Improve Respect for Human Rights? *Journal of Conflict Resolution*, 49(6): 925–953.

Nixon, H.L. 2007. Constructing Diverse Sports Opportunities for People with Disabilities. *Journal of Sport and Social Issues*, 31(4), November: 417–433.

Nolan, A. 2009. Addressing economic and social rights violations by non-state actors through the role of the state: a comparison of regional approaches to the obligations to protect. *Human Rights Law Review*, 9(2): 225–254.

Oliver, D. and Fedtke, J. 2007. *Human Rights and the Private Sphere: a comparative study.* London: Routledge.

Patel, S. 2011. *The European Dimension of Sport as a Medium for Enhancing Participation.* Oral presentation given at the 'Sport & EU Conference' hosted by Nottingham Trent University, Nottingham, UK, in July 2011.

Reaves, R. 2001. 'There's no crying in baseball': Sports and the legal and social construction of gender. *Journal of Gender, Race and Justice*, 283, Spring: 1–24.

Rehman, J. 2010. *International Human Rights Law.* Harlow: Pearson Longman.

Roy E.C. 2007. Aiming for Inclusive Sport: the legal and practical implications of the United Nation's Disability Convention for Sport, Recreation and Leisure for People with Disabilities. *Entertainment and Sports Law Journal* [online], 5(1). Available at www2.warwick.ac.uk/fac/soc/law/elj/eslj/issues/volume5/number1/roy [accessed 16/07/08].

Savulescu, J. and Foddy, B. 2010. Le tour and failure of zero tolerance: time to relax doping controls. *Practical Ethics* [online]. Available at: www.practicalethics.ox.ac.uk [accessed 06/08/11].

Smallwood, J. 2012. Anti-corruption training to be mandatory for counties. *BBCi.* [online], 22 February. Available at: www.bbc.co.uk/sport/0/cricket/17133632 [accessed 02/08/12].

Smith, A. 2011. All Bets Are Off: match fixing in sport: some recent developments. *Entertainment and Sports Law Journal* [online], 9(1). Available at: www2.warwick.ac.uk/fac/soc/law/elj/eslj/issues/volume9/number1/smith/ [accessed 02/08/12].

Solomon, L.M., Mordkoff, D.S. and Noll, R.C. 2009. Physical Enhancement of Human Performance: Is Law Keeping Pace with Science? *Gender Medicine*, 6(1): 249–256.

Stone, D. H. 2005. The Game of Pleasant Diversion: can we level the playing field for the disabled athlete and maintain the national pastime in the aftermath of PGA Tour, Inc v Martin: an empirical study of the disabled athlete. *St Johns Law Review*, 79(2): 377–403.

Van Hilvoorde, I. and Landeweerd, L. 2008. Disability or Extraordinary Talent- Francsco Lentini (three legs) Versus Oscar Pistorius (no legs). *Sport, Ethics and Philosophy*, 2(2): 97–111.

Weston, M.A. 2005. The Intersection of Sports and Disability: analysing reasonable accommodations for athletes with disabilities. *Saint Louis University Law Journal*, 50: 137–163.

Williams, M. 2013. A pragmatic solution for gender equality in Canadian elite sport. *International Sports Law Journal*, 13: 18–34.

World Anti-Doping Agency (WADA). 2009. *The World Anti-doping Code* [online]. Available at: www.wada-ama.org/en/resources/the-code/2009-world-anti-doping-code [accessed 12/11/11].

World Anti-Doping Agency (WADA). 2010. *Athlete Biological Passport Operating Guidelines* [online]. Available at: www.wada-ama.org/en/resources/athlete-biological-passport/athlete-biological-passport-abp-operating-guidelines [accessed 05/12/10].

Index

For Product Safety Concerns and Information please contact our EU representative GPSR@taylorandfrancis.com
Taylor & Francis Verlag GmbH, Kaufingerstraße 24, 80331 München, Germany

www.ingramcontent.com/pod-product-compliance
Ingram Content Group UK Ltd.
Pitfield, Milton Keynes, MK11 3LW, UK
UKHW011011180926
475701UK00004B/673
* 9 7 8 0 4 1 5 3 7 7 1 1 9 *